ALA GUIDE TO
SOCIOLOGY & PSYCHOLOGY
REFERENCE

A L A   G U I D E   T O
SOCIOLOGY &
PSYCHOLOGY
R E F E R E N C E

American Library Association

Chicago / 2011

Printed in the United States of America

15 14 13 12 11   5 4 3 2 1

While extensive effort has gone into ensuring the reliability of the information in this book, the publisher makes no warranty, express or implied, with respect to the material contained herein.

ISBN: 978-0-8389-1025-2

Library of Congress Cataloging-in-Publication Data
ALA guide to sociology & psychology reference / American Library Association.
    p.   cm.
  Includes bibliographical references and indexes.
  ISBN 978-0-8389-1025-2 (alk. paper)
  1. Sociology—Reference books—Bibliography. 2. Sociology—Bibliography. 3. Sociology—Electronic information resources. 4. Psychology—Reference books—Bibliography. 5. Psychology—Bibliography. 6. Psychology—Electronic information resources. I. American Library Association. II. Title: ALA guide to sociology and psychology reference.
  Z7164.S68A53 2011
  [HM585]
  301—dc22   2010019969

Book design by Karen Sheets de Gracia in Helvetica and Times.
Composition by Publication Services, Inc.

♾ This paper meets the requirements of ANSI/NISO Z39.48-1992 (Permanence of Paper).

ALA Editions also publishes its books in a variety of electronic formats. For more information, visit the ALA Store at www.alastore.ala.org and select eEditions.

CONTENTS

PART TWO > PSYCHOLOGY

SERIES INTRODUCTION

AS THE PUBLISHER of the essential *Guide to Reference Books*, first printed more than a century ago, as well as *Reference Sources for Small and Medium-Sized Libraries* and *Fundamental Reference Sources*, the American Library Association has long been a source for authoritative bibliographies of the reference literature for practicing librarians, library educators, and reference service trainers. The ALA Guide to Reference series continues that tradition with expertly compiled, discipline-specific, annotated bibliographies of reference works. The volumes in the series draw their content from the successor to *Guide to Reference Books*, the online *Guide to Reference* (www.guidetoreference.org), and thus serve as snapshots of the evolving content of the online *Guide*.

Although compiled in North America for use largely in North American libraries serving institutions of higher education, the series volumes will also be valuable to public and school librarians, independent researchers, publishers, and book dealers, as well as librarians outside North America, for identifying sources that will answer questions, directing researchers, creating local instructional materials, educating and training LIS students and reference staff, and inventorying and developing reference collections. Because these guides provide a usably comprehensive, rather than exhaustive, repertory of sources as the foundation for reference and information services in today's North American higher education research settings, English-language works figure prominently. Works in other languages are included, however, as categories require them and as higher education curricula in North American colleges and universities suggest their inclusion.

The reader will find entries for works that are, for the most part, broadly focused; works on individual persons or works that are narrowly focused geographically or chronologically are not included. Selection criteria favored titles published in the last fifteen years; the reader will want to consult earlier printed bibliographies and indexes, such as the numerous print editions of *Guide to Reference Books*, for many earlier and still important works.

Together, the volumes in this series include works that can most usefully satisfy the vast majority of demands made on a reference service, while not altogether excluding "exotic" or little-known works that will meet only the unusual need. The hope is that the works included will directly meet 80 percent of the needs that librarians have for reference sources and, in the remaining 20 percent of cases, will lead to other works that will suffice.

Librarians today have a broader definition of that much-mooted and ambiguous term *reference work* than ever before. The volumes in this series therefore include the traditional array of encyclopedic, bibliographic, and compendious works as well as websites, search engines, and full-text databases. Because of current reference practice and user preferences, the bibliographies in the series include those online sources that have replaced their printed versions for most librarians under most circumstances. The annotations for such sources describe the relationships between online and print versions.

In addition to providing classified annotated bibliographies, every volume includes editors' guides that orient readers to each discipline, its scope and concerns, and the kinds of sources available for working in it. The editors' guides will be useful, therefore, to the generalist librarian and LIS student as background to the bibliographies or as intellectual frameworks for addressing reference questions.

We at ALA Publishing hope you find the series helpful and welcome your comments at guidetoreference@ala.org. To get the full benefit of the comprehensive compilation in a wide range of subject areas, we also encourage you to subscribe to the online *Guide*, where you have access to updated entries (especially current Web resources), annotations, and user comments.

CONTRIBUTORS

UNDER THE DIRECTION of general editors Robert Kieft (2000–2009) and Denise Bennett (2009–), many librarians have contributed their time and their knowledge of reference literature to this series. A comprehensive list of these contributors appears under the About section of the online *Guide to Reference* (www.guidetoreference.org).

SOCI

1

OLOGY

EDITORS' GUIDE

GIVEN THAT SOCIOLOGY takes as its field of study the entire sweep of human society, it follows that interdisciplinary explorations are frequent and that the borders of the field are both dynamic and imprecise. These tendencies enrich the number and variety of today's reference materials. Growth in the field combined with the rise of the Internet and digital publishing has substantially expanded the range and type of resources available.

Examples of the diverse published tools reflecting cross-disciplinary approaches include works in Social Psychology, Sociolinguistics, and Economic Sociology (*The Handbook of Economic Sociology* [361]). Sociological methodology draws on work done in numerous other fields of study such as Anthropology, Cognitive Studies, and even Literary Theory. Sociologists also work in many subfields defined by specific populations and social conditions: Aging and Gerontology, Ethnic and Racial Studies, Marriage and Family Issues, Population and Demography, social problems (including Substance Abuse and Crime), Social Services and Welfare, Urban Affairs (also rural Affairs), and Women's Studies and Gender. Each of these areas is represented by specialized reference publications, from subject-specific dictionaries to methodological handbooks.

The presentation of sociology reference materials has been most obviously changed by the appearance of digital tools, including networked online sources. These resources include online versions of traditional indexes to periodicals and scholarly journals—notably Sociofile, the digital successor to *Sociological Abstracts* (53)—but extend to entirely new resources, such as online statistical data sets and websites maintained by a variety of institutions, associations, and advocacy groups. The Web allows a wider scope for new perspectives, offering information previously difficult if not impossible to obtain. The audience for web publications includes not only university-affiliated students and scholars but also practitioners and the general public, extending the definition of "reference" sources and requiring greater scrutiny in terms of authority and bias. Online resources also represent previously marginalized viewpoints based on race, ethnicity, gender, and global or non-Western perspectives.

Three types of works dominate reference publishing in sociology: Encyclopedias, Dictionaries, and Handbooks. According to Alan Sica in *International Encyclopedia of the Social and Behavioral Sciences* (14), "The purpose of an encyclopedia is to summarize and codify knowledge in a given field. This is in contrast to a handbook, which offers essays on cutting-edge research in a field, or a dictionary, which provides short, to-the-point definitions of key concepts in a field" (pp. 4497–4504).

Reference publishing in the field also follows the outlines noted by Tze-Chung Li in *Social Science Reference Sources: A Practical Guide* (39): "The present interest of sociologists focuses on three areas: the study of groups, institutional analysis, and the study of social structure in general" (p. 416). Li also notes the systematic and empirical nature of sociology in comparison to more abstract approaches such as philosophy, leading to greater interest in mathematical formulations in analysis and methodology. At the same time, sociology's grounding in concrete social systems and situations leads to the examination of real-world social problems, lending a certain practical tone.

Digitization and the Internet have transformed access to the reference resources. Thanks to the Web, the potential audience for information now includes the general public and a wide range of practitioners, so that more materials reflect interdisciplinary or popular approaches. Relevant web-based tools include database-supported indexes such as Sociofile, statistical resources (sometimes compiled using freely available data from sources such as American Factfinder [http://www.factfinder.census.gov]) and advocacy sites for interest groups or professional associations. Web-based publishing has cleared a path for materials representing previously marginalized viewpoints, whether based on geography, gender, or ethnicity.

Sociology is blessed with a large number of one-volume dictionaries and multivolume encyclopedias, including landmark social science sets such as Smelser's *International Encyclopedia of the Social and Behavioral Sciences* (14). Guides and handbooks offer summaries to readers on particular aspects of sociological study (e.g., the *Blackwell Companion to Medical Sociology* [35]). The handbook is a typical and prominent format in sociology, assembling essays on current topics from recognized scholars as a convenient introduction to major issues and a jumping-off point for identifying significant readings.

Digitized online information has reduced the importance of published directories and statistical compilations. The Web offers continuously updated contact information for most organizations and institutions, and many individuals. Online data sets, including storehouses such as the U.S. Census Bureau's American Factfinder (http://www.factfinder.census.gov) website allow retrieval of many statistical figures on demand.

Indexing to scholarly periodicals is also now dominated by digitized formats: online access to content via the Sociofile database is faster, more up-to-date and powerful than use of the previous print-format *Sociological Abstracts*. Except for older compilations covering decades not yet well-digitized, most one-volume single-subject bibliographies have ceased to be significant because users can retrieve and export their own custom-designed lists of entries on given subjects.

Particularly for conditions in the United States, issues of Race and Ethnicity remain major topics of social attention and thus sociological study, and the list of available publications has grown. Encyclopedias and guides supporting African-American Studies now cover a wide range of topics, including historical themes. Works on other American minorities, such as Asian Americans and Hispanic Americans, have grown in number as well. Even more striking is the growth in information sources about Native Americans, for whom relatively little was on hand a decade ago, and about Arab Americans, about whom little had been published.

Sociologists remain interested in topics such as Aging, Childhood, and Marriage, but the greatest expansion of reference tools is associated with recent preoccupations of American society. As a result, major subsections now deal with Disabilities, Immigration, Crime, and Violence. The growth of interdisciplinary approaches has called for new sections on Politics, Social Psychology, Theory as a Methodological Development, and Cyberspace.

Reference content in sociology continues to reflect the influence of key individuals (e.g., Max Weber) who set up schools of thought, established theories, and influenced the growth of the field. The result is a substantial offering of biographical content, or even anthologized summaries of key works by these figures.

Further threads in sociological study and reference publishing concern methodology. Quantitative and Statistical Methods are important underpinnings for many investigations. Self-reflection about the practice of sociological study is also important, providing works that offer advice on ethical concerns, or borrow from the concepts of critical theory.

Finally, many publications and resources covering matters of sexual behavior (including GLBT topics) and of women's studies have been shifted to a new interdisciplinary section on Gender Studies.

—THE EDITORS

1 > GENERAL WORKS

1   **Social stratification: An annotated bibliography.** Graham Charles
      Kinloch. xxvii, 357 p. New York: Garland, 1987. ISBN: 0824098056.
016.3055   Z7164.S64K56; HT609

A 350 p. annotated bibliography on social classes. Publ. in 1987, but still
very relevant to issues of sharpening class lines and widening class divides
in society. Provides a look across and back that is doubly valuable in creating a sense of perspective. Includes indexes.

Atlases and General Overviews

2   **The atlas of American society.** Alice C. Andrews, James W.
      Fonseca. ix, 303 p., ill. New York: New York University Press, 1995.
      ISBN: 0814726267.
301.0973021   HN60.A5

Fifteen chapters on population distribution, social mobility, inequality,
ethnicity, health, education, crime, women, and others, with numerous
maps from both private and U.S. government sources. Includes many
tables, charts, and graphs. A concluding chapter presents a composite
ranking of states based on a mix of 17 indicators of social well-being.
Includes list of sources and overall subject index.

Bibliography

3   **Gender and racial images/stereotypes in the mass media: A
      bibliography.** Joan Nordquist. 72 p. Santa Cruz, Calif.: Reference
      and Research Services, 2001. ISBN: 1892068265.
                                                P94.5.M55

Thoroughly documents portrayals of women and minorities in the mass media. Reaching across various disciplines, and back in time, treats issues of stereotypes and racism. A useful gathering of sources otherwise difficult or impossible to identify.

4   **Max Weber: A comprehensive bibliography.** Alan Sica. ix, 334 p. New Brunswick, N.J.: Transaction Publishers, 2004. ISBN: 0765802090.

016.301092B   Z8957.S53; HM477.G3

Max Weber can be considered the father of the field of sociology. Even a century later, as the discipline evolves and embraces entirely new areas, his influence remains fundamental to the concept that society can be studied, and that culture is measurable. This bibliography provides a portal to help a new generation in the field understand how sociology began with Weber.

5   **Social sciences: An international bibliography of serial literature, 1830–1985.** Jan Wepsiec. x, 486 p. London; New York: Mansell, 1992. ISBN: 0720121094.

016.3005   Z7161.A15; H85.W38

Identifies more than 5,200 periodicals in economics, political science, anthropology, sociology, international and comparative law, education, psychology, history, and geography published worldwide since 1830. Includes some ceased titles. Alphabetical entries indicate title changes, years and place of publication, frequency, and available indexing sources. Appendix 2 is a panoramic history of the major social science disciplines. Subject index.

6   **Sociology in government: A bibliography of the work of the Division of Farm Population and Rural Life, U.S. Department of Agriculture, 1919–1953.** Olaf F. Larson, Edward O. Moe, Julie N. Zimmerman, United States. xxii, 301 p. Boulder, Colo.: Westview Press, 1992. ISBN: 0813385296.

016.307720973   Z7164.S688L37; HT421

By 1953, America was well on its way to moving off the farm and into urban settings, changing all the rules of interest to sociology: race, gender, family, community. Today, urbanization is one of the most defining aspects of evolving culture on a global basis. This bibliography captured rural life just as this process got underway in the United States, and thus provides a remarkable benchmark for life within an agrarian culture. Covering 34 years of publications, bibliography provides access to materials otherwise largely unavailable.

7   **The sociology of religion: An organizational bibliography.**
Anthony J. Blasi, Michael W. Cuneo. xxix, 459 p. New York: Garland, 1990. ISBN: 0824025849.

016.3066   Z7831.B54

Entries for 3,207 books, articles, and dissertations published through 1988 (some 1989 imprints are included), arranged under names of religions, denominations, and small religious bodies and movements. Most have brief annotations. Materials are in Western languages, for the most part English, and largely reflect North American scholarship. Provides convenient access to a substantial body of research. Author and subject indexes.

The authors' *Issues in the sociology of religion: A bibliography* (Garland, 1990) is a companion volume covering literature published through 1984. Entries are listed under issues within three broad categories: structure, processes, and disciplinary conceptualizations. Author and alphabetical contents index. The amount of overlap between the two volumes is unclear; different arrangement and subject access within each volume make each useful.

Dictionaries and Thesauruses

8   **The Blackwell dictionary of sociology: A user's guide to sociological language.** 2nd ed. Allan G. Johnson. xii, 413 p. Oxford, [England]; Malden, Mass.: Blackwell, 2000. ISBN: 0631227660.

301.03   HM425.J64

Gives basic and secondary definitions for the terms used in the field of sociology. Many entries also have one or more readings, as well as bibliographic references for further study; 340 p. of concepts and terms are followed by a separate sociologist's biographic section of another 40 p., which includes about a quarter page of details about an individual's life and work, followed by a listing of major publications.

Well done; good for students at the high school level and above, and useful for scholars in a research setting. A basic, workmanlike dictionary of sociology. Highly recommended for school, general, and research collections, and for the scholar's own bookshelf. Available as an e-book.

9   **The Cambridge dictionary of sociology.** Bryan S. Turner. xx, 688
        p. Cambridge, [England]; New York: Cambridge University Press,
        2006. ISBN: 052183290X.
301.03   HM425

A succinct and well-focused miniature encyclopedia rather than a brief-
definition dictionary, this new volume is worthwhile for both research
and general collections. Entries are signed and range in length from long
paragraphs to about six pages (for "deviance," for example). Numerous
sociologists also have biographical entries of about half a page, along with
entries for concepts, movements, and theories. Scope is broadly international for both people and terms.

10   **Cassell's queer companion: A dictionary of lesbian and gay life
        and culture.** William Stewart, Emily Hamer, Frances Williams. vii,
        278 p. London; New York: Cassell, 1995. ISBN: 030434303X.
306.76603   HQ76.25.S75

Approximately 2,500 brief entries define various terms, concepts, people,
organizations, events, quotations, and phrases pertaining to gay and
lesbian life. Includes cross-references but no index. Although its lack of
bibliographic references and informal (often humorous) tone make this
dictionary more a popular resource than a scholarly one, it can still serve
as a starting point for researchers interested in LGBT slang terminology,
both contemporary and historical.

11   **Collins dictionary of sociology.** 4th ed. David Jary, Julia Jary. x,
        710 p. Glasgow, Scotland, [U.K.]: Collins, 2005. ISBN: 7183992.
301.03

A dictionary with clear definitions and cross-references to related terms.
This Scottish "take" on sociological language provides definitions for a
broad range of terms in sociology and social research. Despite its European framework, this is a practical and useful ready reference title. The
4th ed. (2005) provides good definitions for emerging and evolving terms
related to race, class, gender, immigration, and national frameworks. More
comprehensive than other dictionaries, many of which have become, for
better or worse, small encyclopedias. A very good dictionary that covers at
least twice the number of terms of most other current sociology dictionaries, and does it well.

        Highly recommended for general and research collections, for scholars in
sociology and related fields, and for undergraduate and graduate students.

12   A critical dictionary of sociology. Raymond Boudon, François Bourricaud, Peter Hamilton. xiii, 438 p., ill. Chicago: University of Chicago Press, 1989. ISBN: 0226067289.

301.03   HM17.B6813

Twenty years after the original publication of this 2nd ed., (which the University of Chicago has wisely kept in print), this title still holds its value among the well-populated field of dictionaries of sociology, on two counts. The first: It provides a clear definition within a clear context for a core list of key sociological terms. And the second, especially valuable: It makes reference to the sociological tradition in Britain, France, and Germany, as well as in the United States and Canada. The age and maturity of the field of sociology varies greatly among those national contexts, and this volume goes far in bringing the place of each into a rational overall pattern. Available as an e-book.

13   Dictionary of medical sociology. William C. Cockerham, Ferris Joseph Ritchey. xxvi, 169 p. Westport, Conn.: Greenwood Press, 1997. ISBN: 0313292698.

306.46103   RA418.C655

Positioned at the intersection of arguably the softest of the soft sciences (sociology) and the hardest of the hard sciences (medicine), medical sociology has developed at a rapid pace over the last two decades to richly inform both of its parent disciplines. This dictionary from 1997 defines key terms from the newly-emerging field at that time, but also demonstrates how each discipline informs and expands the other. A useful reference tool and also an informal guide to the newly-created field. Includes bibliographical references and index.

14   Dictionary of sociology. 3rd ed. John Scott, Gordon Marshall. ix, 707 p., ill. Oxford; New York: Oxford University Press, 2005. ISBN: 0198609868.

301.03   HM425

The *Oxford dictionary of sociology* has set the gold standard in the field for clarity and context from the 1st ed. in 1994, to the 2nd ed. in 1998, as well as with this 3rd ed. An international panel of contributors brings weight to the work presented here, which sensibly combines concepts, constructs, and people in one alphabetic structure. "Cash-crop" sits easily beside "Caste," "CATI-Computer Assisted Telephone Interviewing," and "Causal modeling." "Charisma" precedes "Chattel slavery," the "Chicago School," and "Vere Gordon Childe."

Definitions and information about the field of sociology are likely to be found here. Well-done, solid, careful. Suitable for any level of audience, from school to university, from student to scholar. Highly recommended for general and research collections, as well as for scholars, students, and others doing research in the field.

15   Dictionnaire critique de la sociologie. 7th ed. Raymond Boudon, François Bourricaud. xxx, 714 p. Paris: Quadrige/PUF (Presses universitaires de France), 2006. ISBN: 213054424X. ISSN: 0291-0489.

This French work provides long essays on central people and topics in sociology, with cross-references, bibliographies, and a subject index. Bourricaud died before the publication of this edition, so the preface surveying the state of the discipline is by Boudon alone. Sociology is a younger discipline in France, so many of the concepts and theories presented here have a particular freshness.

Annotation contributed by Mary W. George of the Princeton University Library.

Earlier editions available in English translation as *A critical dictionary of sociology* (12).

16   Dreisprachiges Wörterbuch der Soziologie = Trilingual dictionary of sociology. 2000, erw. Aufl. ed. Günter Endruweit. 133 p. Königstein/Ts, [Germany]: Athenäum, 1982. ISBN: 3761040652.

301.03   HM17.E53

Parallel lists of sociological terms in German, English, and French. Separate alphabetic section for each language, with equivalent words or phrases given in the other two. Includes cross-references and a source where each term is fully defined.

Annotation contributed by Mary W. George of the Princeton University Library.

17   Penguin dictionary of sociology. 5th ed. Nicholas Abercrombie, Stephen Hill, Bryan S. Turner. xi, 484 p. London; New York: Penguin Books, 2006. ISBN: 0141013753.

301.03   HM17

Created by two British scholars, this is a true and up-to-date dictionary of sociology. Provides clear definitions of terms likely to raise questions at the college and graduate level, and which can be useful to describe an otherwise querulous concept for scholars working in the field. Entries usually conclude with cross-references to related terms, as well as to readings, which refer to the 45 p. bibliography at the back of the volume.

Selective biographical entries are interspersed with concepts and terms in the main volume. A highly useful volume, very much up-to-date on issues and developments like race, class, and gender. Provides intelligent cross-national references and sensitivity to working in the real world. For example, the entry for "Snowball sample" begins with, "In some research settings, it is impossible to compile a complete list of the population to be studied. For example, studies of prostitutes."

18   The Sage dictionary of health and society. Kevin White. xiv, 242
       p. London; Thousand Oaks, Calif.: SAGE, 2006. ISBN: 0761941150.
306.46103   RA418
Key terms and critical concepts are defined and placed in context in the more than 900 entries in this excellent new dictionary of medical sociology. Coverage is global. Biographical entries are included for those who have made special contributions to the field. Provides framework for understanding how illness and health happen, as well as the influence society has on medicine as it is practiced and as it is experienced by individuals. Includes index.

19   The Sage dictionary of sociology. Steve Bruce, Steven Yearley.
       vi, 328 p. London; Thousand Oaks, Calif.: SAGE, 2006. ISBN:
       0761974814.
301.03   HM425
In the well-populated field of sociology dictionaries, this welcome title provides entries that will resonate with Generation Next students, as well as with forward-looking scholars in sociology and related fields. For example, the entry for "Bureaucracy" begins with Weber's definition and then follows up with Merton's concepts. However, the entry doesn't say much about what bureaucracy is. The entry for "Prejudice" says "the term is normally used for unwarranted negative views of some people or thing." A casual, chatty style is used throughout. Definitions are sound and well-referenced and may make more sense to a younger generation than the definitions in more traditional sociology dictionaries.

20   Thematic list of descriptors -- sociology. UNESCO, [International
       Committee for Social Science Information and Documentation].
       xix, 475 p. London; New York: Routledge, 1989. ISBN: 0415017793.
025.46301   Z695.1.S63T48

This publication from Unesco is both a listing of subject headings in sociology and a thesaurus of sociological terms as they are used internationally. Slight differences in terms can change what is meant substantially. Even from 1989, this work is a grounding reference for understanding sociological writing across national borders.

21 **Thesaurus of sociological indexing terms.** Sociological Abstracts, Inc. Bethesda, Md.: Cambridge Scientific Abstracts, 1986–. ISSN: 1546-5217.

025.49301   Z695.1.S63

In addition to listing the subject terms used to create and search *Sociological Abstracts* (53) (the gold standard index to scholarly literature in sociology for the last 60 years), this thesaurus provides an intellectual road map to the vocabulary and relationships of concepts in the discipline. Begins with Historical Notes, which is followed by the main section that lists terms in alphabetical order. Entry information can include History Note (HN), Used For (UF), Scope Notes (SN), and Broader, Narrower, and Related Terms (BR, NT, and RT). Includes a classification scheme, valuable in an online world where such frameworks can be invisible, to help in understanding how constructs in the field relate. Bibliography.

Directories

22 **Yearbook of international organizations online.** http://www .uia.be/node/52. Union of International Associations. Brussels, Belgium: Union of International Associations. 2000–.

314.2   JX1904

A subscription database made up of four components:

At its core is International Organizations Online (www.uia.be/sites/uia .be/db/db/x.php?dbcode=or&go=), a guide to more than 60,000 international nongovernmental organizations (INGOs) and intergovernmental organizations (IGOs) and selected subsidiary bodies. Covers all known IGOs, but the inclusion of NGOs is dependent on numerous criteria. Entries range from a few words in length to more than 10,000.

Biography Profiles Online (www.uia.be/sites/uia.be/db/db/x.php ?dbcode=bi&go=) consists of biographical entries on more than 20,000 individuals holding or having held significant positions in organizations profiled in International Organizations Online.

Statistics Online contains graphs and detailed tables on various aspects of IGOs and INGOs, such as their geographic distribution, fields of activity, dates founded, structure, language use, publishing output, and interrelationships. Periods covered vary; one time series begins in 312 CE.

Bibliography Online consists of bibliographic references to titles mentioned in International Organizations Online and to studies on IGOs and INGOs by scholars throughout the social sciences. Its value to users having access to such databases as WorldCat (www.oclc.org/worldcat) and Worldwide Political Science Abstracts (Cambridge Scientific Abstracts, 2001–) is questionable.

Issued annually in print as the *Yearbook of international organizations* (K. b. Sanr, 1967–) and on CD-ROM as the *Yearbook plus of international organizations and biographies* (K. b. Sanr, 1996–).

Encyclopedias

23   **The Blackwell encyclopedia of sociology.** George Ritzer. 11 v. (cxxiv, 5650 p.), ill. Malden, Mass.: Blackwell, 2007. ISBN: 1405124334.
301.03   HM425

The 11 v. (some 6000 p.) of this comprehensive new encyclopedia include 1,800 signed essays which provide thorough coverage of classic theories, themes, and concepts in sociology. Coverage of recent developments in the field, as well as broad international coverage of new theories and concepts, make this a necessary title for research libraries and an important one for general collections. Bibliographical and cross-references, timeline, lexicon, and index. Available in electronic form.

24   **Encyclopaedia of the social sciences.** Edwin Robert Anderson Seligman, Alvin Saunders Johnson. 15 v. New York: Macmillan, 1930–1935.
303   H41.E6

The first great multi-vol. summary of the field, followed by the *International encyclopedia of the social sciences* (30) in 1968, and *International encyclopedia of the social and behavioral sciences* (29) in 2001.

Coverage extends beyond psychology, education, business, economics, sociology, and government to include some unexpected areas such as agriculture, public health, and transportation. Obviously no longer current, but valuable for background and the foundation knowledge of the 1930s. Begins with essays on the development of social thought and institutions, and the state of the social science disciplines in the European countries, Latin America, Japan, and the United States. Signed articles with bibliographical references follow in alphabetical order; some are lengthy. About half of the articles are biographies of significant figures. Classified list of articles, classified list of biographies, index, and index of contributors.

25 **Encyclopedia of American social movements.** Immanuel Ness, Stephen Eric Bronner, Frances Fox Piven. 4 v. (xxix, 1557 p.), ill. Armonk, N.Y.: Sharpe Reference, 2004. ISBN: 0765680459.
303.484097303   HN57.E594

Sixteen sections cover major U.S. social movements, from antislavery to global justice. "Each section is edited by an expert in the field and includes an introduction; articles on the critical themes, aspects, and events of the social movement or movements; biographical portraits of the key leaders and figures; excerpts from primary sources and historical documents; bibliography and references; and illustrations"—*Introd.* Expanded bibliography for each section and general index in the final volume.

26 **Encyclopedia of food and culture.** Solomon H. Katz, William Woys Weaver. 3 v., ill. (some color). New York: Scribner, 2003. ISBN: 0684805685.
394.1203   GT2850.E53

Nimbly covers an enormous scope of no less than food and nutrition and their place in history and culture on a global basis. Some 600 signed articles in three volumes range in length from 250 to 10,000 words. As an example of coverage, the 75 entries under the letter "C" begin with Cabbage, include Julia Child, and then move on to Civilization and Food; Social Class; Climate and Food; Cocktail Party; Cocktails; Codex Alimentarius; Coffee; Food Coloring; and finish with Cucumbers, Melons and Other Cucurbits; Evolution of Cuisine; Curds; Curry; Custard and Puddings; and Cutlery. Throughout, content is enriched by 450 photos and other illustrations, recipes, menus, especially useful timelines, many bibliographic and cross-references, and a necessary navigation device: A thorough index. Available as an e-book.

27 **Encyclopedia of sociology.** 2nd ed. Edgar F. Borgatta, Marie L. Borgatta. 5 v. (xxxix, 3481 p.), ill. New York: Macmillan Reference USA, 2000. ISBN: 0028648536.
301.03   HM425

A true encyclopedia in the field of sociology, broadly defined, and beautifully executed. The 397 lengthy, signed, and alphabetized entries reflect changes in both the world and the field of sociology since the 1st ed. in 1992. Includes 66 articles that are entirely new, while those retained from the 1st ed. are substantially rewritten. Articles range from three to 17 pages in length and conclude with cross-references and substantial bibliographies that vary in length. Index of more than 200 pages. Electronic sources, including websites, throughout. Thorough and detailed coverage of the field, useful for both the knowledgeable scholar and the student working at an introductory level. Available as an e-book.

28   **International encyclopedia of sociology.** Frank Northen Magill, Héctor L. Delgado, Alan Sica. 2 v. (xxii, 1573 p.). London; Chicago: Fitzroy Dearborn, 1995. ISBN: 1884964451.

301.03   HM17.I53

A useful and workmanlike general encyclopedia in sociology. Signed entries vary in length from a few sentences to several pages. Some international coverage, but a strong focus on matters in the United States at a very general level. Most appropriate for students at the middle and high school levels. Includes bibliographical references and index.

29   **International encyclopedia of the social and behavioral sciences.** http://www.elsevier.com/wps/find/bookdescription. cws_home/601495/description#description. Neil J. Smelser, Paul B. Baltes ScienceDirect. Amsterdam [Netherlands]; [Miamisburg, Ohio]: Elsevier; ScienceDirect. 2002–.

This major reference work is conceived around 37 broad topical sections, including entries from traditional disciplines such as anthropology, economics, education, geography, history, law, linguistics, management, philosophy, political science, and sociology, as well as cross-disciplinary areas of study such as aging, environment and ecology, gender studies, logic of inquiry and research design, and statistics. More than 4,000 signed entries average some four pages in length and provide overviews, reviews of future directions, and bibliographies. Includes 147 biographies of deceased "towering figures." Subscribers have access to ongoing regular updates and additional new articles. Also published in print format in 26 volumes: v. 25 is a list of contributors and name index; v. 26 is a classified list of entries by field and extensive subject index connecting related topics.

30   International encyclopedia of the social sciences. David L. Sills,
      Robert King Merton. v. 1–19, ill. [New York]: Macmillan, [1968]–
      1991. ISBN: 0028955102.

300.321   H40.A2I5

A milestone work of reference, still valuable as a record of social science
learning up to the 1960s. Complemented but not entirely replaced by
the *International encyclopedia of the social and behavioral sciences* (29) of
2001.

Primary emphasis is on anthropology, economics, geography, history, law, political science, psychiatry and psychology, sociology, and statistics. Signed articles are arranged in alphabetical order and often run to
10 pages or more, allowing in-depth discussion and space for substantial
bibliographies. Includes over 600 biographical entries.

Vol. 18 is the 1979 *Biographical supplement* (Free Press, 1979) with
215 additional biographies. Vol. 19 appeared in 1991 as a *Social science
quotations* suppl. Additional foundations for social science thought in
the 20th cent. also can be found in the *Encyclopaedia of the social sciences* (24).

31   **Key contemporary concepts: From abjection to Zeno's paradox.**
      John Lechte. x, 222 p. London; Thousand Oaks, Calif.: SAGE, 2003.
      ISBN: 0761965351.

301.03   HM425

Without pretending to cover the whole field of sociology, or even all of
society, this brief but well-written and thorough encyclopedia manages to
survey concepts that define culture at the present time. Essay-style definitions. Selection and style tend to be casual, but sound.

For example, the letter "F" covers "Family," "Fantasy/Phantasy," "Fan-
tasm," "Fractal," "Freedom," and "Fuzzy logic." A fun read, but also an
important survey of what the world is about, societally-speaking.

32   **Social issues in America: An encyclopedia.** James Ciment. 8 v., ill.
      Armonk, N.Y.: M.E. Sharpe, 2006. ISBN: 0765680610.

361.97303   HN57.S624

Some 150 social issues in the United States are treated in detailed and
signed essays in this eight volume encyclopedia. Arrangement is alphabetical. Representative topics:

- Taxes and Tax Reform; Term Limits; Terrorism, Domestic; Terrorism, Foreign; Terrorism, War on; Tobacco; Tort Reform; Toxic Waste; Traffic Congestion
- Unemployment; Unions; Urban Sprawl
- Voluntarism and Volunteering; Voting Issues
- Waste Disposal; Water Pollution; Weapons of Mass Destruction; Welfare and Welfare Reform; Wilderness Protection; Women's Rights
- Xenophobia and Nativism

The perspective is mainstream, useful for general readership. Popular culture topics are given serious and balanced treatment.

33 World of sociology. Joseph M. Palmisano. 2 v., ill. Detroit: Gale, 2001. ISBN: 0787649651.

301.03   HM585

Comprehensive coverage of the field of sociology and other closely-related disciplines in some 1,250 entries. Biographical entries are provided for both major and lesser-known sociologists, along with information on women and minorities, to provide a balance sometimes lacking in surveys of the field. Language is clear and at a level accessible to upper-level high school and college students. Includes some 350 illustrations, a timeline, as well as bibliographical references and index.

Guides

34 Alternative lifestyles: A guide to research collections on intentional communities, nudism, and sexual freedom. Jefferson P. Selth. xii, 133 p. Westport, Conn.: Greenwood Press, 1985. ISBN: 0313247730.

016.3067   HQ971.S45

More than two decades after its publication in 1985, this volume is still interesting, in a research context, as a manual to the social mores of the time—what was considered to be on the edge and on the fringes. It describes 36 major U.S. collections of the mid-1980s, which totaled 120,000 volumes, 15,000 periodicals, 125,000 audiovisual items, over 3 million photographs, and many ephemeral materials. Introductory pages to the three sections described by the title provide definitions and scope. Entries, which vary in length from two to ten pages, and are arranged alphabetically by title, include contact information and collection details from that time. Extensive indexes. In the ensuing years, at least one of the cited major research collections has disappeared, but as an inventory this manual continues to offer a snapshot and perspective for researchers.

35   **The Blackwell companion to medical sociology.** William C. Cockerham. xiii, 528 p., ill. Oxford, U.K.; Malden, Mass.: Blackwell, 2001; repr. 2005. ISBN: 0631217037.

306.461   RA418.B5736

Global and comprehensive survey of the emerging field of medical sociology. Twenty-six signed chapters draw out topics in Western medicine to show how sociological theory and analysis enrich the clinical understanding of each area. A second section covers countries in every corner of the globe: Canada, Mexico, Brazil, countries in both Western and Eastern Europe, Africa, the Arab world, Israel, Australia, Japan, and China. Cultural constructs from the discipline of sociology inform medical practice and understanding. A thoroughly useful textbook for understanding the field. Includes bibliographical references and index.

36   **A guide to writing sociology papers.** 6th ed. Roseann Giarrusso. xv, 230 p. New York: Worth Publishers, 2007. ISBN: 9780716776260.

808.066301   HM585

This 6th ed. of a classic resource is the latest to provide guidance at a basic, but thorough, level. Intended for students new to the field and for those wanting to be sure their work is well-grounded and papers soundly constructed. Useful for teaching research and writing for other fields at the undergraduate level, too, and even for reviewing basic techniques for graduate students, especially those who are teaching undergraduates for the first time.

37   **Iconic America: A roller-coaster ride through the eye-popping panorama of American pop culture.** Tommy Hilfiger, George Lois. New York: Universe, 2007. ISBN: 9780789315731.

Some 350 symbols of popular culture have been gathered together in this lighthearted but important look at what resonates in the psyche of Americans today. A collaboration of fashion designer Tommy Hilfiger and advertising superstar George Lois. Barbie, Mickey Mouse, and Monopoly are mixed in with the Declaration of Independence in an entertaining catalog of things that matter, even if we aren't quite sure why. Index.

38   **Lost sociologists rediscovered.** Mary Ann Romano. x, 268 p. Lewiston, N.Y.: Edwin Mellen Press, 2002. ISBN: 0773470832.

301.0922   HM478.L67

The lives of eight critical social thinkers and activists, each born in the 19th century, are carefully documented to show that their work and influence qualifies each to be classified as founding members of the then-new discipline of sociology. Their names and dates are:

- Jane Addams, 1860–1935
- Walter Benjamin, 1892–1940
- W.E.B. Du Bois, 1868–1963
- Harriet Martineau, 1802–76
- Pitirim A. Sorokin, 1889–1968
- Flora Tristan, 1803–44
- George E. Vincent, 1864–1941
- Beatrice Webb, 1858–1943

This work serves to bring them back into an appropriate perspective as pioneers in the field. Includes bibliographical references and index.

39   **Social science reference sources: A practical guide.** 3rd ed. Tze-chung Li. xxvii, 495 p. Westport, Conn.: Greenwood Press, 2000. ISBN: 0313304831.

016.3   Z7161.A1; H61.L5

Identifies key resources in anthropology, business, economics, education, geography, history, law, political science, psychology, and sociology, with additional coverage of statistical publ., government documents, and periodicals. For each subject area, describes major guides to the literature, bibliographies, indexes, encyclopedias, directories, and similar tools. Excludes most pre-1980 imprints, for which the 2nd ed. remains the authority. Includes publ. appearing into 1999, thus information about many digital and online resources has become dated. Name/title and subject indexes. Available as an e-book.

40   **The social sciences: A cross-disciplinary guide to selected sources.** 3rd ed. Nancy L. Herron. xxv, 494 p., ill. Englewood, Colo.: Libraries Unlimited, 2002. ISBN: 1563088827.

016.3   Z7161; H61.S648

Annotated bibliography of reference tools in the fields of political science, economics, business, history, law and justice, anthropology, sociology, education, psychology, geography, and communication, as well as publ. that cover the social sciences at large. Following an essay on the nature of published information for a given subject, entries typically cover guides and handbooks, dictionaries and encyclopedias, biographical compilations, directories, bibliographies, indexes, and statistical tools, as well as atlases, chronologies, voting records, and other discipline-specific works when present. Electronic formats are mentioned, reflecting the state of access at the time of publ. (2002). Annotations are substantial paragraphs. Title, author, and subject indexes. Available as an e-book.

41   Sociology: A guide to reference and information sources. 3rd ed. Stephen H. Aby, James Nalen, Lori Fielding. xi, 273 p. Westport, Conn.: Libraries Unlimited, 2005. ISBN: 1563089475.

016.301   Z7164.S68A24; HM585

Begins with two general sections: social science reference and sociology. Followed by 25 specific subdisciplines, which range from more traditional areas like industrial sociology and rural sociology, to newer fields like medical sociology, and even recently reinvented fields, including urban sociology. Includes a full catalog of different types of reference works. Among them are:

- Bibliographies
- Biographies
- Data and Statistics
- Dictionaries and Encyclopedias
- Directories
- Guides
- Handbooks and Yearbooks
- Indexes, Abstracts, and Databases
- Journals
- Organizations
- Websites

A basic listing that is selective and well-focused. A fundamental tool for sociology reference, including referral to larger collections. Index.

Handbooks

42   **Handbook of clinical sociology.** 2nd ed. Howard M. Rebach, John
G. Bruhn. xvi, 437 p. New York: Kluwer Academic/Plenum, 2001.
ISBN: 0306465124.

301   HM585.H35

Clinical sociology brings practical applications, which are based on the
theoretical constructs of sociology, to bear on the social problems in the
world today. This thoroughly revised 2nd ed. of the classic work in the field
is organized into sections on theory and practice, cases for interventions,
types of sociological practice, and social problems that can be addressed.
Also includes detailed information on acquiring credentials as a clinical
sociologist. Intended for students, sociologists, instructors, as well as those
in clinical disciplines. Index.

43   **Handbook of contemporary developments in world sociology.**
Raj P. Mohan, Don Martindale. xviii, 493 p. Westport, Conn.:
Greenwood Press, 1975. ISBN: 0837179610.

301.09   HM19.H23

This 1975 landmark publication creates a detailed picture of the discipline
of sociology in countries around the world as sociology, and everything
else, found itself on the brink of globalization. Discusses what sociology
meant for different regions of the world and particular countries after
the dust of World War II had more or less settled after 1945. Lays a solid
foundation for understanding the development of the field in each region
in the intervening 30 years. Still valuable today.

44   **Handbook of modern sociology.** Robert E. Lee Faris. viii, 1088 p.,
ill., map. Chicago: Rand McNally, [1964].

301.082   HM51.F3

In 1964, this was a landmark publication that created a conceptual and
practical framework for what sociology was, how it had developed, and
where it was going. More than 40 years later, it is still useful for its clear
summary of the discipline on which innovation and expansion have flourished, its attention to classical theory, and treatment of the foundation for
later development.

45   **Handbook of sociology.** 2nd ed. Neil J. Smelser. 824 p. Newbury
Park, Calif.: Sage, 1988. ISBN: 0803926650.

301   HM51.H249

Published in 1988, this was the first general handbook of sociology since Robert E. L. Faris's 1964 *Handbook of modern sociology* (44). Individual chapters by experts treat nearly all of the discipline's major fields, summarize trends in empirical research, and discuss "problems and issues that have persisted in the field."—*Introd.* Substantial bibliographies. Still useful two decades later as a solid foundation of classical theory.

46 **A handbook of the sociology of religion.** Michele Dillon. xiii, 481 p. Cambridge, U.K.; New York: Cambridge University Press, 2003. ISBN: 0521806240.

306.6 BL60.D54

Handbook covers a traditional view of religion as integral to particular cultures, and uses religion as a window onto those cultures. Especially useful for looking at the culture of the late 20th century, poised for change into a globalized world. Includes bibliographical references and index. Available as an e-book.

47 **The international handbook on the sociology of education: An international assessment of new research and theory.** Carlos Alberto Torres, Ari Antikainen. vi, 415 p., ill. Lanham, Md.: Rowman and Littlefield, 2003. ISBN: 0742517691.

306.43 LC189.I53

The 20th century has been called the "Century of Education" as globalization and urbanization have progressed and communication has made the world a much smaller place. The role of the state has been critical in promoting a broad-based education for many more people in society. In this overarching survey, 18 essays in three sections document the role of society and social theory in education.

The first section on Social Theory and Methodology examines Social Capital, Ethnography, and Development of Quantitative Techniques. Section two provides International Perspectives. The final section, on Critical Issues, deals with topics that include Civil Society, Women in Education, North and South Contrasted, and Citizenship in School Textbooks. Comparisons are drawn across national borders on major issues, including access, school choice, equity, and educational performance. Includes bibliographical references and index.

48 **Sage handbook of sociology.** 3rd ed. Craig J. Calhoun, Chris Rojek, Bryan S. Turner, Sage Publications, Inc. xv, 590 p. London;

Thousand Oaks, Calif.: Sage Publications, Inc., 2005. ISBN: 0761968210.

301   HM586.S24

Covers the theory and methods which are the framework and foundations of the field, identifies its key subdisciplines, and describes the important debates which provide the creative tension for future work. This 2005 ed. is the third published by Sage; the emphasis is on new directions, leaving coverage of classical theory to the 1964 Handbook (Rand McNally), and coverage of modern foundations to the 1988 Handbook (Sage). This edition is also innovative in including both American and European thinkers and theories. Includes bibliographical references and index.

49 **The Sage handbook of the sociology of religion.** James A. Beckford, N. J. Demerath III. Los Angeles: SAGE, 2007. ISBN: 9781412911955.

At a time of increased attention to matters of faith, the sociology of religion provides a rich source of understanding and explanation. This handbook presents an unprecedentedly comprehensive assessment of the field's past and future. Global in terms of distinguished contributors, topics, and coverage.

The handbook's 35 chapters are organized into eight sections: basic theories and debates; methods of studying religion; social forms and experiences of religion; issues of power and control in religious organizations; religion and politics; individual religious behavior in social context; religion, self-identity, and the life-course; and case studies of China, Eastern Europe, Israel, Japan, and Mexico.

Each chapter establishes benchmarks for the state of sociological thinking about religion in the 21st century and provides a rich bibliography for pursuing its subject further. Stretches the field conceptually, methodologically, comparatively, and historically. Promises to be an indispensable source of guidance and insight for both students and scholars for years to come.

Annotation contributed by Robert Wuthnow of the Department of Sociology, Princeton University.

50 **21st century sociology: A reference handbook.** Clifton D. Bryant, Dennis L. Peck. 2 v., ill. Thousand Oaks, Calif.: SAGE, 2007. ISBN: 1412916089.

301   HM585

Handbook in two extensive volumes which provides a sweeping, yet detailed, survey of sociology as a coherent whole. Draws especially on developments

GENERAL WORKS

27

from the last quarter of the 20th century; covers research and theory in both new and traditional areas. Long-established topics include race, education, criminology, work, and both rural and urban sociology. Evolving fields include diverse topics ranging across the environment, the military, medicine, health, sports, recreation, food, and eating. Recommended as a comprehensive and encyclopedic survey of the field, making good sense of a larger whole.

Indexes; Abstract Journals

51   **C.R.I.S.: The combined retrospective index set to journals in sociology, 1895–1974.** Annadel N. Wile, Arnold Jaffe, Evan I. Farber. 6 v. Washington: Carrollton Press, 1978. ISBN: 0840801947.

016.3   Z7161.C17H1

Covering the 60 years before modern indexing became available for journals in sociology with the advent of *Sociological abstracts* (53) in 1954, CRIS provides access to articles that reflect sociological thought as it developed over this time. Provides a portal to the sociological thought of an earlier and formative time. Provides access to articles in sociology, broadly defined, for the era before subject indexes became available. Since a classed bibliography is so rare today, it can be useful to outline the organization used here:

v. 1,   Anthropology, applied sociology, culture, death and death rates, differentiation and stratification, group interactions;

v. 2,   Institutions: in general, bureaucratic structures, family and formal voluntary organizations;

v. 3,   Institutions: health and medical systems and structures, industrial systems and structures, law and legal systems, military systems and structures, political institutions, religion;

v. 4,   Knowledge, research in sociology, rural systems and structures, sex roles, social change and economic development;

v. 5,   Social disorganization, social ecology, sociology as a profession, theorists (A-Z), theory of sociology, urban systems and structures;

v. 6,   Author index (A-Z).

52   **SocINDEX.** http://www.ebscohost.com/. EBSCO Publishing. Ipswich, Mass.: EBSCO Publishing. 2005–.

HM1

Born digital in 2005, SocINDEX is an abstract and full-text database with coverage of modern sociology and closely-related fields. Provides coverage of both theoretical and applied work, including many links to full text. Some coverage of related topics such as employment (business) and gender (law). Limited coverage of years before 2005. Offers entire contents of 1,000 core journals and selective items from another 3,000 titles. Also indexes monographs and other types of materials. The only source for full text of papers presented at American Sociological Association conferences from 2000 forward. Non-English language articles are included. Advanced searches must be entered as special code.

53   **Sociological abstracts.** http://www.csa.com/factsheets/socioabs-set-c.php. Leo P. Chall, [Sociological Abstracts]. San Diego, [Calif.]: Sociological Abstracts. 1952–. ISSN: 0038-0202.
301   HM1.S67

Comprehensively indexes the world's literature in sociology and related disciplines, both theoretical and applied, from 1952 to the present. Originally published in paper format, but the online version is now preferred, sometimes also referred to as SocioFile. Online coverage extends back to 1952, providing quick searching over all years, with a significant and increasing number of links to full text.

Provides indexing and abstracts for over 1,800 journals, conference papers presented at five major sociological association meetings, numerous dissertations, book reviews, and selected sociology books. Journals are in 30 different languages from about 55 countries, covering sociological topics in fields including anthropology, economics, education, medicine, community development, philosophy, demography, political science, and social psychology. Journals published by sociological associations, groups, faculties, and institutes, and periodicals containing the term "sociology" in their titles, are abstracted fully, irrespective of language or country of publication. Non-core journals are screened for articles by sociologists and/or articles of immediate interest or relevance to sociologists.

Descriptors are drawn from the *Thesaurus of sociological indexing terms* (21).

Quotations

54   **Dictionary of quotations in sociology.** Panos Demetrios Bardis. xiv, 356 p. Westport, Conn.: Greenwood Press, 1985. ISBN: 0313237786.
301.0321   HM17.B37

"Presents the nature, origin, development, and current status of general sociological concepts through direct quotation."—*Pref.* Cross-cultural, interdisciplinary, and historical in coverage. Entries appear in chronological order under alphabetically-arranged subject headings such as alienation, class struggle, ideology, methodology, power, division of labor, and violence. Each entry provides author, source title, and date of publication. Includes bibliographical references and indexes.

55 **Key quotations in sociology.** Kenneth Thompson. 207 p. London; New York: Routledge, 1996. ISBN: 0415135176.
301.03   HM17

Dictionary arrangement of key sociological terms makes up the first part of this volume, with definitions drawn from the writings of important sociological figures of the last 50 years or so. Length of entries varies from a single sentence to several paragraphs. Part two covers 22 key social thinkers of this time period, with emphasis on British and French sociologists. Creates a context for understanding key concepts. Includes bibliographical references and indexes. Available as an e-book.

56 **The Max Weber dictionary: Key words and central concepts.** Richard Swedberg, Ola Agevall. xvi, 344 p., ill. Stanford, Calif.: Stanford Social Sciences, 2005. ISBN: 0804750947.
301.03   HM425.S94

A sampler drawn from the complex writings of the father of sociology. Remarkably fresh nearly a century after Max Weber's life, bridging the gap between his time and ours. Provides a convenient understanding of the roots of sociology.

57 **Social science quotations: Who said what, when, and where.** David L. Sills, Robert King Merton. xxiii, 437 p. New Brunswick, N.J.: Transaction, 2000. ISBN: 0765807203.
300.3   H41.S64

Organized alphabetically by the name of the person quoted. Provides year of birth and death, and a brief statement of nationality and occupation. Quotations range in length from a sentence to a paragraph. Cites the source publ. Index by subject keywords and personal name.

2 › THEORY, METHODS, AND STATISTICS

Atlases and General Overview

58   Methods in behavioral research. 9th ed. Paul C. Cozby. xv, 410 p., ill. New York: McGraw-Hill Higher Education, 2007. ISBN: 9780073531816.

150.72   BF76.5.C67

This is the 9th (and latest) ed. of the standard textbook on methods in the behavioral sciences. Worth a place on the reference shelf because it tells at least something about everything in the field, and does so in a cogent and comprehensive fashion.

Dictionaries and Thesauruses

59   The A–Z of social research: A dictionary of key social science research concepts. Robert L. Miller, John D. Brewer. xv, 345 p., ill. London; Thousand Oaks, Calif.: Sage, 2003. ISBN: 0761971327.

300.72   H62.A5124

Broadly relevant essays on social science research methods and concepts, intended also to function as a textbook for students. Entries in alphabetical order explain topics from historical methods and geographic information systems to statistical interaction and sampling/probability. Presents the advantages, limitations, context, and importance for terms, with citations to additional readings (books and articles).

60   The Sage dictionary of social research methods. Victor Jupp, Sage Publications, Inc. xii, 335 p. London; Thousand Oaks, Calif.: Sage Publications Inc., 2006. ISBN: 0761962972.

300.72   H62.S274

A one-vol. encyclopedia covering major concepts in social research. Over 200 signed articles in alphabetical order on concepts such as sampling, ethnography, the interview, the experiment, and postmodernism. Each article includes a short definition, a discussion of distinctive features, an evaluation of its significance, cross-references to associated concepts, and citations to additional readings. Subject and author indexes.

Encyclopedias

61 **Encyclopedia of social theory.** Austin Harrington, Barbara L. Marshall, Hans-Peter Müller. New York: Routledge, 2006. ISBN: 0415290465.

301.03   HM425.E46

Contains 479 signed entries by international scholars that range in length from one or two paragraphs to six pages or more. Covers social theory from multidisciplinary and international perspectives. Social theory can be obscure and unintelligible in other hands, but these authors are knowledgeable and make the material lucid, comprehensible, and interesting. Includes chronology, bibliographical references, and index.

A comparative note: Less than a third of the entries are also covered in the Sage *Encyclopedia of social theory* (62) published in 2005, although that work is stronger in its biographical entries.

62 **Encyclopedia of social theory.** George Ritzer. 2 v. (xxxviii, 1–982). Thousand Oaks, Calif.: Sage Publications, 2005. ISBN: 0761926119.

301.01   HM425.E47

A highly useful Reader's Guide begins each of the two volumes of this encyclopedia, whose greatest strength is in its biographical emphasis. Some 300 signed entries by international scholars range in length from a paragraph to several thousand words. Many theorists are covered, in alphabetically arranged entries, with extensive and useful detail provided on their life and work. This information is often difficult to locate otherwise. Includes chronology, master bibliography, and overall index. A useful basic resource on social theory for beginning researchers.

Comparative note: The Routledge title of the same name from 2006, provides more coverage of schools of thought in social theory, but not the biographical range and depth found here. Available as an e-book.

63 **The Sage encyclopedia of social science research methods.** Michael S. Lewis-Beck, Alan Bryman, Tim Futing Liao. 3 v., ill. Thousand Oaks, Calif.: Sage, 2004. ISBN: 0761923632.

300.72   H62.L456

Defines and explains terms and concepts in social science research methodology. Some 1,000 entries in alphabetical order, ranging in length from a paragraph to multiple pages depending on their importance, complexity, or extent of the material in question. Concepts covered range from simple topics like the bar graph to the complex, such as partial least squares regression. List of entries, reader's guide by related topics, list of contributors. General bibliography, index. Available as an e-book.

Guides

64   **Bibliography and the sociology of texts.** D. F. McKenzie. 130 p., ill. Cambridge, U.K.; New York: Cambridge University Press, 1999. ISBN: 0521642582.

Z1001.M398

This work makes the case that the form of information influences the understanding of what is recorded. Material form, whether manuscript, print, sound, graphics, film, or electronic media, can have a strong relationship with the meaning derived from that text or other form of information. Further, as a text is transcribed or translated into different formats, the meaning can consequently shift and change. Presents a unifying concept of the meaning of recorded information that can be applied to a wide range of cultural documents.

Also available as an e-book through the ebrary and NetLibrary subscription services.

65   **Foundations of social theory.** James Samuel Coleman. xvi, 993 p., ill. Cambridge, Mass.: Belknap Press of Harvard University Press, 1990. ISBN: 0674312252.

301.01   HM24.C63

The classic work on social theory. Often cited in methods and theory scholarship in the social sciences, Coleman's genius in this manual for sociological theory is in the clarity and brevity with which he treats a range of constructs in social theory. A slight but essential reference volume that should be retained among the later, and more expansive, publications on the topic. Invaluable.

66   **Handbook of measurement issues in family research.** Sandra L. Hofferth, Lynne M. Casper. xv, 497 p., ill. Mahwah, N.J.: Lawrence Erlbaum Associates, 2007. ISBN: 080585617X.

306.85072   HQ10.H24

Twenty-three chapters address quality issues in data collection, as well as measurements and models in quantitative research on families and children. Based on papers presented to a 2003 conference on family demography, and drawing from the fields of sociology, economics, family studies, and child development. Measurement issues with gay and lesbian couples are included. Indexes and extensive bibliographical references.

67   **Handbook of sustainable development planning: Studies in modelling and decision support.** M. A. Quaddus, Muhammed Abu B. Siddique. xii, 347 p., ill. Cheltenham, U.K.; Northhampton, Mass.: Edward Elgar, 2004. ISBN: 1840648791.

338.927   HC79.E5H319

At the intersection of the sociology of urban and regional studies, economic sociology, and the sociology of organizations, lies development planning. In today's world, it is widely believed that sustainable development is essential. This handbook begins with an analysis of the current state of such work and suggests further directions. Part I, chapters 1–4, reviews the modeling of sustainability in terms of planning and development, and also reviews the current literature. Part II, chapters 5–14, looks at modeling as applied to environmental disaster, mining, energy management, land and water management, agri- and aquaculture, and infrastructure. Part III, chapter 15, concludes with future directions. Subject index. Available as an e-book.

68   **Sequential analysis: A guide for behavioral researchers.** John Mordechai Gottman, Anup Kumar Roy. ix, 275 p., ill. Cambridge, [England]; New York: Cambridge University Press, 1990. ISBN: 0521346657.

302.018   HM251.G695

Sequential analysis is a powerful social science research tool, especially for social psychology. It looks for recurring sequential patterns in social interactions in order to study both individuals and groups. This guide was the first to present an integrated approach to understanding sequential analysis. Historical approaches to the field are covered, including stationarity, order, homogeneity, pooling data across subjects, and autocorrelation in inferring cross-correlation. Provides examples of applications in behavioral research. Reviews various computer programs that can be used in this data analysis.

69   **The undergraduate researcher's handbook: Creative experimentation in social psychology.** Ralph J. McKenna. xi, 292

p., ill. Needham Heights, Mass.: Allyn and Bacon, 1995. ISBN: 0205155375.

302.072   HM251.M268

This step-by-step handbook on conducting research projects is sensible and sound. Provides guidance for both the actual research and the corollary supporting work, which includes time management, creation of a resume, keeping records, writing skills, presentation, and even a sample e-mail. Tips on selecting a mentor to help in the process are also provided. Handbook provides solid guidance across the board, as it contains strategies and tools applicable to a broad range of classes and subjects. Includes bibliographical references and indexes. Quite useful, and not just for social psychology. Recommended for advanced high school and undergraduate-level use. Valuable for general and college collections that serve adult students, in both distance learning and community college settings.

Handbooks

70   **Analyzing social settings: A guide to qualitative observation and analysis.** 4th ed. John Lofland. xxi, 282 p., ill. Belmont, Calif.: Wadsworth/Thomson Learning, 2006. ISBN: 0534528619.

301.072   HM571

In its 4th ed., this continues to be the classic field manual for social science research. Teaches three critical areas: gathering, focusing, and analyzing data. Includes illustrations from classic sociological fieldwork, from *Street corner society* to *Tally's corner.* How-to approach makes the methods of qualitative data collection and analysis very clear. First published in 1971, title has changed with the times and now includes a helpful discussion of the use of evolving computer technology in the gathering and analysis of field data. Now covers institutional review boards, newly-created on most college campuses. Bibliographical references and index.

71   **Classical and modern social theory.** Heine Andersen, Lars Bo Kaspersen. xi, 524 p. Malden, Mass.: Blackwell, 2000. ISBN: 0631212876.

301.01   HM606.D36K53

In one volume of highly readable essays, nearly every social theory any student or researcher might want to build on, or may chance to encounter, is described in cogent terms. A clear encyclopedic handbook on social theory. Highly recommended for research collections.

72   **Essential guide to qualitative methods in organizational research.** Catherine Cassell, Gillian Symon. xviii, 388 p., ill. London; Thousand Oaks, [Calif.]: SAGE Publications, 2004. ISBN: 0761948872.

302.35072   HM786.E87

A thorough handbook that covers all aspects of qualitative methods in organizational research. Interviews, analysis, case study research, and soft system research are among the topics explored. The 30 articles, with footnotes, focus on the individual discipline in which the research is framed, as well as the care necessary to design and conduct research. Describes a wide range of methods and their applications. Forward-looking techniques include using life histories and both in-person and electronic interviews. A wide range of individual research methods are covered, including the 20 statement test, research diaries, and ethnography. Bibliographical references and index.

73   **A handbook for action research in health and social care.** Richard Winter, Carol Munn-Giddings, Cathy Aymer. xvi, 281 p., ill. London; New York: Routledge, 2001. ISBN: 0415224837.

362.072   HV11.W597

Action research, closely allied to practice, can be used in the fields of social work, medical care, nursing, and community work to investigate various aspects of care. Clear definitions are provided and case studies are included to make the suggestions practical. Includes bibliographical references and index. Available as an e-book.

74   **Handbook of contemporary European social theory.** Gerard Delanty. xxv, 419 p., ill. London; New York: Routledge, 2006. ISBN: 0415355184.

301.094   HM477.E85

The recent rise of the new and relatively unified Europe has seen the creation of a multidisciplinary matrix of diverse social theories. This handbook examines the changes through contributed articles in five thematic sections: 1) Disciplinary Traditions, 2) National Traditions (including German, French, British, Italian, Spanish, Nordic, East Central Europe, and Russian social theories), 3) Intellectual Traditions, 4) Themes and Narratives, and 5) Global Perspectives, which relates European social theory to that of Asia, the United States, and Latin America. One of the most useful works on social theory to be published in recent years, and not just for Europe. Index. Available as an e-book.

75   **Handbook of research methods in social and personality psychology.** Harry T. Reis, Charles M. Judd. xii, 558 p., ill. New York: Cambridge University Press, 2000. ISBN: 0521551285.

302.072   HM1019.H36

An important and comprehensive handbook that covers research methodology in social psychology in some 15 signed essays. Titles of essays are descriptive: "Nasty data: Unruly, ill-mannered observations can ruin your analysis." The concluding chapter on quantitative synthesis alone is worth its price. Includes bibliographical references and indexes.

76   **The multilevel design: A guide with an annotated bibliography, 1980-1993.** Harry J. M. Hüttner, Pieter van den Eeden. viii, 276 p. Westport, Conn.: Greenwood Press, 1995. ISBN: 0313273103.

016.30072   Z7161.A15H88; H62

Multilevel research is a fundamental construct in social science research. It acknowledges that individuals belong to groups, which in turn have relationships with other groups, and those in turn form larger groups, and so on. Research must deal with groups at all appropriate levels for true validation. This useful guide explains this construct in six clear and well-written chapters. An annotated bibliography of sources follows, divided into useful sections that cover books and journal articles written from 1980 through 1993. Author, title, and subject indexes.

77   **Participant observation: A guide for fieldworkers.** Kathleen Musante DeWalt, Billie R. DeWalt. ix, 285 p. Walnut Creek, Calif.: AltaMira Press, 2002. ISBN: 0759100446.

305.800723   GN346.4

Which guiding principles and practical approaches are the most effective in fieldwork that uses participant observation with human subjects? This basic guide offers a strategy and methodology for beginning such work and collecting useful data. How can investigation be structured so it doesn't mask or interfere with what is being measured? What are ethical concerns in dealing with human subjects?

78   **The Sage handbook of methods in social psychology.** Carol Sansone, Carolyn C. Morf, A. T. Panter. xxvii, 528 p., ill. Thousand Oaks, [Calif.]: Sage Publications, 2004. ISBN: 076192535X.

302.01   HM1019.S24

Basic handbook of the methodological framework for social psychology is made up of signed chapters in three sections. First section examines the research process and suggests ways to focus on the goals to be accomplished; second section outlines structures and strategies for design and analysis, with statistical analysis at a basic level. Third section looks at ethical considerations and cross-disciplinary enrichments that can be achieved. Includes bibliographical references and indexes.

79 **Tricks of the trade: How to think about your research while you're doing it.** Howard Saul Becker. xi, 232 p. Chicago: University of Chicago Press, 1998. ISBN: 0226041239.

300.72 H91

Drawing on a wide range of fields in the humanities and social sciences, a strategy is offered for beginning research or for strengthening one's research in the social sciences. The "tricks of the trade" apply to both quantitative and qualitative research and draw on four steps. The first is to use imagery to see where research might go; the second offers ways to sample data in order to get as much variety as possible in the data being collected; the third is to find concepts that will organize what is found; and finally, the fourth is to use logic to consider the implications of the research. Such strategies can seem obvious and intuitive to experienced researchers; for neophytes, this advice provides a starting point in what can otherwise seem an overwhelming process.

Statistics

80 **Dictionary of statistics and methodology: A nontechnical guide for the social sciences.** 3rd ed. W. Paul Vogt. xix, 355 p., ill. Thousand Oaks, Calif.: Sage Publications, 2005. ISBN: 0761988548.

300.15195 HA17.V64

Intended for specialists in the social and behavioral sciences who are not trained in statistics. Defines statistical and methodological terms used in the social sciences. Definitions tend to be verbal rather than mathematical. Available as an e-book.

81 **The Sage dictionary of statistics: A practical resource for students in the social sciences.** Duncan Cramer, Dennis Howitt. x, 188 p. London; Thousand Oaks, Calif.: Sage Publications, 2004. ISBN: 0761941371.

519.503 HA17.C73

Defines significant terms in statistics. Includes see and see also references for related words and phrases. A compact dictionary that includes links to Internet sites.

3 > SOCIAL CONDITIONS AND SOCIAL WELFARE

General Works

Handbooks

82   **Human development reports.** United Nations Development Programme. ill. New York: Oxford University Press, 1990–. ISSN: 0969-4501.

306.305   HD72.H85

In 1990, under the aegis of the U.N.'s Development Programme Office, the first annual global *Human development report* was published. It created a furor because the social indicators (they were added to traditional national economic measures) revealed glaring problems among the citizenry of most countries in the world. In the years since 1990, hundreds of national, regional, and city-level *Human development reports* have been created. Each contains a lengthy narrative focused on some aspect of human development, and extensive, carefully gathered and vetted statistical measures.

This series is one of the more comprehensive and useful reports on the social and economic situation of the world's people at all levels. In addition to the main report, as well as some of the regional or national reports that are available for purchase in paper, the U.N. Development Programme's website offers both the global and the current regional, national, and local *Human development reports* in PDF format, at no cost, at: http://hdr.undp.org/. Website also offers a data search capacity.

Also available are CD-ROM compilations of the global reports spanning 15 years or more.

The *Human development reports* in all their permutations are valuable for reference work on a broad range of social and economic issues around the globe.

Aging and the Elderly

Atlases and General Overview

83   **Data collections from the National Archive of Computerized Data on Aging.** National Archive of Computerized Data on Aging (U.S.). Summer 1993–; v., Annual. Ann Arbor, Mich.: Interuniversity Consortium for Political and Social Research, 1993–.

Largest library of electronic data on aging in the United States offers materials for secondary analysis on major issues of scientific and policy relevance. NACDA supports intellectual vitality in the gerontological sciences. Print publication annually or twice annually from 1993 through 2002; electronic resource, CD-ROM 2003 and following. On the Web at http://www.icpsr.umich.edu/NACDA.

Bibliography

84   **Aging well: A selected, annotated bibliography.** W. Edward Folts. x, 156 p. Westport, Conn.: Greenwood Press, 1995. ISBN: 0313287716.

016.30526   Z7164.O4A37; HQ1061

Identifies important resources in the study of aging and the elderly up until the publication of this title. Since this sits on the leading edge of the era of full-text and electronic indexes, which began to cover in a comprehensive way the study of gerontology, there is permanent reference value in this title in any serious research collection. Don't send it to storage.

85   **Annotated bibliography on productive ageing in Asia and the Pacific.** United Nations. vii, 181 p. Bangkok, [Thailand]: Economic and Social Commission for Asia and the Pacific, United Nations, 1996.

Z7164.O4A54; HQ1064.A78

Older people in many cultures of Asia and the Pacific are held in high regard. What are the effects associated with this circumstance, and how do older people in this region remain highly productive well into their senior years? Includes indexes.

86   **The Black aged in the United States: A selectively annotated bibliography.** 2nd ed. Lenwood G. Davis. xiv, 277 p. New York: Greenwood Press, 1989. ISBN: 0313259313.

016.3052608996073   Z1361.N39D354; E185.86

More than 600 entries identify books, journal articles, dissertations, theses, and government documents dealing with aging among African Americans up until the date of this publication in 1989. Historical notes recount aging issues among enslaved African Americans. Directory of homes for elderly black persons is given for the years 1860 to 1988. A part of African American history that is difficult, if not impossible, to find elsewhere.

87   **Drug abuse and the elderly: An annotated bibliography.** Douglas H. Ruben. xxii, 247 p. Metuchen, N.J.: Scarecrow Press, 1984. ISBN: 0810816776.

016.3622920880565   Z7164.N17R82; HV5801

Although more than 20 years old, this bibliography provides a useful window onto a broad range of literature on alcohol and drug use among elderly Americans. As a cross-disciplinary field, and at a time when elder issues were not often well-respected, references lead to the literature that was being produced for a then rather neglected field. Modern online indexes and full-text resources seldom reach back this far or link to the broad range of materials found here.

Directories

88   **Resource directory for older people: NIH publication no. 01–738.** National Institute on Aging. 111 p. [Bethesda, Md.]: U.S. Department of Health and Human Services, Public Health Service, National Institutes of Health, 2001 update.

362.6302573   HV1450.R47

A fully-annotated directory of 67 organizations and associations that provide information and services for the elderly in America, and to social workers and medical professionals who care for them. Each entry includes full contact information, including address, phone, fax, e-mail, and website. Entries include numerous professional medical associations; a number of federal agencies including Labor, Justice, Transportation, and

Veterans Affairs; advocacy groups such as the Medicare Rights Center; wellness groups such as the National Association for Health and Fitness; nutrition advocacy programs, including Meals on Wheels; and to help pay for it all, the Senior Job Bank, to give a sampling of the coverage. Appendixes list state agencies and ombudsman offices. Index.

Also available electronically at http://www.aoa.gov/eldfam/how_to _find/resourcedirectory/resource_directory.aspx.

Encyclopedias

89   **Encyclopedia of ageism.** Erdman Ballagh Palmore, Laurence G. Branch, Diana K. Harris. xviii, 347 p. Binghamton, N.Y.: Haworth Pastoral Press; Haworth Reference Press, 2005. ISBN: 0789018896.

305.2603   HQ1061.E63

Ageism, defined broadly in this work as discrimination against the elderly, is seen by some as pervasive in American culture and harmful to all ages in society. This encyclopedia deals with some 125 aspects of ageism in signed essays written by 60 contributors. Places some emphasis on the negative and even dangerous aspects of getting old in a mixture of popular culture, legal frameworks, medical treatment of the elderly, and so on. One small section of index entries includes, in alphabetical order, Suicide, Tax breaks, Television, Terms preferred by older people, Theories of aging, Transportation, Types of ageists, and so on. This is a remarkably complete and useful reference work on discrimination against the elderly.

90   **Encyclopedia of aging.** David J. Ekerdt. 4 v., ill. New York: Macmillan Reference USA, 2002. ISBN: 0028654722.

305.2603   HQ1061.E534

A basic, interdisciplinary gerontology encyclopedia for general readers. Entries cover a broad range of sociological, psychological, legal, economic, medical, biological, and public policy subjects. Includes source documents, cross-references, bibliographies at the end of each article, and a list of articles grouped by topical areas. Not so comprehensive as to be overwhelming, this is a basic resource which can serve as a good starting point for some researchers, even for middle and high school students, as well as for older levels. Available as an e-book.

91   **Encyclopedia of aging.** 4th ed. Richard Schulz. 2 v., 720 p. New York: Springer, 2006. ISBN: 0826148433.

305.2603   HQ1061.E53

From the 1st ed. in 1987, this encyclopedia has provided a thorough presentation of a wide range of items, issues, and facts dealing with aging. Now in its 4th ed., it documents in thoughtful essays many aspects of the lives of older persons, as well as issues and services for the elderly. Made up of some 600 essays, including 200 that are entirely new, with others significantly updated. Multidisciplinary, covering relevant materials from biology, physiology, genetics, medicine, psychology, nursing, social services, sociology, economics, technology, and political science. Extensive listing of further resources, cross-references, and thorough index. Definitive work on gerontology and geriatrics. A must-have reference title for general and research collections. Available as an e-book.

92   **Encyclopedia of gerontology.** 2nd ed. James E. Birren. 2 v. Oxford, U.K.; San Diego, Calif: Academic Press/Elsevier, 2007. ISBN: 0123705304.

RC952.5.E58

1st ed., 1996.

Alphabetical arrangement of 181 articles on all aspects of aging, the aged, old age, with topics such as theories of aging, biological, behavioral, social, and environmental influences on aging, etc. Written in a standard format, each chapter includes a brief table of contents, a glossary of words with definitions as used in the chapter, and brief bibliography. Cross-references; subject index. Intended for students and professionals.

Other well-regarded, but less recent or comprehensive gerontology encyclopedias are Ekerdt's 2002 *Encyclopedia of aging*, or Schulz' 2006 *Encyclopedia of aging* (4th ed., 2006).

93   **Encyclopedia of health and aging.** Kyriakos S. Markides. 650 p. Thousand Oaks, Calif: Sage Publications, 2007. ISBN: 9781412909495.

613.043803   RA777.6.E534

Resource on health and aging in the United States and abroad. "Reader's Guide" lists entries by key themes and topics, with entries contributed from different disciplines (e.g., biology, epidemiology, health psychology, public policy, sociology, and others) related to health and aging: aging and the brain; diseases and medical conditions; drug-related issues; function and syndromes; mental health and psychology; nutritional issues; physical status; prevention and health behaviors; sociodemographic and cultural issues; studies of aging and systems of care. Also addresses economic issues and provides recent research results and facts on health and aging. Includes further readings, bibliographical references, a list of online resources, and index. Appropriate for academic, various types of health sciences libraries, and public libraries.

94   **Encyclopedia of retirement and finance.** 2nd ed. Lois A. Vitt, E. Craig MacBean, Jürg K. Siegenthaler, Institute for Socio-Financial Studies. 2 v., ill. Westport, Conn.: Greenwood Press, 2003. ISBN: 0313324956.

305.2603   HQ1064.U5E524

Dealing with the financial aspects of retirement, aging, and being old, this is an updated version of the 1996 *Encyclopedia of financial gerontology*. Some 185 signed entries in alphabetic format are grouped into nine sections: Advisers, Advice and Support; Economic and Income Security; Employment, Work and Retirement; Family and Intergenerational Issues; Financial Investments and Insurance; Health Care and Health Coverage; Housing and Housing Finance; Legal Issues; and Quality of Life and Well-Being. Especially useful are entries dealing with Family, Ethical and Legal Issues, and Housing, Health Care and Security concerns. Cross-references. Includes bibliographical references and extensive index. Highly recommended for both general and research collections. Available as an e-book.

95   **The graying of America: An encyclopedia of aging, health, mind, and behavior.** 2nd ed. Donald H. Kausler, Barry C. Kausler. xiv, 479 p. [Champaign], Ill.: University of Illinois Press, 2001. ISBN: 0252026357.

305.2603   HQ1064.U5K39

Contains some 470 entries in alphabetical order, most of them added or revised since the 1st ed. This 2nd ed. became the basis for another title (really the 3rd ed. of *Graying of America*) published in 2007 as *Essential guide to aging in the twenty-first century: Mind, body, and behavior* (100). Subject index.

Guides

96   **Alcoholism and aging: An annotated bibliography and review.** Nancy J. Osgood, Helen E. Wood, Iris A. Parham. xi, 250 p. Westport, Conn.: Greenwood Press, 1995. ISBN: 0313283982.

016.3622920846   Z7721.O83; HV5138

Covering the time period 1965 through 1995, authorities from several disciplines identify materials that deal with alcoholism in the elderly. Senior alcoholism is reported to be a serious and underreported problem. Includes a 50 p. literature review, with abstracts for over 300 sources of various materials: books, chapters, journal articles, and other works. Bibliography, cross-references, and index.

97   **Building library collections on aging: A selection guide and core list.** Mary Jo Brazil. x, 174 p. Santa Barbara, Calif.: ABC-CLIO, 1990. ISBN: 0874365597.

025.2761267   Z688.A58B7

Covers the basic principles of organizing a library collection of materials on aging. Includes index.

Handbooks

98   **Aging well: The complete guide to physical and emotional health.** Jeanne Y. Wei, Sue Levkoff. x, 373 p., ill. New York: Wiley, 2000. ISBN: 047132678X.

613.0438   RA777.6.W43

Popular, well-rounded, and thorough work on the steps the elderly and their care givers can take to enhance their health and longevity. Also available in Chinese translation, 2005.

99   **The Cambridge handbook of age and ageing.** Malcolm Lewis Johnson, Vern L. Bengtson, Peter G. Coleman. xxvi, 744 p., ill. Cambridge, [U.K.]; New York: Cambridge University Press, 2005. ISBN: 0521533708.

305.26   HQ1061.C315

Some 80 chapters contributed by authors from 16 countries on five continents focus on the behavioral and social sciences; also covers biological and medical aspects of aging. Key topics include theories of aging, demography, physical aspects of aging, mental processes and aging, nursing and health care for older people, the social context of aging, cross-cultural perspectives, relationships, quality of life, gender, and financial and policy for aging and the elderly. Cross-national perspective. Bibliographies, index. Available as an e-book.

100   **The essential guide to aging in the twenty-first century: Mind, body, and behavior.** [3rd ed.] Donald H. Kausler, Barry C. Kausler,

Jill A. Krupsaw. xiii, 516 p. Columbia, [Mo.]: University of Missouri Press, 2007. ISBN: 9780826217073.

305.2603   HQ1064.U5K30

Really the 3rd ed. of the *Graying of America*, this volume builds on the strengths of that former title, presenting the biological and psychological aspects of aging in a concise and non-technical way that is still clear and takes the reader seriously. Includes nearly 588 entries, including 172 new ones and 150 which have been substantially revised. This volume has added important research from the last five years, for example, the interaction of health issues (such as hearing) on the health of a spouse or partner, the importance of getting enough sunlight and sleep, and what makes a quality nursing home. Includes bibliographical references and indexes. A comprehensive handbook to growing old with strength and grace. Available as an e-book.

101   The handbook of aging and cognition. 3rd ed. Fergus I. M. Craik, Timothy A. Salthouse. New York: Psychology Press, 2007. ISBN: 9780805859904.

155.6713   BF724.85.C64H36

Everyone gets forgetful eventually, right? The answer is that it depends. This careful and well-researched handbook details in factual and exact terms what does and does not happen to cognitive ability in the aging process, with and without complications of illness and disease. Includes much new theory and research from the last seven years since the previous edition. Includes bibliographical references and indexes. Available as an e-book.

102   Handbook of aging and mental health: An integrative approach. Ya'akov Lomrants. xix, 539 p., ill. New York: Plenum Press, 1998. ISBN: 0306457504.

618.97689   BF724.8.H35

The social, psychological, and physical aspects of aging are covered in a comprehensive fashion in this well-researched handbook on aging and all aspects of health. Includes bibliographical references and index.

103   Handbook of aging and the family. Rosemary Blieszner, Victoria Hilkevitch Bedford, Lillian E. Troll. xxiii, 509 p., ill. Westport, Conn.: Greenwood Press, 1995. ISBN: 0313283958.

305.26   HQ1061.H3353

In what is delicately termed the second half of life, this handbook examines the role that families play in the life of an older person, even as that person becomes truly old. Siblings, grandparenting, legal issues, and cultural diversity are among the diverse topics covered. The family is the first and also the last social network in most people's lives. Being older, if anything, strengthens that importance. Friends who are as close as family count, too. Includes bibliographical references and index.

104   Handbook of aging and the social sciences. 6th ed. Robert H.
     Binstock, Linda K. George, Stephen J. Cutler. xxv, 514 p., ill.
     Amsterdam, [Netherlands]; Boston: Academic Press, an imprint of
     Elsevier, 2006. ISBN: 0120883880.
305.26   HQ1061.H336

What can the social sciences tell us about getting old? A number of answers are provided from various disciplines in this comprehensive handbook. Twenty-five signed chapters are drawn from the fields of anthropology, bioethics, demography, economics, epidemiology, law, political science, psychology, and sociology. Includes bibliographical references and indexes.

105   Handbook of Asian aging. Hyunsook Yoon, Jon Hendricks. xvi, 495
     p. Amityville, N.Y.: Baywood, 2006. ISBN: 089503316X.
305.26095   HQ1064.A78H35

What are the special considerations for older populations in Asia? Does the traditional respect, verging on veneration, for the elderly translate into care by family and governmental agencies? How adequate is the support provided to older people in Asia? And how do elderly Asians view their own aging? Interesting answers are suggested for these questions in this handbook, and a survey of the situation of the elderly in Asia is presented. Includes bibliographical references and index.

106   Handbook of communication and aging research. 2nd ed. Jon
     F. Nussbaum, Justine Coupland. xvii, 596 p., ill. Mahwah, N.J.:
     Lawrence Erlbaum Associates, 2004. ISBN: 0805840702.
305.26   HQ1061.H3365

Aging as reflected in sociolinguistics, and shown in a variety of cultural contexts, informs the social aging focus of this handbook. Deals with stereotypes of older persons in the media. Also describes the place of electronic communication in keeping seniors active and connected with their families and in their communities. What does it mean to get older? To be older? Available as an e-book.

107   The handbook of elder care resources for the federal workplace.
U.S. Office of Personnel Management. 68 p., ill., map. Washington: U.S. Office of Personnel Management, Office of Workforce Relations, Family-Friendly Workplace Advocacy Office, 2000.

HV1461

Useful handbook spells out guidelines for federal employees to care for elderly relatives and others close to them. Includes bibliographical references.

108   Handbook of emotion, adult development, and aging. Carol Magai, Susan H. McFadden. xxi, 470 p., ill. San Diego, [Calif.]: Academic Press, 1996. ISBN: 0124649955.

152.4   BF531.H316

What happens to the ability to feel and respond in emotional terms as aging occurs? This remarkable handbook presents answers with a multi-disciplinary perspective on emotional development and issues for adults, extending into midlife and senior years. Well-documented signed chapters are divided into five sections: Part one covers theoretical perspectives including biological, discrete emotions, ethological, humanistic, and psychosocial. Part two (affect and cognition) deals with the role of emotion in memory, problem solving, and internal perceptions of self and gender. Part three (emotion and relationships) deals with sibling, parent, and child relationships, friends and romantic partners, and reactions to loss at all ages. Part four (stress, health, and psychological well-being) treats coping, along with religion, personality, and quality of life. Part five (continuity and change in emotion patterns and personality) covers emotion over the entire lifespan. Includes bibliographical references and index. Available as an e-book.

109   Handbook of the biology of aging. 6th ed. Edward J. Masoro, Steven N. Austad. xx, 660 p., ill. Amsterdam, [Netherlands]; Boston: Elsevier Academic Press, 2006. ISBN: 0120883872.

612.67   QP86.H35

Aging happens in various ways, the physical being one of the most fundamental. This handbook provides a solid foundation for understanding changes the body goes through as it ages. A good starting place for serious study of what aging means in other ways. Includes bibliographical references and index.

110 **Handbook of the life course.** Jeylan T. Mortimer, Michael J. Shanahan. xx, 728 p., ill. New York: Kluwer Academic/Plenum Publishers, 2003. ISBN: 0306474980.

305.2   HQ799.95.H36

Life Course Studies, a recent construct in social psychology, examines the sequence of roles played out in the ages of a lifetime. In this handbook, 59 authors have contributed 34 chapters organized around seven themes of the Life Course. Content includes essays, reports on empirical research, and presentation of various analytical models. Some work reported is classic, while other is new and original. Includes both historical and cross-national perspectives. Classic themes include considerations of the role of gender, class, and race. A remarkable synthesis of heavy theory immediately related to events and transitions in individual lives. Includes bibliographical references and index. Available as an e-book.

111 **Handbook of the psychology of aging.** 6th ed. James E. Birren, K. Warner Schaie, Ronald P. Abeles. xxi, 564 p., ill. Amsterdam, [Netherlands]; Boston: Elsevier Academic Press, 2006. ISBN: 0121012646.

155.67   BF724.55.A35H36

Twenty signed essays delve into the psychology of aging from a variety of perspectives. Beginning with questions raised by theoretical issues in aging, articles discuss cognitive neuroscience, lifespan theory, how reading and language relate to aging, as well as what can be learned from problem solving, motivation, and even attitudes toward aging. Volume concludes with consideration of wisdom, memory, and religion in later life. Readable essays that present some weighty material in comprehensible form. A useful volume for both general and research collections.

112 **Handbook on ethical issues in aging.** Tanya F. Johnson. xii, 420 p. Westport, Conn.: Greenwood Press, 1999. ISBN: 0313287260.

174.2   HV1451.H35

In whose best interest are ethical issues about aging framed? Beginning with this overarching question, ten signed essays examine matters of diversity, religion, and spirituality in creating an ethical framework for considering issues of aging. Medicine, quality of care, and terminal care are also discussed. The final three chapters deal with impaired judgment, mental health, and personal safety. A thoughtful and well-referenced volume that explores the gray interdisciplinary worlds of ethics and the elderly, and manages to shed some welcome light on areas where they intersect. Includes bibliographical references and indexes. Available as an e-book.

Internet Resources

113 **AgeLine.** http://www.ebscohost.com/thisTopic. php?marketID=1&topicID=23. AARP (American Association of Retired People). Ipswich, Mass.: EBSCO. 2004–.

HQ1061

AgeLine is a comprehensive index, with abstracts. Provides coverage of the scholarly and professional literature on aging and age-related matters, including the delivery of health care to the older population and its costs, and various public policy issues. Covers 1978 to the present, with selected coverage from 1966–77. Materials include books, chapters from books, journal articles, dissertations, videos, and a surprisingly broad range of gray literature. Does not include book reviews, editorials, newspapers, individual conference papers, and statistical data.

Full text is linked when available, and ordering information is provided for priced publications. Publications indexed in this database use *Thesaurus of aging terminology*, a controlled vocabulary of subject terms, currently in its 8th ed.

Formerly a free database provided by the American Association of Retired People (AARP), AgeLine is now only available via subscription through EBSCOhost. Website provides clear user information for the database and excellent guidance for those, of any age or academic level, writing about aging matters. Also of note is AARP's companion Internet Resources on Aging at http://www.aarp.org/internetresources/.

Appropriate for school, general, and research collections.

Alcoholism and Drug Abuse

Bibliography

114 **Alcohol and other drug abuse among homeless individuals: An annotated bibliography.** M. Susan Ridgely, Caroline T. McNeil, Howard H. Goldman, National Institute on Alcohol Abuse and

Alcoholism (U.S.). ix, 37 p. Rockville, Md.: U.S. Department of Health and Human Services, Public Health Service, Alcohol, Drug Abuse, and Mental Health Administration, National Institute on Alcohol Abuse and Alcoholism, [1990].

Z7721.R53; HV5140

Actual circumstance is examined against the classic stereotype of the homeless person as a "wino" or a "druggie." The homeless are often a difficult population to study, as are alcoholics and those addicted to drugs, especially because of the privacy concerns so strongly held today. This bibliography covers a time when research subjects were more readily available. Unfortunately, since this work was published, little has changed in the severity of both homelessness and alcoholism as social problems, so it remains relevant.

115   **Alcohol and reproduction: A bibliography.** Ernest L. Abel. xix, 219 p. Westport, Conn.: Greenwood Press, 1982. ISBN: 0313234744.
016.6183   Z6671.2.F46A26; RG629.F45

The effects of alcohol and drug abuse on unborn children are covered thoroughly. Documents how alcohol and drugs affect the bodies of women who abuse them. Provides a solid block of references for a time before online indexes and full-text databases really covered this difficult topic. Useful both for content and as social history.

116   **Alcohol and sexuality: An annotated bibliography on alcohol use, alcoholism, and human sexual behavior.** Timothy J. O'Farrell, Carolyn A. Weyand, Diane Logan. xii, 131 p. Phoenix, Ariz.: Oryx Press, 1983. ISBN: 0897740408.
016.61669   HV5201.S48O33

Building on the popular culture model that alcohol frees sexual inhibitions, the materials referenced in this bibliography document the effects, both short- and long-term, on both attitudes and abilities in sexual behavior. More than two decades after its original publication, still a useful source.

117   **Alcohol and the family: A comprehensive bibliography.** Grace M. Barnes, Diane K. Augustino. xiii, 461 p. New York: Greenwood Press, 1987. ISBN: 031324782X.
016.362292   Z7721.B364; HV5132

Alcoholism's effect on the social and economic relationships in the family are covered in detail in the materials referenced in this bibliography. What are the immediate and long-term effects on the children of alcoholics? What are the psychological implications of alcoholism? How does treatment work for the family? Some of the referenced studies might be blocked today because of modern privacy concerns, so this listing from a more open time is still very useful.

118   **Alcohol and youth: A comprehensive bibliography.** Grace M. Barnes, Robert J. Brown. xvi, 452 p. Westport, Conn.: Greenwood Press, 1982. ISBN: 0313231362.
016.362292088055   Z7721.B37; HV5824.Y68

Youth in North America are in grave danger from alcoholism, and alcohol use is dangerously widespread among them. Risk factors, overall considerations, and particular groups and ages are covered in detail. Because this print work covers material up to the time when cross-disciplinary online indexes began, it is an excellent companion to the earlier time period. Should be retained in reference collections of research libraries.

119   **Alcohol in the British Isles from Roman times to 1996: An annotated bibliography.** David W. Gutzke. xvii, 266 p. Westport, Conn.: Greenwood Press, 1996. ISBN: 0313294208.
016.394130941   Z7721.A42; HV5446

Alcohol has had a strong presence in the British Isles for at least 2,000 years, as the many references provided in this title attest. Annotations identify those items of particular interest. Bibliography and index.

120   **Alcohol use and world cultures: A comprehensive bibliography of anthropological sources.** Dwight B. Heath, A. M. Cooper. xv, 248 p. Toronto: Addiction Research Foundation, 1981. ISBN: 0888680457.
016.39413   Z7721.H4; HV5035

The cultural context of alcohol, at the social level, and at the alcoholic level, is examined in great detail in societies around the world. Comparisons are drawn among cultures, and references lead to a wealth of material that can strengthen research and understanding of alcohol use, in a broad sense, in various cultures. Worth keeping even 25 years after publication both for content and as a fill-in for the time before online indexes and full-text databases began, and before they expanded international coverage, which is still rather thin in 2007.

121   **Alcoholism and aging: An annotated bibliography and review.**
Nancy J. Osgood, Helen E. Wood, Iris A. Parham. xi, 250 p.
Westport, Conn.: Greenwood Press, 1995. ISBN: 0313283982.
016.3622920846   Z7721.O83; HV5138

Covering the time period 1965 through 1995, authorities from several
disciplines identify materials that deal with alcoholism in the elderly.
Senior alcoholism is reported to be a serious and underreported problem.
Includes a 50 p. literature review, with abstracts for over 300 sources of
various materials: books, chapters, journal articles, and other works. Bibliography, cross-references, and index.

122   **Black alcohol abuse and alcoholism: An annotated bibliography.**
Thomas D. Watts, Roosevelt Wright. xix, 265 p. New York: Praeger,
1986. ISBN: 0030057132.
016.36229208996073   Z7721.W37; HV5292

For the time period before online indexes began full coverage, this print
resource is still valuable for leading researchers to documentation on
alcoholism among African Americans. The cultural context provided is a
valuable addition to present-day electronic resources. The narrow focus
strengthens the breadth of coverage of alcoholism.

123   **Drug abuse and the elderly: An annotated bibliography.** Douglas
H. Ruben. xxii, 247 p. Metuchen, N.J.: Scarecrow Press, 1984. ISBN:
0810816776.
016.3622920880565   Z7164.N17R82; HV5801

Although more than 20 years old, this bibliography provides a useful
window onto a broad range of literature on alcohol and drug use among
elderly Americans. As a cross-disciplinary field, and at a time when elder
issues were not often well-respected, references lead to the literature that
was being produced for a then rather neglected field. Modern online
indexes and full-text resources seldom reach back this far or link to the
broad range of materials found here.

124   **Jewish alcoholism and drug addiction: An annotated bibliography.**
Steven L. Berg. xviii, 160 p. Westport, Conn.: Greenwood Press,
1993. ISBN: 031327603X.
016.3629089924   Z7721.B45; HV5185

The cultural aspects of Jewish life that can affect the onset and treatment
of alcoholism and drug abuse are considered in detail. Incidence of substance abuse among Jews is included. Indexes.

125 **Message in a bottle: Theoretical overview and annotated bibliography on the mass media and alcohol.** Nicholas Dorn, Nigel South. ix, 178 p. Aldershot, Hants, England; Brookfield, Vt.: Gower, 1983. ISBN: 0566006219.
016.362292   Z7721.D67; HV5035

The mass media's depiction of alcohol consumption has sometimes been problematic both as to accuracy and effect. This work begins with an overview of media and alcohol, and then provides an annotated bibliography that leads to a wealth of further materials. The first wake-up call, in 1983, for the media to become aware of its role and responsibility in alcohol reporting and education, and still relevant today.

126 **Substance abuse among ethnic minorities in America: A critical annotated bibliography.** Howard M. Rebach. 469 p. New York: Garland, 1992. ISBN: 0815300662.
016.3622908693   Z7164.D78S8; HV5825

This lengthy annotated bibliography offers a rich compilation of references for the study of alcohol and drug abuse among the various ethnic minorities in the United States. Cultural factors from ethnic traditions are suggested, and readings explore the relationship of each ethnic minority to the mainstream culture, as an enabling or even causative factor.

127 **Work and alcohol abuse: An annotated bibliography.** John J. Miletich. xvii, 263 p. New York: Greenwood Press, 1987. ISBN: 0313256896.
016.33125   Z7164.C81M619; HF5549.5.A47

Extensive annotated bibliography references the effect of alcoholism on both the alcoholic and the place of employment. Incidence of alcoholism in various job categories and professions is covered, and the effects of work-based alcohol treatment are included. The legal framework for dealing with alcoholism at work has shifted in the two decades since original publication, and new job situations have arisen, but for the topics covered here this is still a solid resource.

Dictionaries and Thesauruses

128 **The alcohol and other drug (AOD) thesaurus: A guide to concepts and terminology in substance abuse and addiction.** 3rd ed. National Institute on Alcohol Abuse and Alcoholism. 4 v. [Rockville,

Md.]: U.S. Department of Health and Human Services, Public
Health Service, 2000.

HV5804

A multilevel dictionary that can be searched by broad outline, quick hierarchy, detailed outline, or annotated hierarchy for a focus on alcohol and
other drugs. Clicking down to get to the actual definitions can be cum-
bersome, but the correct level yields a careful and detailed definition and
context. Highly useful in both research and popular collections.

129   The A-Z encyclopedia of alcohol and drug abuse. Thomas
Nordegren. 682 p. Parkland, Fla.: Brown Walker Press, 2002. ISBN:
158112404X.

616.86003   RC564.N667

Alcohol and narcotics dictionary on a grand scale. Alphabetic entries range
over international usage relating to illegal drugs. This title is especially
valuable to explain and put into context up-to-date listings and coverage
of both mod and slang terms dealing with alcoholism and drug abuse.

**130   Intoxication in mythology: A worldwide dictionary of gods, rites,
intoxicants and places.** Ernest L. Abel. vii, 212 p. Jefferson, N.C.:
McFarland, 2006. ISBN: 078642477X.

394.14   BL303.A24

Alcohol consumption to the point of intoxication has deep cultural
roots, which are traced in world mythology in this thorough and well-
researched work. From the Mayan god of intoxication, Acan, to Zagreus,
an early version of the Greek god Dionysus, encyclopedic coverage of
the historical bases of drinking to excess on a global basis. Bibliography
and index.

Directories

**131   Directory, non-governmental organizations and drug abuse
prevention, treatment and rehabilitation.** 4th ed. [United
Nations]. v, 269 p. New York: United Nations, 2003. ISBN:
9211481651.

HV5801

This 4th ed., publ. in 2003, updates the United Nation's global listing of
non-governmental organizations (NGOs) working to prevent drug abuse
and to treat those addicted to drugs.

132 **National directory of drug and alcohol abuse treatment programs.**
[Department of Health and Human Services, Substance Abuse and
Mental Health Administration, Office of Applied Studies]. Rockville,
Md.: U.S. Department of Health and Human Services, Substance
Abuse and Mental Health Administration, Office of Applied Studies,
2000–.
362.291802573   HV5825.N323

Comprehensive directory of U.S. treatment programs for alcoholism and
drug abuse. Updated on an annual basis; year of issue lags two to three
years behind the calendar date.

Encyclopedias

133 **Alcohol and temperance in modern history: An international
encyclopedia.** Jack S. Blocker, David M. Fahey, Ian R. Tyrrell. 2 v., ill.
Santa Barbara, Calif.: ABC-CLIO, 2003. ISBN: 1576078337.
362.29203   HV5017.A43

Some 500 signed alphabetic entries from a wide range of authorities detail
the global production and consumption of alcohol, and the rise of temperance movements from 18th century to the present. Chronology begins
with 15th century. Multinational perspectives from many countries deal
with individual and societal effects of alcohol. Bibliographies. Appendixes
cover some primary documents and give annotated listings of Internet
resources. Available as an e-book.

134 **Encyclopedia of drugs, alcohol and addictive behavior.** 2nd ed.
Rosalyn Carson-DeWitt. 4 v. (lx, 1863 p.), ill. New York: Macmillan
Reference USA, 2001. ISBN: 0028655419.
362.2903   HV5804.E53

This 2nd ed. of the 1995 landmark encyclopedia on alcoholism and drug
abuse updates information found there, and also has added entries on
addictive behaviors such as eating disorders and compulsive gambling.
Definitive and comprehensive, with signed entries usually from two to
four pages in length, with bibliographies. Multidisciplinary perspective
includes behavioral and pharmacological aspects, as well as legal issues.
Discusses drug abuse and the economics of production, trade, and sales in
various countries. In addition, there are extensive listings of organizations
that deal with various aspects of alcoholism, drug abuse, and addictive

behaviors. The sweeping coverage and certain authority of the 1st ed. has been preserved and enhanced. Available as an e-book.

135   **The encyclopedia of drugs and alcohol.** Greg Roza. vii, 199 p., ill.
      New York: Franklin Watts, 2001. ISBN: 0531118991.
615.103   RM301.17.R698

Useful for both middle school and high school students, this juvenile-level encyclopedia covers 250 common over-the-counter, prescription, and recreational drugs, both legal and illegal. The history, uses, and effects of drugs are described in entries that range in length from a few paragraphs to about a page. Entries also cover related topics such as binge drinking, and crime and illnesses related to drugs. Both slang and descriptive terms are defined. Especially helpful for this age group is "Where to Go for Help" that identifies organizations and websites focused on, or including, substantial amounts of assistance for young people.

136   **Prevention primer: An encyclopedia of alcohol, tobacco, and
      other drug prevention terms.** Center for Substance Abuse
      Prevention, U.S. Department of Health and Human Services,
      Public Health Service, Substance Abuse and Mental Health
      Services Administration. iii, 135 p. [Rockville, Md.?]: Center for
      Substance Abuse Prevention, 1994.
362.2903   HV5804

The special terms used by and with alcoholism and drug abuse are covered thoroughly. Encyclopedic essays place the terms into both field and theoretical contexts. An especially useful work for students, social workers, law enforcement, journalists, and anyone trying to understand the cultural context of the use of illegal drugs, and of alcoholism.

Guides

137   **Alcoholism in the workplace: A handbook for supervisors.** U.S.
      Office of Personnel Management. 14 p. Washington: U.S. Office of
      Personnel Management, Office of Workforce Relations, 2001.
                                                                HF5549.5.A4

An up-to-date and broad-ranging practical guide for dealing with alcoholism in the workplace in the United States. Includes the supervisor's role, signs to look for, leave and attendance, performance problems, relationships at work, and behavior at work.

Full text available online at the U.S. Office of Personnel Management website at: http://www.opm.gov/Employment_and_Benefits/WorkLife/ OfficialDocuments/ HandbooksGuides/Alcohol/index.asp.

138 **Cultural competence for social workers: A guide for alcohol and other drug abuse prevention professionals working with ethnic/ racial communities.** Joanne Philleo, Frances Larry Brisbane, Leonard G. Epstein, Center for Substance Abuse Prevention (U.S.). xiv, 218 p. [Rockville, Md.]: U.S. Department of Health and Human Services, Public Health Service, Substance Abuse and Mental Health Services Administration, Center for Substance Abuse Prevention, [1995].

HV5824.E85C85

Provides a conceptual framework and offers practical suggestions for working with various ethnic groups. Particular consideration is given to work with major individual groups: African Americans, Hispanics, Native Americans, and Asian Americans. The concept of cultural competence is offered as the ability to deal with the cultural aspects of treatment for drug and alcohol abuse.

139 **Dangerous drugs: An easy-to-use reference for parents and professionals.** 2nd ed. Carol L. Falkowski. xvi, 292 p., [8] p. of plates, ill. (some color). Center City, Minn.: Hazelden, 2003. ISBN: 1568389817.

362.29   HV4998.F35

A thorough, useful, and up-to-date popular treatment on alcoholism and drug abuse. Focus is on young people and the family. Defines various types of addictions and substances causing them. Very practical. In addition to alcohol and the myriad ways that it can affect various individuals, sections detail hallucinogens, inhalants, stimulants, sedatives, hypnotics, etc. Breadth and repetition strengthen this work. Highly recommended.

140 **Drug abuse and addiction media guide.** National Institute on Drug Abuse. v, 48 p. Bethesda, Md.: National Institutes of Health, 2001.

HV5825

Popular misconceptions in the media about the effects of drug abuse and addiction are countered in this useful handbook based on solid scientific research. Begins with an overview and goes on to describe in detail health consequences of drug abuse. Also includes a glossary, statistical sources, and a list of advocacy programs.

Handbooks

141 **Alcoholism sourcebook: Basic consumer health information about alcohol use, abuse, and dependence, featuring facts about the physical, mental, and social health effects of alcohol addiction, including alcoholic liver disease, pancreatic disease, cardiovascular disease, neurological disorders, and the effects of drinking during pregnancy; along with information about alcohol treatment, medications, and recovery programs.** 2nd ed. Amy L. Sutton. xviii, 653 p., ill. Detroit: Omnigraphics, 2007. ISBN: 0780809424.

362.29286   RC565.A4493

Thorough and detailed popular coverage of all aspects of alcoholism, especially in relation to children, youth, families, and recovery. Answers questions such as: What are the biochemical aspects of alcoholism? How does alcoholism affect adolescents and young people? Drug abuse is covered only slightly. Glossary of terms, directory of government and private information resources, list of substance abuse agencies by state. Includes bibliographical references and index. Solid reference value.

142 **Blacks Against Drunk Driving: A culture-based handbook to promote traffic safety awareness and action, DOT Report No. HS 809 032.** National Black Alcoholism and Addictions Council. iv, 35 p., ill. (some color). Washington: U.S. Department of Transportation, National Highway Traffic Safety Administration, 2000.

Thorough handbook provides cultural context for preventing driving under the influence among African Americans. Elements that can lead to drunk driving are discussed, and ways to identify and prevent its occurrence are suggested.

143 **Complete handbook for combating substance abuse in the workplace: Medical facts, legal issues, and practical solutions.**

William F. Banta, Forest S. Tennant. xxvi, 592 p., ill. Lexington, Mass.: Lexington Books, 1989. ISBN: 0669178799.

658.3822   HF5549.5.D7B36

A mainstream handbook in rather formal terms on the situation and treatment of alcoholism and drug abuse in the workplace. Employee assistance programs are described, and government policy is covered. Provides access to cross-disciplinary materials before the advent of the major online indexes which cover these topics and materials. Bibliography.

144   Comprehensive handbook of drug and alcohol addiction.
Norman S. Miller. xx, 1330 p., ill. New York: Dekker, 1991. ISBN: 082478474X.

616.86   RC564.C652

A solid reference book on the mainstream elements in alcoholism and drug abuse, with the current state of illegal drugs in 1991. Worth looking forward to the updated and expanded 2nd ed. slated to be released after the end of 2007.

145   Drug abuse handbook. 2nd ed. Steven B. Karch. 1267 p., ill. Boca Raton, [Fla.]: CRC Press/Taylor and Francis, 2007. ISBN: 0849316901.

615.19   RM316.D76

Ranging from criminal and legal aspects of drug abuse, to pharmacology, sports and workplace issues, and postmortem measures, handbook covers both societal and biochemical aspects. Bibliography and index. Available as an e-book.

146   Handbook of drug abuse prevention: Theory, science, and practice. Zili Zloboda, William J. Bukoski. New York: Springer, 2006. ISBN: 9780387324593.

Prevention of drug abuse involves reduction of risk factors and enhancement of protective factors. Groups of diverse age, gender, or ethnicity may be involved, along with a wide range of substances. Some 50 signed essays explore these topics. Bibliographies and index.

147   International handbook on alcohol and culture. Dwight B. Heath. xxiv, 391 p. Westport, Conn.: Greenwood Press, 1995. ISBN: 0313252343.

394.13   HV5035.I57

Essays on alcohol use in 27 individual countries. Alphabetic entries range from Australia to Zambia and cover cultures with widely differing cultural backgrounds. Entries are signed, and scholars come from a variety of disciplines. Essays present a global perspective.

Internet Resources

148 **Help and hope for children of alcoholics and other substance abusers.** http://www.coaf.org/. Children of Alcoholics Foundation (U.S.). New York: Children of Alcoholics Foundation. 2007.

A toolbox of useful references for understanding the alcoholic and the alcoholic's family, and for helping the survival of the children of alcoholics and those abusing other substances. Up-to-date bibliographies. Extensive online guides, lists of contacts, links to a number of other Internet sites, and online discussion groups. Resources for alcoholics and their families, in age-appropriate language for younger children, for teens, and for adults. A rich reference source for up-to-date information on alcoholism and the family.

Childhood and Adolescence

Atlases and General Overview

149 **Atlas—child and adolescent mental health resources: Global concerns.** World Health Organization. [Geneva, Switzerland]: World Health Organization, [2005]. ISBN: 9240680071.

Not restricted to the developing world, concerns about the mental health of children and youth are unfortunately justified in most countries of the world. Different problem situations threaten the mental health of the young across the globe. Atlas presents the situation graphically on a worldwide basis. Includes bibliographical references. Also available electronically.

150 **The progress of Canada's children and youth: 2006.** Louise Hanvey. 80 p., ill. Ottawa, Ont., [Canada]: Canadian Council on Social Development, 2006. ISBN: 0888105290.

An annual Canadian publication; provides a comprehensive accounting of children and youth in Canada through a wealth of narrative and statistical information. Available in hard copy or on the Web at http://www.ccsd.ca/pccy/2006/.

151   **The state of the world's children.** UNICEF. ill. Oxford; New York:
       Oxford University Press for UNICEF, 1980–. ISSN: 0265-718X.
362.71091724   HQ792.2.S73

From its beginnings as a slight pamphlet in 1980, this annual UNICEF
publication has become a weighty flagship publication on the world's children through narrative accounts and statistical measures. In print from
Oxford University Press or on the Web at http://www.unicef.org/publica-
tions. A valuable reference source for both general audiences and research
collections, kept scrupulously up-to-date.

Bibliography

152   **A bibliography of family placement literature: A guide to
       publications on children, parents and carers.** 2nd ed. John
       Sudbery, Martin Shaw, British Association for Adoption and
       Fostering. viii, 371 p. London: BAAF, 2005. ISBN: 1903699304.
016.3627330941   HV875.58.G7

A listing of references on adoption and foster care for children in the
United Kingdom. A useful counterpoint to United States customs and
practices. Index.

153   **Scholarly resources for children and childhood studies: A
       research guide and annotated bibliography.** Vibiana Bowman.
       viii, 289 p., ill. [Lanham, Md.]: [Scarecrow Press], 2007. ISBN:
       9780810858749.
305.23072   HQ767.85

A thoughtful and thorough guide to the emerging field of the study of
children and their culture. Beginning with a chapter that defines the field,
the basis of research with children is covered. Further chapters explore
childhood from a wealth of other disciplines: anthropology, art, business
and economics, education, English language and literature, history, psychology, and sociology. Resources from U.S. government documents and
the Internet are also listed in detail.

Directories

154   **National directory of children, youth and families services.** [s.n.].
       Longmont, Colo.: Marion L. Peterson, 1991–. ISSN: 1072-902X.
362.702573   HV741.N3157

In 2007, this standard annual reference publication for professionals working with at-risk children and their families is in its 28th year. An estimated 45,000 listings cover social services, child abuse protection, health/mental health services, substance abuse, juvenile justice/probation, treatment centers, educational services, national organizations, federal and state government services. Provides information for not only each U.S. state, but also down to the county level. Also available online at http://www.contexomedia.com.

Encyclopedias

155   **Child welfare for the twenty-first century: A handbook of practices, policies, and programs.** Gerald P. Mallon, Peg McCartt Hess. xviii, 764 p. New York: Columbia University Press, 2005. ISBN: 0231130724.

362.70973   HV741.C516

The historic evolution of child welfare services is traced in this thorough and engaging encyclopedic handbook. Begins by redefining children as being in need of shelter from adult responsibility in society, and moves through the need for safety from abuse and neglect in family situations. Handbook documents the need to preserve and strengthen the family. Adoption is explored in many venues, including for Native American and Alaska native children where it is especially sensitive. Birth mothers, special living arrangements for children in need of shelter, the role of law, and improved agency structure and function are all covered in detail. A thoughtful and highly recommended discussion of how and why child welfare exists in the world today. Includes bibliographical references and index. Available as an e-book.

156   **The encyclopedia of child abuse.** Robin E. Clark, Judith Freeman Clark, Christine A. Adamec. New York: Facts on File, 2007. ISBN: 0816066779.

HV6626.5.C57

What constitutes child abuse? What causes children to be abused? How does society, and particular subcultures internationally, decide what is abuse and what is discipline? What laws protect the child from abuse and punish its occurrence? And what is the effect on children who are abused? These questions are answered in some 400 entries which update topics from earlier editions, including current critical issues like bullying, clergy abuse, sexual trafficking, and foster care. Excellent coverage by state, including "Grounds for termination of parental rights." Advocacy organizations are listed. Extensive cross-references, bibliographical references, index.

157 **Encyclopedia of children, adolescents, and the media.** Jeffrey Jensen Arnett. 2 v. (xxxvii, 886, I–70 p.), ill. Thousand Oaks, Calif.: Sage Publications, 2007. ISBN: 1412905303.
302.23083   HQ784.M3

Cautionary perspective informs 460 extensive, signed entries, which describe the effect of media on children and adolescents. Traditional, new, and emerging media are covered, along with an international focus. Topical entries include advertising, advocacy groups, books and print media, computers and electronic media, cross-cultural perspectives, developmental stages, gender and sexuality, media education, media effects, media use, movies, music, public policy, research methods, television, theories, and violence and aggression. The history of children's content in media is covered in several entries; for example, the evolution of forms and characters in comic books. Extensive index.

158 **Encyclopedia of children and childhood: In history and society.** Paula S. Fass. 3 v., ill. New York: Macmillan Reference USA, 2004. ISBN: 0028657144.
305.2303   HQ767.84.E53

A fresh new encyclopedia whose three volumes cover a very broad range of topics that define children and childhood in a remarkably comprehensive way. Includes both childhood and adolescence, and makes reference to traditional and current language, culture, media, and experience. The first two volumes contain 445 signed entries that vary in length from a few sentences to several pages and are drawn from many disciplines. Each includes a bibliography and cross-references. The third volume is a collection of primary source documents on childhood, ranging from Teddy Roosevelt's letter of advice to his son in 1901, to the U.N.'s landmark Declaration of the Rights of the Child in 1959. Many illustrations throughout. A new classic reference documenting what it means to be a child, to care for a child today, or to study the meaning of childhood in today's society. Available as an e-book.

Guides

159   **Remembered childhoods: A guide to autobiography and memoirs of childhood and youth.** Jeffrey E. Long. xxv, 495 p. Westport, Conn: Libraries Unlimited, 2007. ISBN: 9781591581741.
016.920   Z5304.C5; CT25L66

Lists of autobiographies and memoirs arranged in chapters on regions, experience (travel, nature, disease/disability, abuse, ethnic heritage), and adult occupation. Covers English-language works, including translations into English. Each citation has a few subject terms. Indexes of subjects, settings (geographical), authors/titles.

Handbooks

160   **America's children: Opposing viewpoints.** Carol Wekesser. 263 p., ill. San Diego, Calif.: Greenhaven Press, 1991. ISBN: 0899084613.
362.70973   HV741.A733

Handbook that poses useful and provocative questions about common assumptions on child welfare in America, and ways that it can and should be improved. Deals with issues of education, abuse, poverty, and health.

161   **Annual children's law institute.** [Practising Law Institute]. New York: Practising Law Institute, 2002–. ISSN: 1554-6837.
346   KF479.Z9C49

The Children's Law Institute is an annual conference on the state of law for children in the United States, presented by the Practising Law Institute in New York City. Each conference produces an excellent state-of-the-art publication that captures the sense of the materials presented at that conference. The result is a thorough handbook covering the legal framework that protects and governs children's behaviors in the United States. Whether a child is in need of supervision for the good of society, or needs a sheltered environment for protection against missing or inappropriate caregivers, the material discusses in detail what the law can provide. Examples of the thoughtful and useful nature of this reference work include social issues such as improved family visitations, dealing with families whose children are in foster care, and tips for families providing foster care. The Tenth Annual Children's Law Institute was held in 2007.

162   **Blackwell handbook of early childhood development.** Kathleen
McCartney, Deborah Phillips. xv, 663 p., ill. Malden, Mass.;
Oxford, [U.K.]: Blackwell, 2006. ISBN: 1405120738.

305.231   BF721.B44

Covering ages 2 to 7, this handbook provides a comprehensive summary
of research in the field of child development. Thirty substantial signed
essays delve into basic questions, including early brain development and
the weight of parental influence on young children. Developmental psychology is explored through topics like conceptual frameworks; biological
and physiological development; cognitive development; language and
literacy development; and social, emotional, and regulatory development.
Covers other issues influencing the care and education of young children
like poverty, family systems, orphanages, media, and going to school. A
basic handbook to help researchers from many disciplines comprehend
the inner world of young children. Available as an e-book.

163   **Children law: An interdisciplinary handbook.** Charles Prest,
Stephen Wildblood. xli, 1036 p. Bristol, [U.K.]: Family Law, 2005.
ISBN: 0853089442.

346.42017   KD772.P74

Volume documents the legal framework governing the protection and
allowed behavior of children in the United Kingdom. Includes bibliographical references.

164   **Handbook on child support enforcement: Answers to your
questions.** United States, Office of Child Support Enforcement. 69,
[11], 1–6 p. Washington: U.S. Department of Health and Human
Services, Administration for Children and Families, Office of Child
Support Enforcement, 2005.

HV741

This updated handbook covers a myriad of details about the questions
surrounding child support in the United States today. A legal situation,
child support is fraught with difficulties in enforcement, including the
situation of a non-custodial parent who flees or kidnaps the child from
the custodial parent. A difficult situation for both law and society, issues in
child support are clarified in many areas in this thorough work. List provided of Tribal Grantee, Regional, and State Child Support Enforcement
Offices. Available electronically at http://www.acf.hhs.gov/programs/cse/
pubs/2005/handbook_on_cse.pdf.

165   Missing and exploited children: How to protect your child.
Margaret C. Jasper. ix, 217 p. [Dobbs Ferry, N.Y.]: Oceana
Publications, 2006. ISBN: 019532157X.

KF9323.Z9J37

This handbook in the *Legal almanac series* takes a clear-eyed and well-
documented view of a parent's worst nightmare: the abduction, disap-
pearance, and possible subsequent harm of their child. Practical steps are
spelled out to prevent a child's abduction in numerous circumstances.

**166   The safe child handbook: How to protect your family and cope
with anxiety in a threat-filled world.** John S. Dacey, Lisa B. Fiore.
xii, 206 p., ill. San Francisco: Jossey-Bass, 2006. ISBN: 0787986887.
649.10289   HQ770.7.D33

Handbook covers in detail various dangers children can face in modern
society, including weather emergencies, kidnapping, terrorism, harmful
media, child abuse by trusted individuals, alcohol and drug abuse, violence
in school, and dangers which can be present in the home. Beyond physical
dangers, how can a family's life be more serene, and what are the best ways
to cope with the "What if" fears of family members? Appendix lists Internet sites by type of threat. Bibliography, index. Available as an e-book.

Statistics

167   America's children: Key national indicators of well-being. Federal
Interagency Forum on Child and Family Statistics (U.S.). ill.
Washington: Federal Interagency Forum on Child and Family
Statistics, 1997–. ISSN: 1930-6938.
305.2313305.23   HQ792.U5A535

Annual U.S. government publication, begun in 1997, serves as a report
card for America on statistical measures of its children and adolescents,
documenting the effectiveness of their care. In 2007, 38 key indicators
were used to draw this picture.

Since 2004, only available on the Internet at: http://www.childstats.
gov/americaschildren/. Intended for a general audience.

168   Children in the states. Children's Defense Fund (U.S.). vi, 115 p.
Washington: Children's Defense Fund, 2001.
362.7   HV741

Updated on the Web by the Children's Defense Fund, this is a valuable compilation of state-level data on children. Data are listed as "most recent"; more specific attribution and dates of sources would strengthen this source. Still, very worthwhile to understand the particular situation of children in a certain state. Web address is http://www.childrensdefense. org/.

169 **Statistical handbook on the world's children.** Chandrika Kaul. xxi, 544 p., ill. Westport, Conn.: Oryx Press, 2002. ISBN: 1573563900.

305.23021 HQ767.9.K38

Statistics on children can be difficult to find. This title fills that niche and provides a useful compilation of statistics on children drawn from many sources and on a wide range of topics. Statistics are organized topically into chapters on Demographics; Education; Health and Nutrition; Disease, Hunger and Malnutrition; HIV-AIDs; Economics; Family, Social and Behavior; and Crime, Violence and War. Global coverage. Includes bibliographical references and index.

Crime and Deviance

Atlases and General Overview

170 **Atlas of crime: Mapping the criminal landscape.** Linda S. Turnbull, Elaine Hallisey Hendrix, Borden D. Dent. xxiii, 270 p., ill., maps. Phoenix: Oryx Press, 2000. ISBN: 1573562416.

364.9730904 HV6783.A85

Both a geographic handbook and an atlas, this title includes some 30 signed essays on the place of geography in understanding crime in the United States. Approx. 170 graphics include maps, charts, and tables. A remarkable resource presenting graphical depictions of crime that are not otherwise easily available, if at all. Includes bibliographical references and index.

Bibliography

171 **Annotated bibliography on women offenders, prisons, jails, community corrections, and juvenile justice.** http://nicic.org/ Downloads/PDF/Library/021385.pdf. Peggy Ritchie, National

Institute of Corrections Information Center. Longmont, Colo.:
U.S. Department of Justice, National Institute of Corrections
Information Center, 2006.

A comprehensive modern bibliography of resources for understanding
and managing women in prison situations. One of a number of worthwhile bibliographies found on the National Institute for Corrections website at http://nicic.org/.

172   Crime and punishment in America: A historical bibliography.
ABC-CLIO Information Services. xii, 346 p. Santa Barbara, Calif.:
ABC-CLIO Information Services, 1984. ISBN: 0874363632.
016.364973   Z5703.5.U5C7; HV6789

Covers a broad range of mainstream crime, including violent crime,
political crime, and criminal justice administration. Especially useful for
references from a time before online and full-text databases made access
to publications on crime and criminal justice more readily available.
Work in this field is from several disciplines and often falls between the
mainstream themes in each one, and therefore can otherwise be lost in
paper indexes.

173   Criminal justice bibliography. Marvin Marcus. i, 53 l. Atlanta:
School of Urban Life, Georgia State University, [1971].
016.364973   KF9223.A1M37

An exhaustive traditional bibliography covering all aspects of criminal
justice, from entry into the system, police and corrections officers, law
and courts, prisons, parole, and so on. An especially valuable resource for
capturing references to this literature for the time before online indexes
and full-text services began providing coverage of this multidisciplinary
field. Gives a picture of the sociology of law when it was a different field
than it is three decades later. Title should not be relegated to a storage
library.

174   Delinquency and juvenile justice: An international bibliography.
Clayton A. Hartjen, S. Priyadarsini. x, 600 p. Westport, Conn.:
Praeger, 2004. ISBN: 0313320985.
016.36436   Z5703.4.J88H376; HV9069

International coverage of research from 1975 through 2001 on juvenile
justice, judicial and correctional agencies, and delinquency and crimes
committed by youth. Broad coverage from countries around the world;

topics are subdivided into categories by country. Entries are annotated. Subject and author indexes. Available as an e-book.

175 **Lynching and vigilantism in the United States: An annotated bibliography.** Norton H. Moses. xix, 441 p. Westport, Conn.: Greenwood Press, 1997. ISBN: 0313301778.
016.364134   Z5703.5.U5M67; HV6457

Provides a window onto articles and publications detailing the dark history of mob violence in America. Lynching is often intertwined with hate crimes. Bloody citizen action in the form of vigilantism is also covered. A useful reference to the literature of the harm that can happen when the rule of law breaks down in extremely fraught situations.

176 **The sociology of law: A bibliography of theoretical literature.** 3rd ed. A. Javier Treviño. 212 p. Lewiston, N.Y.: E. Mellen Press, 2003. ISBN: 0773465855.
016.340115   K366.T74

What is the meaning of law in broader society? How does society create, influence, and interpret the legal systems it has created and participates in? This 3rd ed. of the standard handbook in the sociology of law explores basic constructions in the field and documents classic theorists: Karl Marx, Emile Durkheim, Donald Black, and others. Feminist jurisprudence is also discussed. Includes a concluding section on Law and Society in Global Perspective, then surveys this relationship in the United States, Brazil, the United Kingdom, the Netherlands, Poland, Scandinavia, Germany, France, China, Korea, and Japan. Volume concludes with a 34 p. dictionary of sociolegal terms and an author index.

Dictionaries

177 **The concise dictionary of crime and justice.** Mark S. Davis. ix, 286 p. Thousand Oaks, Calif.: Sage Publications, 2002. ISBN: 0761921753.
364.03   HV6017.D38

Dictionary of some 2,000 criminal justice terms gives complete and up-to-date definitions. Where there are misconceptions or controversies about a term, those are explained clearly. Cross-references are made to related terms. In a field where legal terms mix with street culture and shorthand terms among law enforcement professionals, this is a useful and welcome reference volume. Includes bibliographical references.

Encyclopedias

178 **The encyclopedia of American law enforcement.** Michael Newton.
New York: Facts On File, 2007. ISBN: 0816062900.

363.2097303   HV8133.N48

With special strengths in historical coverage and biographic content, some
600 entries in an alphabetic arrangement thoroughly cover American
police and law enforcement from the 17th century to the present. The
place of law enforcement in the development and function of the larger
society is drawn out in numerous entries. Civil rights and social issues
are covered, and women in law enforcement are discussed. Both major
federal law enforcement agencies, and some at the state level, are listed in
directory format. Black-and-white photographs. Cross-references, bibliography, index.

179 **Encyclopedia of crime and punishment.** David Levinson. 4 v.
(xxxv, 1876, 38 p.), ill. Thousand Oaks, Calif.: Sage Publications,
2002. ISBN: 076192258X.

346.03   HV6017.E524

Encyclopedia in four volumes and 430 signed entries covers crime and
punishment in an exhaustive fashion. Well-written entries, and a broad
range of articles, cover diverse topics over time and throughout the culture. All of the expected topics, including profiles of individual major prisons, as well as broader coverage of topics like torture, money laundering,
and so on. Well-deserved recipient of numerous awards when published,
this remains a classic reference on crime and punishment. Extensive bibliographies, index. Available as an e-book.

180 **Encyclopedia of DNA and the United States criminal justice
system.** Louis J. Palmer. vii, 464 p., ill., maps. Jefferson, N.C.:
McFarland, 2004. ISBN: 0786417358.

614.1   RA1057.55.P34

When the American criminal justice system began to use DNA analysis
around 1985, a quiet but profound revolution was begun in connecting
the guilty to their crimes and freeing the innocent who had been wrongly
accused and, in many cases, convicted. DNA analysis is most often used in
cases of sexual assault criminal convictions.

This encyclopedia traces the development of DNA "fingerprinting"
and the dramatic role it has played in criminal justice in the United States.

Entries relate DNA analysis to microbiology, population genetics, statistics, and the legal rules for the admissibility of scientific evidence. Also includes all state and federal laws that govern the use of DNA analysis in the courts, along with useful summaries. The opinions from key cases dealing with DNA evidence are included. Also provides a list of convicted sex offenders who were freed on the basis of DNA analysis, as well as entries for the organizations that work to free innocent individuals. A remarkably comprehensive and engaging reference book. Includes bibliographical references and index.

181   Encyclopedia of gangs. Louis Kontos, David Brotherton. Westport, Conn.: Greenwood Press, 2007. ISBN: 9780313334023.

364.10660973   HV6439.U5E53

This thoroughly researched new reference work lives up to its name, with encyclopedic coverage of the world of gangs, on a global basis, from the perspectives of myriad disciplines. The best-known and largest gangs on an international basis begin this catalog of a special criminal subculture. Gang culture is then described in entries with myriad details, including symbols, drugs, prison, graffiti, clothing, and so on. Everyday aspects of gang life are covered in chapters on media, workers, gender relations, schools, labels. International coverage includes gang activity in Australia, Brazil, China, France, Germany, Canada, Japan, and South Africa, among other countries. Various initiatives to counteract gangs and associated violence are also covered. Entries are signed. Includes bibliographical references and index. Available as an e-book.

182   Encyclopedia of prisons and correctional facilities. Mary Bosworth. 2 v. (xli, 1334 p.), ill. Thousand Oaks, Calif.: Sage Publications, 2005. ISBN: 076192731X.

365.97303   HV9471.E427

Some 400 signed entries in two volumes provide a comprehensive treatment of both the history and current state of U.S. prisons and correctional facilities. Topics are far-ranging and include juvenile justice, prison architecture, privatization, key legal statutes, theories of punishment, security and classification, and sentencing policy and laws. Entries are often framed in terms of social issues such as race, gender, and class. Biographies and detailed descriptions of major prisons are included. An appendix provides a directory of every federal prison in the United States. Includes bibliographical references and index. Available as an e-book.

183   **Encyclopedia of war crimes and genocide.** Leslie Alan Horvitz, Christopher Catherwood. New York: Facts on File, 2006. ISBN: 0816060010.

364.13803   HV6322.7.H67

Alphabetic arrangement of more than 450 entries covering the history of crimes against humanity in both peace and war. Entries for organizations working against such crimes include Amnesty International, Freedom House, and the International Committee of the Red Cross. Perpetrators and rescuers are covered, including Klaus Barbie, François "Papa Doc" Duvalier, Saddam Hussein, as well as Desmond Tutu and Simon Wiesenthal. Topics include apartheid, biological weapons, collateral damage, ethnic cleansing, and ghost prisoners. Full text of key primary documents. Black-and-white photographs and illustrations. Cross-references, bibliography, index. Thorough coverage of a chilling but compelling and very difficult subject.

184   **Encyclopedia of white-collar and corporate crime.** Lawrence M. Salinger. 2 v. (xxviii, 974 p.), ill. Thousand Oaks, Calif.: Sage Publications, 2005. ISBN: 0761930043.

364.16803   HV6768.E63

Comprehensive and well-written encyclopedia of some 500 entries dealing with all aspects of white-collar crime. Historical content is provided, along with definitions, laws, and cases, as well as companies and personalities involved in high-profile cases. Government, political scandals, and regulation are covered, as well as scams and swindles. Chronology of notable events. Numerous cross-references, bibliographical references, and index. Available as an e-book.

185   **Encyclopedia of white-collar crime.** Jurg Gerber, Eric L. Jensen. Westport. Conn.: Greenwood Press, 2006. ISBN: 0313335249.

364.168097303   HV6768.E65

More than 500 entries giving history, definitions, law, investigations, prosecutions, biographical sketches, and events. Arranged in 17 topics: business fraud and crimes, companies, consumers, countries and regions, criminology and justice, financial and securities fraud, government, laws, medical and healthcare fraud, people, political scandals, pollution, products, regulation, scams and swindles, war profiteering, and work-related crimes. Includes cross-references, further readings, and a chronology of events.

SOCIAL CONDITIONS AND SOCIAL WELFARE

186   **Guns in American society: An encyclopedia of history, politics, culture, and the law.** Gregg Lee Carter. 2 v. (xxxiv, 756 p.), ill. Santa Barbara, Calif.: ABC-CLIO, 2002. ISBN: 1576072681.
363.33097303   HV7436.G8783

A remarkably encyclopedic coverage in two volumes of some 500 entries on all aspects of guns in American society. Groups working in the areas of gun control are included, from the American Civil Liberties Union to the John Birch Society. Assault weapons, ammunition, the effect of available guns on crime, decisions in key court cases on guns, mail order guns, trigger locks, and other numerous topics. Not only are weapons covered, but their impact on society, and the attitudes and actions of disparate groups concerned with them are documented. Includes bibliographical references and index. Available as an e-book.

Guides

187   **Student party riots.** Tamara D. Madensen, John E. Eck. viii, 64 p. Washington: U.S. Department of Justice, Office of Community Oriented Policing Services, 2006.

HV7936.C83

Dealing effectively with student parties that cross over into the violence of riots is one of the most challenging tasks for law enforcement that police high school or college campuses, with the risk of destruction of property, harm to other students and people, widespread abuse of alcohol and drugs, and sexual misconduct. This handbook offers practical advice for controlling and quelling such behavior without damage to the civil rights of students or the relationship between the campus and surrounding areas.

Available online at http://www.cops.usdoj.gov/pdf/Student_Party.pdf.

Handbooks

188   **The Cambridge handbook of Australian criminology.** Adam Graycar, Peter N. Grabosky. xx, 380 p., ill. Cambridge, [U.K.]; New York: Cambridge University Press, 2002. ISBN: 0521818451.
364.994   HV7173.5.C34

Handbook that provides an interesting counterpoint to American criminal justice. Along with the expected entries on courts, policing, and criminal law, also includes matters of gender, race, class, the elderly, indigenous people, and restorative justice. Extensive bibliographical references and index.

189 Developing policies to prevent injuries and violence: Guidelines for policy-makers and planners. Doris Schopper, Jean-Dominique Lormand, Rick Waxweiler. ix, 74 p. Geneva, [Switzerland]: World Health Organization, 2006. ISBN: 9241593504.

Discusses the relationship between government policy and the violence of wounds and other injuries to individuals. Defining crime and deviant behaviors in such a way as to protect citizens from harm is made real and literal in this compelling public health manual.

Available as a PDF document at: http://www.ihs.gov/MedicalPrograms/ PortlandInjury/PDFs/WHODevelopingPoliciesInjuries.pdf.

190 Handbook of restorative justice: A global perspective. Dennis Sullivan, Larry Tifft. xvii, 574 p., ill. London; New York: Routledge, 2006. ISBN: 0415353564.

364.68   HV8688.H36

Thorough handbook begins with essays that describe the ways in which the concept of restorative justice has been created in current day law and society; continues with a discussion of the needs of the victim and the ways in which restorative justice can actually function. The situation of overwhelming human rights violations is discussed in this light, and the concept of "transitional justice" is presented. Final sections include a critical commentary on restorative justice, and transformational justice as part of structural change. Includes bibliographical references and index. Available as an e-book.

191 Handbook of transnational crime and justice. Philip L. Reichel. xvi, 512 p., ill., maps. Thousand Oaks, Calif.: Sage Publications, 2005. ISBN: 0761926224.

364.135   HV6252.H36

This thorough handbook begins by providing a historical framework for understanding transnational crime, and then looks at questions of justice and measures international criminal activity. Eight chapters detail various specific transnational crimes: terrorism, money laundering, traffic in plundered antiquities, computer crime, environmental crime, drug trafficking, human smuggling, and crimes against humanity. The next six chapters look at how society responds to such crimes, beginning with a comparative overview of policing courts and corrections, which is an extraordinary reference in itself, since this is very difficult to locate otherwise. The origins of Interpol are traced, and additional chapters look at cooperation of law enforcement between countries, trials of international cases, and concerns about human rights and judicial fairness in some countries.

Individual chapters then discuss organized crime activities by each region of the world. Volume concludes with chapters on international juvenile justice and on symbolic law, isolationism, and the death penalty. This well-done and remarkable resource provides much information, especially in the later chapters, which is not found in other sources. Includes bibliographical references and index.

192   Handbook of youth and justice. Susan O. White. xi, 442 p., ill. New York: Kluwer Academic/Plenum Publishers, 2001. ISBN: 0306463393.

364.360973   HV9069.H312

Handbook covers the protection, or lack of protection, of juveniles in the justice system in 21 signed chapters contributed by specialists from numerous disciplines. Discusses victimization of children and youth, pornography, and death by violence. Girls are discussed as a special case of victimization. Cross-cultural comparisons are drawn from Western and Eastern Europe and the United States in looking at delinquency. Examines the growth of delinquents into adult criminals. Finally, the reliability of children's memories is considered, and the effectiveness of remaking family structures to improve the lives of at-risk children and youth is discussed. A thorough and wide-ranging handbook that provides fresh insight into the situation of youth and justice. Includes bibliographical references and index.

193   Hate crimes: A reference handbook. 2nd ed. Donald Altschiller. xi, 247 p. Santa Barbara, Calif.: ABC-CLIO, 2005. ISBN: 1851096248.

364.15   HV6773.52

Begins with the history of hate crime legislation and goes on to cover various U.S. federal and state laws dealing with hate crimes, including United States Supreme Court decisions. Describes targeted groups, including African Americans, Arab Americans, Asian Americans, Jewish Americans, Muslim Americans, and gay, lesbian, and transgendered people. Deals with hate crimes on a global basis. Includes a chronology of hate crimes. A biographical section describes the work against hate crimes of 17 individuals. Statistics on hate crimes, various venues where hate crimes occur, and hate in cyberspace are all covered. Concludes with a directory of organizations working against hate crimes. Provides lists of print and nonprint resources. A thorough and useful reference compilation. Available as an e-book.

194   Illicit trafficking: A reference handbook. Robert J. Kelly, Jess Maghan, Joseph Serio. xv, 260 p. Santa Barbara, Calif.: ABC-CLIO, 2005. ISBN: 1576079155.

364.135   HV6252.K45

A remarkably detailed and lengthy handbook defining the activities, economics, players, and victims both inside and outside the activity and consequences of illegal trade. Includes armaments, small arms, larger armaments, nuclear materials, and illicit drugs. Also human cargo: immigrants outside the rules of countries they are leaving, and especially outside the rules of countries they wish to enter, and forced migration, especially of women and children, for domestic work and prostitution, the new slave trade. International organized crime, militia, or terrorist groups are often involved.

There are tremendous negative ramifications for society: illicit trafficking often brings in the tools and goods which fuel the business of drug crime, family violence, street crime, organized crime, and even crimes against humanity. Illicit trafficking by its nature is a clandestine and hugely profitable business. This handbook sheds a welcome and unusual light on it. Available as an e-book.

195   Profiling and criminal justice in America: A reference handbook. Jeffrey B. Bumgarner. xii, 299 p. Santa Barbara, Calif.: ABC-CLIO, 2004. ISBN: 1851094695.

363.2308900973   HV9950.B86

Handbook looks at both side of the question of whether profiling is ever justified, and if so, how it can be used without being abused. Biographical entries are included for individuals who have made significant contributions to the debate on profiling. Contains key cases and state statutes dealing with profiling. References and index. Available as an e-book.

Cyberspace and the Internet

Encyclopedias

196   The Internet: A historical encyclopedia. Hilary W. Poole, Laura Lambert, Chris Woodford. 3 v., ill. Santa Barbara, Calif.: ABC-CLIO, 2005. ISBN: 1851096590.

004.678   TK5105.875.I57

Three volume encyclopedia looks at the people and societal framework involved in the development of the Internet and provides a firm grounding in how cyberspace evolved and who its prime movers and shakers were. A thorough and comprehensive survey of the development and current state of the Internet in well-written essays. Vol. 1 contains 41 biographical essays; v. 2 deals with the Internet and its effect on society in 35 entries, and provides a section on Internet statistics. Vol. 3 is a detailed chronology of the development of the Internet and its predecessor technologies from 1843 to 2004. All volumes include lists of acronyms and a glossary. Available as an e-book.

197   **24/7: Time and temporality in the network society.** Robert Hassan, Ronald E. Purser. xvii, 284 p., ill. Stanford, Calif.: Stanford Business Books, 2007. ISBN: 9780804751964.

303.4833   HM656

Changes in the concept and uses of temporal measures in the age of the Internet are documented in the 13 signed essays of this encyclopedia. What is the meaning of network time? How does the science of time distance us from feeling present in our world? How has computer time affected the popular culture? How does the clock time of computers and networks control our work lives and our personal realities?

Guides

198   **Internet and the law: Technology, society, and compromises.** Aaron Schwabach. xxxv, 395 p., ill. Santa Barbara, Calif.: ABC-CLIO, 2006. ISBN: 1851097317.

343.7309944   KF390.5.C6S39

The use of the Internet and other computer technology has opened a new area of law and created complex new areas of existing law such as copyright. This guide and encyclopedia explains evolving laws governing use of the Internet and discusses the meaning of these laws, not only for copyright, but also for censorship, hackers, spam, and both personal and property crime on the Internet. Includes a useful compilation of the full text of selected cases, statutes, regulations, and treaties dealing with the Internet. Bibliographies.

199   **The invisible web: Uncovering information sources search engines can't see.** Chris Sherman, Gary Price. xxix, 439 p., ill. Medford, N.J.: CyberAge Books, 2001. ISBN: 091096551X.

025.04   ZA4450

A remarkably rare study of how the Internet works, what can be easily found, and the value of what is "invisible" or must be searched in special ways. In the last two-thirds of the volume, Chapters 10 through 27 each deal with a specific topic: art and architecture, bibliographies and library catalogs, education, entertainment, government information, and so on. For a major tool, and one so much relied upon, the Internet is little documented and not well understood. *The invisible web* goes a long way toward remedying this situation.

Handbooks

200 **Cybercrime: A reference handbook.** Bernadette H. Schell, Clemens Martin. xiv, 247 p. Santa Barbara, Calif.: ABC-CLIO, 2004. ISBN: 1851096833.
364.168   HV6773.S3547

Sobering, thorough coverage of ways in which the Internet can be used by criminals. Beginning with a history of cybercrime, and an index of terms, cyberterrorism and Homeland Security are discussed, as well as categories of cybercrime, system invasions, home and company issues with computer security, software safeguards, and legislative countermeasures. Work by international bodies such as the Council of Europe are discussed, along with recent developments in investigative techniques. Timelines are provided.

201 **The Internet and society: A reference handbook.** Bernadette H. Schell. xx, 311 p. Santa Barbara, Calif.: ABC-CLIO, 2007. ISBN: 1598840312.
303.4833   HM851.S25

A useful and basic handbook on the development and function of the Internet, especially the ways that it can go wrong, including cybercrime, loss of privacy, and security breaches. Covers changes in society that flow from the Internet and related technology, including laws. Recent controversial issues are covered. Some biographical material. Bibliographies and index. Available as an e-book.

202 **The Internet revolution.** Kevin Hillstrom. xxvi, 203 p., ill. Detroit: Omnigraphics, 2005. ISBN: 0780807677.
004.67809   TK5105.875.I57H54

Three sections make up this handbook on the Internet. The first describes how the World Wide Web was created, which covers both the technological steps which built on one another, as well as the events and changes in society, including loosening of government control, which enabled its evolution and the development of e-commerce. Middle section covers biographies of personalities responsible for the Internet's creation and function. Last section is made up of primary documents, including essays, speeches, and papers that were themselves foundations for the Internet's creation and development. A solid reference. Bibliography, chronology, index.

203 **The Oxford handbook of Internet psychology.** Adam N. Joinson. viii, 508 p., ill. Oxford; New York: Oxford University Press, 2007. ISBN: 9780198568001.

303.4833   HM1017.O94

Although focused on the experience of the individual, this could be the handbook on the Internet as social network that the field of sociology has needed. Relevant for understanding society and social interactions, and for important aspects of the subdisciplines of sociology. Some 30 signed essays cover use and experience of the Internet exhaustively, with solid references throughout. Concluding chapters provide thorough coverage on the use of the Internet for both qualitative and quantitative research. Topics in this section include survey design, ethics, and technological matters. Index.

204 **Student guide to research in the digital age: How to locate and evaluate information sources.** Leslie F. Stebbins. xiii, 202 p., ill. Westport, Conn.: Libraries Unlimited, 2006. ISBN: 1591580994.

025.524   ZA3075.S74

A well-organized guide to finding and critically evaluating information resources for college-level research: books and e-books, scholarly and popular articles, primary sources, biographies, legal information, and U.S. government documents and statistics. Also addresses general steps in research and citing sources. Appendixes: subject guide to journal article databases, glossary. Another guide, *The college student's research companion* (Neal-Schuman, 2007), uses the metaphor of a road trip to chart the process of finding and evaluating information.

Death and Dying

Bibliography

205 **The challenge of euthanasia: An annotated bibliography on euthanasia and related subjects.** Don V. Bailey. xvi, 395

p. Lanham, Md.: University Press of America, 1990. ISBN: 0819177113.

179.7   R726.B25

Breaching the bounds of law, society, and religion, euthanasia is controversial. In many cases, it is also illegal when applied to people, at least in the United States. This bibliography draws together a particularly useful group of references, otherwise difficult to identify, for the time period before being well covered by electronic cross-disciplinary and full-text searching. Of permanent reference value. Index.

206   Death and dying in children's and young people's literature: A survey and bibliography. Marian S. Pyles. xii, 173 p. Jefferson, N.C.: McFarland, 1988. ISBN: 0899503357.

809.89282   PN1009.5.D43P9

The depiction of death in literary works intended for children speaks not only of the ways that society expects children to understand, but also reflects broader concepts of death itself. This volume looks at how death has been treated historically in children's literature, and then provides extensive bibliographical entries dealing with the topic. A worthwhile reference for material published before electronic multidisciplinary and full-text databases enabled their ready identification. Index.

207   The dying child: An annotated bibliography. Hazel B. Benson. xxi, 270 p. New York: Greenwood Press, 1988. ISBN: 0313247080.

016.155937   Z6671.52.T47B46; RJ249

A thorough listing of references drawn from many disciplines for the time period 1960 through 1987. Entries are arranged in thematic groups, by age of child, the response of the family, responsibility of caregivers, and the physical care of the dying child. Entries include abstracts and indicate number of references used. Author and subject indexes. Especially valuable for its coverage of the time period before full-text and multidisciplinary indexes were commonly available.

208   Near-death experiences: An annotated bibliography. Terry K. Basford. ix, 182 p. New York: Garland, 1990. ISBN: 082406349X.

016.1339013   Z6878.P8B37; BF1045.N4

Are things commonly seen by those who are perilously close to death or perhaps even clinically dead (the Light, guides in the form of friends, family, and pets who are predeceased), but who then return to life—are they hallucinations or remarkable views into the world of life after death? This extensive bibliography presents references which speak to both sides of this controversial topic. Index.

Dictionaries and Thesauruses

209   **Death dictionary: Over 5,500 clinical, legal, literary, and vernacular terms.** Christine Quigley. xi, 195 p. Jefferson, N.C.: McFarland, 1994. ISBN: 0899508693.

306.903   HQ1073.Q54

Definitions for some 5,500 words and phrases directly associated with death and dying are provided. Disciplines providing terms include sociology, history, archeology, theology, the dramatic arts, and even the military. Entries from 65 cultures and nine religions. Thesaurus and bibliographical references.

Encyclopedias

210   **Death and the afterlife: A cultural encyclopedia.** Richard P. Taylor. x, 438 p., ill. Santa Barbara, Calif.: ABC-CLIO, 2000. ISBN: 0874369398.

393.03   GT3150.T25

Comprehensive coverage of funerary practices and beliefs about the afterlife, from the world over. Alphabetic arrangement of entries that vary in length from a few sentences to several pages. Burial of the dead among various major religious and ethnic groups is covered in significant detail: Jews, Muslims, and so on. Also provides extensive answers to questions like: What are the beliefs about life after death among Christians and Buddhists? Where does the concept of the soul fit into Chinese, Greek, and Persian traditions? Includes cross-references, bibliographies, and index. A solid and significant reference work. Available as an e-book.

211   **Encyclopedia of afterlife beliefs and phenomena.** James R. Lewis, Raymond Moody. xxi, 420 p., ill. Detroit: Gale Research, 1994. ISBN: 0810348799.

133.903   BF1311.F8L48

An encyclopedic range of beliefs about life after death drawn from many religions and cultural traditions. Some 250 well-written articles range in length from a few sentences to several pages. Special added focus is on near death experiences, reflected in the biographic entries that include Edgar Cayce and Elisabeth Kübler-Ross. An especially useful reference source for concepts which include, but go beyond, those of most established religions. Bibliographical references and index.

212   The encyclopedia of death and dying. Dana K. Cassell, Robert C. Salinas, Peter A. S. Winn. xxvi, 369 p. ; 24. New York: Facts On File, 2005. ISBN: 0816053766.

306.903   HQ1073.C374

Alphabetic signed entries cover a useful range of topics on death and dying; current topics are included. Biographical entries, non-Christian religious practices are detailed. British focus in coverage and language. Includes bibliographical references and index. Available as an e-book.

213   The encyclopedia of suicide. 2nd ed. Glen Evans, Norman L. Farberow, Alan L. Berman. xxxiii, 329 p. New York: Facts On File, 2003. ISBN: 0816045259.

362.2803   HV6545.E87

Comprehensive coverage in some 500 entries of various sociological, psychological, philosophical, and religious perspectives on the taking of one's own life. Suicide, especially among the young, is a leading cause of death in the United States today, so this 2nd ed., with enriched content, is an especially important source of balanced information on a critical topic. Appendixes provide both United States and international statistics on suicide, which are otherwise difficult to find. Also includes lists of associations, clinics, hotlines, and further resources to aid in suicide prevention. Extensive cross-references, bibliographical references, and index.

214   Macmillan encyclopedia of death and dying. Robert Kastenbaum. 2 v. (xxi, 1017 p.). New York: Macmillan Reference USA, 2003. ISBN: 002865689X.

306.9   HQ1073.M33

Scholarly multidisciplinary resource on all aspects of death and dying and also related contemporary psychosocial issues, such as bereavement, grief and mourning across cultures, etc. Alphabetically arranged signed entries. Useful resource for health professionals and also for general readers. Suitable for academic library collections and large public libraries. An appendix provides information on organizations. Illustrations, bibliographies, and index. Also available as an e-book through netLibrary and Gale Virtual Reference Library (Gale Cengage Learning, 2002–).

Similar recent titles include *Encyclopedia of death and dying* (Routledge, 2002), ed. by Glennys Howarth and Oliver Leaman, publ. 2002, and *Handbook of death and dying* (Sage, 2003), ed. by Clifton D. Bryant, publ. 2003.

Guides

215 **Handbook of bereavement research: Consequences, coping, and care.** Margaret S. Stroebe. xv, 814 p. Washington: American Psychological Association, 2001. ISBN: 155798736X.
155.937072   BF575.G7H355

What does it mean in psychological terms to grieve? Research in this handbook reports on how we deal with loss and grief and focuses on the value of grief as a coping mechanism. Further note is made of the harm that can come from unassuaged expressions of grief, and the nature of appropriate interventions. Includes bibliographical references and indexes. Available as an e-book.

216 **Working with loss, death and bereavement: A guide for social workers.** Jeremy Weinstein. 200 p. Thousand Oaks, Calif.: Sage Publications, 2007. ISBN: 9781412923910.

155.937

Supported by reference to standard social work theory, chapters cover a wide variety of situations where social workers can be called upon to help clients deal with issues resulting from loss and death. The process of grieving is also covered. What is grief? What are the psychological elements being experienced? How can people in this situation be helped? Definitions are provided and methods suggested for working with individuals, families, and communities. Ethical issues are discussed. Case studies, exercises, and references to cultural influences are also provided.

Handbooks

217 **Death and inheritance: the Islamic way: A handbook of rules pertaining to the deceased.** Muhammad Abdul Hai `Arifi, Muhammad Shameem. 264 p. Karachi, Pakistan: Darul Ishaat, 2000.

Islamic law deals specifically with death and inheritance, as recorded in this handbook. In both Arabic and English.

218   Death anxiety handbook: Research, instrumentation, and application. Robert A. Neimeyer. xvi, 284 p. Washington: Taylor and Francis, 1994. ISBN: 1560322829.
155.937   BF789.D4D347

Anxiety about death and dying is examined as a psychological phenomenon, and a scale to measure such anxiety is described. Methods for coping with death anxiety are suggested, and situations which alleviate (near death experiences) and aggravate (being HIV positive) are explored. Death anxiety as manifested by nursing home personnel towards elderly residents is discussed. Various ways to reduce or at least cope with death anxiety are suggested. A competent handbook dealing with a dark and almost taboo topic.

219   Death in the African family: A handbook on how Africans bury their dead. Joe Okoli Enukora, Bisi Ogunbadejo, Mazi People [Africa]. 160 p., ill. London: North London ITeC Press. ISBN: 0952680602.
393.908996   GT3287

Authorized by Africa's Mazi people, this handbook provides a window onto African customs surrounding death and traditional African ceremonies and rites associated with funerals. A useful counterpoint to the Eurocentric perspective found in many reference volumes on death and dying available today. Includes bibliographical references.

220   Grief in children: A handbook for adults. Atle Dyregrov. 119 p. London: J. Kingsley, 1991. ISBN: 185302113X.
155.937083   BF723.G75D9713

This translation from the Norwegian *Sorg hos barn* emphasizes the reality of grief even in very young children. Useful suggestions are offered for helping a child cope with grief, beginning with acknowledgment of their loss.

221   Handbook for mortals: Guidance for people facing serious illness. Joanne Lynn, Joan K. Harrold. xiv, 242 p., ill. Oxford; New York: Oxford University Press, 2001; 1999. ISBN: 0195146018.
362.175   R726.8

The finality of death underlies the detailed information presented here on dealing with serious, even terminal, illness in personal and family situations. The value of improving physical comfort, of open channels of communication with doctors and other caregivers, and the importance of gaining knowledge about the illness are emphasized. Planning ahead is discussed, and the question of hastening death is raised. The special cases of the death of a child, and sudden death, are also covered. Includes bibliographical references and index. A significant and compassionate addition to reference sources dealing with death and dying. Available as an e-book.

222   Handbook of adolescent death and bereavement. Charles A. Corr, David E. Balk. xvii, 420 p., ill. New York: Springer, 1996. ISBN: 0826192408.
155.9370835   BF724.3.D43H26

The complex world of adolescents, with their family, friends, and teachers, requires a special framework for dealing with death and loss for this age group. What are the special considerations for understanding the loss of an adolescent? When an adolescent experiences loss through death, how can we help him or her cope? What works well for and with adults, and even children, may not be effective with adolescents. A thoughtful handbook, which includes bibliographical references and indexes.

Note companion volume by the same authors addressing these questions for children, *Handbook of childhood death and bereavement* (223).

223   Handbook of childhood death and bereavement. Charles A. Corr, Donna M. Corr. xiii, 384 p., ill. New York: Springer, 1996. ISBN: 082619320X.
155.937083   BF723.D3H36

Childhood is such a dangerous time in terms of serious threats to health and well-being, and our connection with children is of such a special nature, that losing a child can be overwhelming. The other type of childhood loss, where a child loses through death a family member, close friend, or pet, can be extremely difficult for the child to deal with. Such grief is real, and needs to be taken seriously, with help offered to the child. For adults dealing with the loss of a child, and helping children deal with the grief of loss, this handbook offers practical and useful suggestions for understanding the situations and for taking positive steps. Includes bibliographical references and indexes.

Note companion volume by the same authors addressing these issues for adolescents, *Handbook of adolescent death and bereavement* (222).

224   **Helping bereaved children: A handbook for practitioners.** 2nd ed.
Nancy Boyd Webb, Kenneth J. Doka. xxiv, 408 p., ill. New York:
Guilford Press, 2002. ISBN: 1572306327.
155.937083   BF723.G75H34

This thorough and compassionate handbook uses case studies to explain
how grief is experienced by children at certain ages, and in particular circumstances, and what works to help them through it. The death of grandparents, godparents, siblings, through suicide, the violent death of parents,
and sudden death in school are all considered as experienced by a child.
Further material is presented on counseling for bereaved children, and
the uses of art and storytelling to help children cope with death. A special
entry is included for how children coped with the losses of 9/11. Includes
bibliographical references and index. Available as an e-book.

225   **Hospice and palliative care handbook: Quality, compliance, and
reimbursement.** T. M. Marrelli. xvii, 524 p., ill. St. Louis: Mosby-
Year Book, 1999. ISBN: 0815135572.
362.1756   RA1000.M37

This technical handbook, now in its 2nd ed., explains what a hospice is, how a
hospice operates at the highest standards, and how costs for hospice care can
be reimbursed. A useful reference source for families and friends, and even
patients themselves, in understanding a relatively new option for dealing with
a known end-of-life time. Includes bibliographical references and index.

226   **The international handbook of suicide and attempted suicide.**
Keith Hawton, Kees van Heeringen. xviii, 755 p. New York: Wiley,
2000. ISBN: 0471983675.
362.28   HV6545.I59

A practical handbook offering guidelines for professionals dealing with suicidal
individuals. Based on exploring the psychological, biological, and epidemio-
logical circumstances of suicidal behavior. Coverage is both comprehensive and
up-to-date. The most effective preventative interventions and clinical treatments
are suggested. Also valuable in a general collection where readers are looking
for serious answers to understand what is happening to family members and
friends. Includes bibliographical references and index. Available as an e-book.

227   **Medical examiners' and coroners' handbook on death registration
and fetal death reporting.** 2003 rev. ed. National Center for Health

Statistics (U.S.). ix, 130 p., ill. (some color). Hyattsville, Md.: U.S. Department of Health and Human Services, Centers for Disease Control and Prevention, National Center for Health Statistics, [2003].

614.10973   RA405.A3M435

What is death, and how is it recorded in society today? This handbook provides technical and legal answers.

Quotations

228 **Last words: A dictionary of deathbed quotations.** Bernard Ruffin. vii, 261 p. Jefferson, N.C.: McFarland, 1995. ISBN: 0786400439.

082   PN6081.R84

Some 2,000 last quotes from a broad range of individuals make up this thought-provoking reference work. Included are statesmen (Sir Winston Churchill's, "I'm bored of it all."), show business personalities (W.C. Fields's curse of most of the world), and scientists (Thomas Edison's, "It is very beautiful over there."). Entries include short biographical notes on the person quoted, and set the quotation in context. Quotes are drawn from accounts in newspapers, magazines, biographies, and firsthand reports. Includes bibliographical references and index.

229 **Light on aging and dying.** Helen Nearing. xii, 153 p. San Diego, [Calif.]: Harcourt Brace, 1998; c1995. ISBN: 0156004968.

305.26   PN6084.O5L54

What do life and death really mean? What were the last words spoken that reflect values and strength? Compilation of cheerful, but wise and thoughtful, commentaries on the value of life, and the meaning of passing from it.

Disabilities and the Disabled

Atlases and General Overview

230 **Americans with Disabilities Act of 1989: Hearings before the Committee on the Judiciary and the Subcommittee on Civil and Constitutional Rights of the Committee on the Judiciary, House of Representatives, One Hundred First Congress, first session on H.R. 2273... August 3, October 11 and 12, 1989.** United States,

[Congress]. 446 p., ill. Washington: U.S. Government Printing Office, 1990.

344.730324; 347.304324   KF27.J8

The expert testimony recorded in these hearings presents a valuable snapshot of persons with disabilities in America at the end of the 1980s, as well as an understanding of the purposes for which the Americans with Disabilities Act of 1989 was crafted. Worthwhile as a reference for why disabilities legislation was needed.

Bibliography

231   **Americans with Disabilities Act: Annotated bibliography of resources.** http://www.ada.gov/lodblind.pdf. United States, Department of Justice. 1 v. (various pagings). Washington: American Association of Retired Persons, [1995?].

016.34273087; 016.34730287   KF480.A1A48

Created by the American Association of Retired Persons under a contract with the Department of Justice, this annotated bibliography provides a thorough listing of references dealing with disabilities five years out from the passage of the Americans with Disabilities Act in 1990. This landmark federal law prohibits discrimination based on disabilities and it changed the landscape of public accommodations, employment, education, and many other areas.

232   **A brief information resource on assistance animals for the disabled.** http://www.nal.usda.gov/awic/companimals/assist.htm. Kristina Adams, Stacy Rice, Animal Welfare Information Center, USDA. Beltsville, Md.: National Agricultural Library, 2003.

"Today, animals provide therapeutic benefits to humans with physical and mental illnesses as well as provide assistance to people with disabilities."—*Introd.* This focused bibliography provides print and Internet publications, along with websites of major organizations promoting animals as helpers for both physically and mentally disabled persons. Wide range of information, including legal and regulatory materials. Covers dogs, horses, monkeys, and so on. Sources can be otherwise difficult to locate.

Dictionaries and Thesauruses

233   **Dictionary of developmental disabilities terminology.** 2nd ed. Pasquale J. Accardo, Barbara Y. Whitman, Shirley K. Behr. xxiv,

451 p., ill. Baltimore, Md: Paul H. Brooks Publ., 2002. ISBN: 155766594X.

618.9285889003   RJ135.A26

1st ed., 1996.

Interdisciplinary resource, with terminology from medicine, genetics, mental retardation, pediatrics, psychology, social work, physical therapy, and others. Provides concise definitions for neurodevelopmental disorders and developmental disabilities, with brief descriptions of medical syndromes. Includes tests and published instruments, key legislation, associations and organizations, and public laws relating to disabilities. Synonyms and and acronyms, with cross-references to full name of acronym. Includes bibliographical references.

Encyclopedias

234   **The autism encyclopedia.** John T. Neisworth, Pamela S. Wolfe. xxvii, 306 p. Baltimore, Md.: Paul H. Brookes, 2005. ISBN: 1557667950.

616.85882003   RC553.A88A847

The incidence of autism in the U.S. population has increased exponentially in the last few decades. The reasons for this are still being debated and researched, but this careful and comprehensive encyclopedia goes far towards helping explain how autism affects the individual, and the ways in which family, friends, community, and schools can appropriately respond to the autistic person. Written to be authoritative, but with a clarity that makes the information largely comprehensible to the nonspecialist, 125 contributors from many disciplines have provided some 500 essays on a comprehensive range of topics as they relate to the person with autism. More than 20 pages of references are highly useful for further reading and study. A remarkably useful reference title for both general and research collections.

235   **Encyclopedia of disability.** Gary L. Albrecht. 5 v., ill. Thousand Oaks, Calif.: Sage Publications, 2006. ISBN: 0761925651.

362.403   HV1568.E528

"Conceived as an effort to bring current knowledge of and experience with disability across a wide variety of places, conditions, and cultures to both the general reader and the specialist."—*Introd.* In the first four volumes of this landmark new reference work, more than 500 scholars have contributed some 1,000 entries, which span history far back into antiquity up to the present time, cover cultures and peoples from all over the world, and delve into topics both expected and unexpected, with clarity, insight, and extensive documentation. Entries range from one paragraph to ten pages, and conclude with a bibliography of both print and electronic resources. The fifth and final volume includes a wealth of primary documents drawn from religious texts, including the Bible, literature and poetry, medicine, diaries, and legislation, all divided into three time periods: the ancient world; historical time from 1500 to 1800; and the modern era from 1945 to the present. Documents are annotated and lavishly illustrated. A superb resource at both basic and advanced levels. Available as an e-book.

236   Gallaudet encyclopedia of deaf people and deafness. John V. Van Cleve, Gallaudet College. 3 v., ill. New York: McGraw-Hill, 1987. ISBN: 0070792291.

362.420321   HV2365.G35

Comprehensive coverage in three volumes of all aspects of deafness and deaf people, from a broad range of disciplines. Some 275 signed entries trace the personal experience and societal context of deafness through history and at the present time. Entries are thorough and insightful, helping those who do not have hearing loss to understand more fully the world of the deaf. The reference value of this work has, if anything, been increased as deaf people have been mainstreamed into society.

237   Sports and the physically challenged: An encyclopedia of people, events, and organizations. Linda Mastandrea, Donna Czubernat, Ann Cody. xxx, 173 p., ill. Westport, Conn.: Greenwood Press, 2006. ISBN: 0313324530.

796.019603   GV709.3.M37

Provides 169 entries describing significant people, terms, events, equipment, legislation, and organizations in the history of disability sports. Opens with a timeline of firsts, beginning with the 1870s participation of schools for the deaf in sporting events and covers both large events like the Special Olympics and local opportunities such as handicapped horseback riding and swimming programs. Alphabetically arranged, entries range from a paragraph to about two pages, some with bibliographies. Index.

Guides

238   An ADA guide for local governments. http://www.usdoj.gov/crt/ada/emergencyprepguide.htm. U.S. Department of Justice, Civil

Rights Division, Disability Rights Section. Washington: U.S. Department of Justice, Civil Rights Division, Disability Rights Section.

Governments at local and state levels, including local fire departments and emergency rescue teams, can be faced with a sudden need to provide emergency assistance to disabled persons, as well as the able-bodied, in emergencies from various causes. Among the most dramatic are tornadoes, hurricanes, floods, and wildfires.

This handbook offers ways to prepare in advance to help evacuate and shelter disabled persons. Identifying who needs special help is highly recommended. Shelters need to have barrier-free design, and transport must be available to accommodate various types of disabilities. How can the disabled person and their families and friends help local officials be prepared? What are useful steps to build a partnership with those who can provide emergency aid? A useful reference to ensure that when the unexpected happens, both the disabled person and the emergency team will be ready.

239 **Americans with Disabilities Act.** http://www.ada.gov/lodblind.pdf. U.S. Department of Justice, Civil Rights Division, Disability Rights Section. Washington: U.S. Department of Justice, Civil Rights Division, Disability Rights Section, 2001.

KF480.A33

What accommodations must be made by places of lodging for those who are blind or have difficulty seeing? This guide spells out appropriate measures to take to welcome such guests and to be in compliance with the 1989 Americans with Disabilities Act and later related regulations.

240 **Empowering people with severe mental illness: A practical guide.** Donald M. Linhorst. xii, 353 p. New York: Oxford University Press, 2006. ISBN: 019517187X.

362.20425   HV3006.A4L56

The movement to mainstream individuals who suffer from mental illness in the United States has bypassed those with more severe forms of mental disabilities. This provocative handbook suggests ways in which those with severe mental illness can also be empowered to live full and relatively independent lives, including matters of treatment, planning, housing, employment, and so on. Includes bibliographical references and index. Available as an e-book.

241 **A field guide for the sight-impaired reader: A comprehensive resource for students, teachers, and librarians.** Andrew Leibs, Richard Scribner. xxv, 247 p. Westport, Conn.: Greenwood Press, 1999. ISBN: 0313309698.

011.63   HV1731.L45

What are the requirements and resources available for the sight-impaired reader? This field guide outlines resources and offers guidance for programs to enable this special category of reader. Available as an e-book.

242 **Frequently asked questions about service animals.** Easter Seals Project ACTION (Accessible Community Transportation in our Nation). Washington: Easter Seals Project ACTION, 2007. http://projectaction.easterseals.com/site/DocServer/Service_Animal_FAQs.pdf.

636.7

Beginning with clear definitions, this seven page pamphlet provides a succinct guide to how service animals must be accommodated on public transit, including what questions can be asked of the disabled person traveling with a service animal, what to do about any allergies of the driver or others, and where the animal may ride. A brief but essential reference for understanding disability accommodation.

243 **Getting down to business: A blueprint for creating and supporting entrepreneurial opportunities for individuals with disabilities.** P. R. Lind and Company. 63 l. [Washington, D.C.]: [President's Committee on Employment of People with Disabilities], 2000.

HD2358.5.U6G47

What are the special considerations in U.S. policy that enable business opportunities for persons with disabilities? This guide outlines positive steps that can and must be taken.

244 **A guide for people with disabilities seeking employment.** Social Security Administration. 1 folded sheet (8 p.). Washington: Social Security Administration, 2000.

HD7256.U5

A quick fact sheet outlining assistance with employment for disabled persons, as guaranteed by the 1989 Americans with Disabilities Act and successor regulations.

245   **Multicultural aspects of disabilities: A guide to understanding and assisting minorities in the rehabilitation process.** 2nd ed. Willie V. Bryan. xii, 336 p. Springfield, Ill.: C. C. Thomas, 2007. ISBN: 9780398077082.

362.408900973   HV1569.3.M55B79

Beginning with an overview of how culture influences our perceptions of disability, this thorough handbook then deals with disability in various groups. Rehabilitation, discrimination, and minorities are treated in separate essays. Specific ethnic groups are discussed: African Americans, Asian and Pacific Americans, Hispanic and Latino Americans, Native Americans. Chapters deal with special considerations in working with the disabled among women and the elderly. Specific therapies and family counseling are each considered in the context of establishing helping relationships. Bibliographical references and indexes.

246   **101 accessible vacations: Travel ideas for wheelers and slow-walkers.** Candy Harrington, Charles Pannell. New York: Demos Medical Publishing, 2008. ISBN: 9781932603439.

910.873   HV3022.H36

This guide to vacation and leisure spots accessible to disabled persons is certainly useful for its stated purpose of helping individuals plan their activities. It also provides a remarkable measure of the greatly expanded extent of accommodations now available to disabled people in vacation areas, some quarter century since the Americans with Disabilities Act became law in the United States.

Handbooks

247   **Accessibility handbook for transit facilities: Americans with Disabilities Act of 1990.** Commerce Clearing House. 1 v. (various pagings), ill. Chicago: Commerce Clearing House, [1992].

343.73093087; 347.30393087   KF2179.A32

Ready access to public transportation—buses, trains, subways—was one of the most radical entitlements provided to the disabled in the landmark 1989 Americans with Disabilities Act. Three years into the implementation of that new law, this handbook documents exactly what was meant by barrier-free design. Useful for understanding what the law intended for public transit, and for a snapshot of what the situation with public transit had been up until this point. Permanent reference value.

**248   ADA handbook: Employment and construction issues affecting
your business.** Martha R. Williams, Marcia L. Russell. vi, 185 p., ill.
Chicago: Real Estate Education, 1993. ISBN: 0793105951.

344.730159; 347.304159   KF3469.W55

Handbook deals with the accommodations in the built environment of the
workplace, place of business, or public space that must exist or be made to
comply with the Americans with Disabilities Act. Also covered are considerations of more general accommodations as condition of employment. A
useful, practical, and down-to-earth take on how the ADA plays out in the
real world. Includes bibliographical references and index.

249   Americans with Disabilities Act handbook. [U.S. Department
of Justice, Equal Employment Opportunity Commission]. 1 v.
(various pagings), ill. Washington: [U.S. Department of Justice,
Equal Employment Opportunity Commission], [1991]. ISBN:
0160358477.

346.73013; 347.30613   KF480.A32A2

Just as the regulations and interpretations that flowed from the passage of
the 1989 Americans with Disabilities Act were beginning to settle in 1992,
the Department of Justice created this handbook to explain what the ADA
meant in practical terms. Nearly two decades after passage, this careful and
detailed handbook still provides solid guidance for the intent and extent
of that landmark legislation.

250   Americans with Disabilities Act handbook. 4th ed. Henry H.
Perritt. 2 v., forms. New York: Aspen Publishers, 2003. ISBN:
073553148X.

                                                               KF3469.P47

This 4th ed. of Perritt's *Americans with Disabilities Act handbook,* kept
up-to-date with annual supplements (the most recent in 2007 is *2007-1
Cumulative supplement/Volumes 1 & 2,*), is the working document for
exactly how the ADA fits into the business and cultural life of America
today. A useful and definitive two volume reference set covering a shifting regulatory and legal framework that governs protections for disabled
persons in the United States.

251   Dementia, aging, and intellectual disabilities: A handbook.
Mattthew P. Janicki, A. J. Dalton. xxix, 488 p., ill. Philadelphia:
Brunner/Mazel, 1999. ISBN: 0876309163.

618.97683   RC523.D455

The special circumstance of a person who lives with intellectual disability developing Alzheimer's or other dementia is covered in this thorough and insightful handbook. Especially useful are the three case studies of persons in this circumstance. The biology and physiology of dementia are also well-documented. Best practices section gives extensive detail on how best to care for such individuals. Includes a lengthy resource section, glossary, bibliographical references, and index. An essential handbook for the professional, and also highly recommended for general collections to provide solid information for family members or friends of such a disabled person.

252   **Disability, civil rights law, and policy.** Peter David Blanck. 1 v. (various pagings). St. Paul, Minn.: Thomson/West, 2004. ISBN: 0314145141.

342.73087   KF480.D57

The rights that society gives to the disabled are inexorably tangled within, as well as being guaranteed by, law and regulations. This highly useful handbook, kept up-to-date with pocket parts, documents both law and policy as they have evolved in recent years to enable the disabled. The United States and other countries are covered, and the current interpretation of the 1989 Americans with Disabilities Act is presented. Discusses the history of the movement for civil rights for the disabled and the ways that disability must be accounted for in public services, public accommodations, and freedom from discrimination in housing, employment, and education. Implications for social welfare and tax policy are also covered. A useful reference work for both general and research collections, as well as in law libraries.

253   **First response to victims of crime who have a disability: A handbook for law enforcement officers on how to approach and help crime victims who have Alzheimer's disease, mental illness, mental retardation, or who are blind or visually impaired, deaf or hard of hearing.** United States, National Sheriffs' Association. vii, 25 p. Washington: U.S. Department of Justice, Office of Justice Programs, Office for Victims of Crime, 2002.

362.88   HV6250.25.U548

Various disabilities can make it difficult for police and other law enforcement personnel to communicate with or properly evaluate disabled individuals who are victims of crime or who might otherwise come to their attention. This practical and useful handbook provides a thorough foundation for better understanding the situation with disabled persons.

Also an Internet resource at http://www.ojp.usdoj.gov/ovc/publications/infores/firstrep/2002/NCJ195 500.pdf.

254   The golden bridge: Selecting and training assistance dogs for children with social, emotional, and educational challenges. Patty Dobbs Gross. xi, 251 p., ill. West Lafayette, Ind.: Purdue University Press, 2006. ISBN: 155753408X.

362.4083   HV1780.G76

The remarkable encouragement and assistance that dogs can bring to children with autism or other developmental disabilities is detailed in this handbook. Discusses the situation of disabled children and describes how dogs can be introduced into their lives to great benefit. Combines matter-of-fact descriptions with sensitive, yet accurate, terminology. For parents and professionals. This reference is also useful more broadly to understand how assistance dogs may help disabled persons of any age who have mental disabilities.

255   Handbook of attention deficit hyperactivity disorder. Michael Fitzgerald, Mark Bellgrove, Michael Gill. Chichester, West Sussex, England, [U.K.]; Hoboken, N.J.: John Wiley and Sons, 2007. ISBN: 9780470014448.

618.928589   RJ506.H9H3449

A useful handbook that explains how Attention Deficit Hyperactivity Disorder (ADHD) affects the individual and, by extension, the family and the community. Some 20 signed essays deal with ADHD in both children and adults. Various theories for causes are discussed, and pharmacology of treatment, along with behavioral modifications, are presented. The role of genetics is described from several perspectives. An exhaustive and authoritative treatment of ADHD that would be useful in both general and research collections. Includes bibliographical references and index. Available as an e-book.

256   Handbook of communication and people with disabilities: Research and application. Dawn O. Braithwaite, Teresa L. Thompson. xviii, 555 p., ill. Mahwah, N.J.: Lawrence Erlbaum Associates, 2000. ISBN: 0805830596.

362.4048   HV1569.4.H35

Research in the field of communications includes a broad spectrum of the social and behavioral sciences, and as a relatively new discipline often asks as many questions as it answers. This handbook was the first work to focus in a serious way on the special needs and circumstances of communication among disabled persons, and of communication of disabled persons with those who are not. The first section of five signed chapters discusses "Interpersonal and Relationship Issues." The second section deals with organizational settings, addressing communication in the special education and college campus environments. Beyond the scholarly issues of communication research, this volume is a valuable reference for anyone trying to understand how to improve communication with disabled persons, in any setting. Includes bibliographical references and indexes. Available as an e-book.

257 **Handbook of intellectual and developmental disabilities.** John W. Jacobson, James A. Mulick, Johannes Rojahn. xx, 726 p., ill. New York: Springer, 2007. ISBN: 9780387329307.

618.928588 RJ506.D47H358

As disabled persons have entered the mainstream of society in the last 25 years, the need to understand intellectual disability, termed mental retardation, has increased dramatically. This serious handbook is an in-depth reference for all aspects of mental retardation, autism, and other forms of intellectual disability. Adults are covered especially well, and children are included. Social and vocational skills are discussed; a final essay on ethics and values in working in these areas raises interesting issues for consideration. Includes bibliographical references and index. Available as an e-book.

258 **If you are blind or have low vision, how we can help.** Braille - annual ed. U.S. Social Security Administration. 1 v. of braille. Baltimore: U.S. Social Security Administration, 2006.

Published annually in braille, paper, and Internet versions, this guide outlines programs and assistance available from the U.S. Social Security Administration to the blind and those with low sight. Online at http://www.ssa.gov/pubs/10052.html as a PDF.

259 **Improving access to public transport: Guidelines for transport personnel.** European Conference of Ministers of Transport. 27 p., ill. Paris: ECMT Publications, 2006. ISBN: 9282103579.

HV1568.6.I55

In Europe, as well as elsewhere, preserving the independence of elderly and disabled persons relies in part on a transportation system that is both accessible and user-friendly. Guidelines presented here help operators understand the concerns of elderly and disabled passengers, and suggest ways to respond to their needs. The attitude and skill of the operator, whether it be a driver, captain, or pilot, can go a long way toward accomplishing ready access and making the older or disabled person feel comfortable using the transport. This refreshing European publication includes, but goes beyond, the necessary barrier-free physical environment so often emphasized in American publications. Ready access must be provided, but there is also a strong emphasis on the importance of creating a truly friendly environment for the elderly or disabled passenger all around. Available as an e-book.

260   **Including children with special needs: A handbook for educators and parents.** Diane Schwartz, Susan Semel. Westport, Conn.: Greenwood Press, 2005. ISBN: 0313333777.

371.9046   LC3981.I62

The 1997 Americans with Disabilities Act created in U.S. federal law significant new requirements to protect and enable disabled persons. One of the most significant of these was mandated access to education in the least restrictive environment in public schools, i.e., mainstreaming into regular classrooms. This thorough handbook presents 13 essays on ways to provide a good education and also a positive home environment for all children, disabled and not, by making both schools and homes better for the disabled child. Thoughtful, useful, and practical. Includes bibliographical references and index.

261   **Making Europe accessible for tourists with disabilities: Handbook for the tourism industry.** European Commission, [Directorate General XXIII, Tourism Unit]. 119 p., ill. Luxembourg; Lanham, Md.: Office for Official Publications of the European Communities, 1996. ISBN: 9282773.

HV1568.6.M35

The challenge of creating an accessible environment across a diverse and antique region, with old cities, long-established ports, and airports, is addressed in this broad-ranging handbook. Stresses the importance of improving access in both new and renovated construction as soon and as much as possible. Includes bibliographical references.

262 **Natural environments and inclusion.** Susan Rebecka Sandall, Michaelene Ostrosky. vi, 84 p., ill. Denver: Division for Early Childhood of the Council for Exceptional Children, 2000. ISBN: 1570353425.

HQ778.5.N38

Handbook provides an overview and details on the inclusion of young children with disabilities into mainstream life. Inclusion is a positive term to offset the negativity that can be implied in the concept of "not discriminating" against such children. This handbook offers the perspective that having disabled children be a part of everyday life, in day care, schools, and the home, along with able-bodied children, is a natural and wholesome concept that benefits everyone.

Updates, and an extension of this concept, are provided on the website, Natural Environments and Inclusion (http://www.nectac.org/topics/inclusion/) of the National Early Childhood Technical Assistance Center at the University of North Carolina at Chapel Hill. This site provides links to numerous organizations and projects that promote acceptance of children with disabilities in society.

263 **Oxford handbook of deaf studies, language, and education.** Marc Marschark, Patricia Elizabeth Spencer. xvi, 505 p., ill. Oxford; New York: Oxford University Press, 2003. ISBN: 0195149971.

362.42   HV2380.O88

Volume begins with in-depth review of the role and remarkable contributions of deaf people throughout recorded history. Well-documented and clearly written signed essays by scholars from a broad range of disciplines. Provides an up-to-date and global assessment of the opportunities and circumstances of deaf and hard of hearing people today. Paternalism is avoided, with factual presentation and respect for their many contributions. Covers acquisition and development of language by the deaf, their perception of speech, language and language development, and their hearing perception. Also includes education, literacy, cognition, and cultural, social, and psychological issues. Several essays discuss the origins and use of sign language. Technological advances, including cochlear implants, are presented. Includes bibliographical references and index. Available as an e-book.

264 **People with disabilities on tribal lands: Education, health care, vocational rehabilitation and independent living.** National

Council on Disability (U.S.). vii, 135 p., ill. Washington: National Council on Disability, [2003]. ISBN: 016051438X.

362.40897073   E98.H35P46

The National Council on Disability, an independent U.S. federal agency that advocates for better treatment of the disabled, produced this lengthy report about disabled native peoples living on tribal lands and how they are served, and underserved, by agencies responsible for their welfare. This report was co-authored by several groups of native peoples, and carries the weight of both oversight and tribal concern for disabled members of the native community. Useful for understanding the care needed by these disabled persons, and also as a model for surveying and measuring the adequacy of care for disabled populations.

Also available electronically at http://www.ncd.gov/newsroom/publications/2003/pdf/tribal_lands.pdf.

265   **The rights of people with mental disabilities: The authoritative ACLU guide to the rights of people with mental illness and mental retardation.** Robert M. Levy, Leonard S. Rubenstein, Bruce J. Ennis. x, 370 p. Carbondale, [Ill.]: Southern Illinois University Press, 1996. ISBN: 0809319896.

346.730138; 347.306138   KF480.L48

Even a decade after first publication, this is the classic handbook on civil liberties for persons with mental disabilities in America. Building on the freedoms guaranteed by the 1989 Americans with Disabilities Act, this volume reviews what society can and must do in the case of involuntary commitment, both as to admission and release. Also reviewed are personal autonomy, what really constitutes informed consent, and the person's right to refuse treatment. Discusses freedom from discrimination, the right to treatment and services, and rights in daily life, both in institutions and in the community. Outlines the responsibility of the legal system. Available as an e-book.

Internet Resources

266   **National Council on Disability.** http://www.ncd.gov/. National Council on Disability. Washington: National Council on Disability, 2007.

This independent federal agency provides a proactive and multidisciplinary analysis of the state of disability compliance and access for the disabled in the United States. Major reports are offered for free download in PDF format. Information is kept up-to-date on the site by bulletins, news items, and other materials. Publications make careful and sensitive reference to the perspective of the disabled person and their community. Valuable for a broad range of up-to-date information on the disabled.

Homelessness and Hunger

Atlases and General Overview

267   **17th annual World Food Day teleconference, poverty and hunger: The tragic link.** Ray Suarez, Amartya Sen, Patricia Young, U.S. National Committee for World Food Day. 2 videocassettes (173 min.), sd., col. [Washington, D.C.]: GW Television, 2000.

Nobel laureate Professor Amartya Sen leads a wide-ranging discussion on the relationship of hunger and poverty, on which he has written extensively. The occasion is the 17th annual teleconference on World Food Day in 2000. A compelling case is made that in order to alleviate hunger, poverty at the societal level must be addressed.

Bibliography

268   **Alcohol and other drug abuse among homeless individuals: An annotated bibliography.** M. Susan Ridgely, Caroline T. McNeil, Howard H. Goldman, National Institute on Alcohol Abuse and Alcoholism (U.S.). ix, 37 p. Rockville, Md.: U.S. Department of Health and Human Services, Public Health Service, Alcohol, Drug Abuse, and Mental Health Administration, National Institute on Alcohol Abuse and Alcoholism, [1990].

Z7721.R53; HV5140

Actual circumstance is examined against the classic stereotype of the homeless person as a "wino" or a "druggie." The homeless are often a difficult population to study, as are alcoholics and those addicted to drugs, especially because of the privacy concerns so strongly held today. This bibliography covers a time when research subjects were more readily available. Unfortunately, since this work was published, little has changed in the severity of both homelessness and alcoholism as social problems, so it remains relevant.

269   **An annotated bibliography of research methods used to study the homeless.** Norweeta G. Milburn, Roderick J. Watts, Susan L.

Anderson, Housing and Community Development Studies Center. ii, 143 l. Washington: Housing and Community Development Studies Center, 1986.

HV4043

Working with individuals from any human population offers special challenges today, but especially so with the homeless. There can be special circumstances beyond economic deprivation that lead to homelessness, which may involve perpetrators or victims of substance abuse, psychological impairment, physical abuse, crime, and physical or emotional illness. Within this especially complex framework, the works cited in this bibliography offer important guidance, cautionary notes, and suggestions for ways to reduce the intrusive nature of asking questions for research with the homeless. Still relevant 20 years after its original publication.

270   **The essential reference on homelessness: A fully annotated bibliography.** National Coalition for the Homeless (U.S.). iii, 448 p. Washington: The National Coalition for the Homeless; Homelessness Information Exchange, 1994.
016.36250973   Z7164.H72E88; HV4505

Produced by a national advocacy group for the homeless, this bibliography provides careful annotations to guide the researcher to appropriate materials for better understanding homelessness.

271   **Homelessness: An annotated bibliography.** James M. Henslin. 2 v. New York: Garland, 1993. ISBN: 0824041151.
016.3625   Z7164.H72H46; HV4493

The well-written annotations in this extensive two-volume bibliography provide important guidance for the selection of materials relevant to particular homelessness research needs. This is especially important in homelessness research because it is so complex and cross-disciplinary.

272   **Homelessness: Bibliography.** Barry V. Coyne. 206 p. New York: Nova Science Publishers, 2007. ISBN: 1600213065.
016.3625   Z7164.H72H653; HV4493

Thorough and lengthy compilation of references to books, articles, reports, and so on, on homelessness in its myriad multidisciplinary fields. Good indexing strengthens an excellent reference work.

273   **Homelessness in America, 1893–1992: An annotated bibliography.** Rod Van Whitlock, Bernard Lubin, Jean R. Sailors. 215 p. Westport, Conn.: Greenwood Press, 1994. ISBN: 0313276234.
016.36250973   Z7164.H72H66; HV4505

Identifies books, articles, dissertations, and unpublished works from a century of thought and theory on homelessness in the United States. Entries are presented in 11 topical chapters, including "Families and Children," "Special Populations," and "Alcohol and Drug Abuse." Includes 1,700 sources, 700 with annotations. Author and subject index.

274   **Publications relating to homelessness: A working bibliography.** [U.S. Department of Housing and Urban Development, Office of Policy Development and Research, Division of Policy Studies]. iv, 53 p. Washington: U.S. Department of Housing and Urban Development, Office of Policy Development and Research, Division of Policy Studies, [1990].
016.36250973   Z7164.H72P83; HV4505

This slight volume of some 50 p. offers a listing of publications on the homeless. Documentation on homelessness is not easily identified; this title is a useful addition to that group of reference materials because it covers the time period up to 1990, the date that roughly marks the beginning of electronic indexes and full-text databases. For dates before 1990, this title is one that serves well.

Directories

275   **Food, hunger, agribusiness: A directory of resources.** Thomas P. Fenton, Mary J. Heffron. xvii, 131 p., ill. Maryknoll, N.Y.: Orbis Books, 1987. ISBN: 088344531X.
016.33819   Z7164.F7F46; HD9000.5

Individual chapters on organizations; books; periodicals; pamphlets and articles; audiovisual materials; and catalogs, directories, guides, and curriculum and worship materials. Each chapter also includes an annotated list, a supplementary list, and a list of information sources to locate more materials. Contains organizations, individuals, titles, geographical areas, and subject indexes. "Emphasizes resources on the relationship of hunger to its political and economic origins."—*Foreword*

Encyclopedias

276   **Encyclopedia of homelessness.** David Levinson. 2 v. (xxx, 886 p.), ill. Thousand Oaks, Calif.: Sage Publications, 2004. ISBN: 0761927514.

362.5097303   HV4493.E53

Designed "to correct false images and misconceptions and beliefs from the past by providing readers with a comprehensive, accurate, and up-to-date description of homelessness in the twenty-first century."—*Introd.* Includes 170 entries divided into 11 general topics: Homelessness in the U.S.; Homelessness in U.S. History; Research; Causes; Health Issues; Organizations; Cities and Nations; Services and Service Settings; Housing; Legal Issues, Advocacy, and Policy; Legislation and Programs. Entries are some two pages in length and include bibliographies. Some illustrations. Homelessness in other countries is covered.

The voices of the homeless are given special emphasis. Global coverage beyond U.S. focus. Five appendixes are included: listing of autobiographical and fictional accounts of homelessness, a filmography of works about homelessness, a directory of street newspapers, a documentary history of homelessness, and a master bibliography of publications on homelessness. Extensive index. Available as an e-book.

Guides

277   **America's homeless: Numbers, characteristics, and programs that serve them.** Martha R. Burt, Barbara E. Cohen, Urban Institute. xi, [1], 176 p. Washington; Lanham, Md.: Urban Institute Press, 1989. ISBN: 0877664714.

362.50973   HV4505.B87

From three Urban Institute research projects, brings together findings on the homeless, presenting statistics on their numbers, location, racial characteristics, nutrition, and so on, and a summary of state and national programs intended for their assistance. Verbal descriptions are supplemented by numerous tables. No index, but detailed table of contents includes complete list of statistical tables. A useful snapshot of homelessness as it was measured and perceived in 1989.

278   **A status report on hunger and homelessness in America's cities.**
United States Conference of Mayors. ill. Washington: United States
Conference of Mayors. ISSN: 1088-7970.
362.5097305   HV4505.S735

Since the late 1980s, the U.S. Conference of Mayors has issued an annual
estimation of the number and extent of the homeless and the level of
poverty in the major cities in the United States. Trends in the numbers
of homeless and the assistance provided to them are also indicated at the
city level.

Recent reports may be available electronically on the Conference of
Mayors's website. See for example, http://usmayors.org/HHSurvey2007/
hhsurvey07.pdf.

Handbooks

279   **American homelessness: A reference handbook.** 3rd ed. Mary Ellen
Hombs. xiii, 299 p. Santa Barbara, Calif.: ABC-CLIO, 2001. ISBN:
1576072479.
362.50973   HV4505.H647

The problem of homelessness in America is considered and solutions sought
at both the federal and the state levels. This handbook brings together a wide
and rich array of documentation which sheds much light on the situation of
the homeless, and offers various solutions from all levels. Half of the material is new to this revised 3rd ed. Available as an e-book.

280   **Community relations strategies: A handbook for sponsors of
community-based programs for the homeless.** Rose Anello,
Tillie Shuster, Wanda B. Carroll, Shelter Development Project
(Community Service Society of New York). 38 p., forms. New
York: Shelter Development Project, Community Service Society of
New York, [1985].
659.2936358   HV4505.A63

Providing temporary shelter for the homeless is a first response at the local
level in the community where the homeless are found. However, without
appropriate interface with the local residents and business persons, such
shelters flounder before they can begin. This handbook, more than 20
years after its original publication, still provides a solid and useful framework for establishing appropriate relations between homeless shelters and
the local community.

281 **World hunger: A reference handbook.** Patricia L. Kutzner.
xii, 359 p., ill. Santa Barbara, Calif.: ABC-CLIO, 1991. ISBN:
0874365589.

363.8   HD9000.5.K883

Gives a broad overview of the many dimensions of world hunger, focusing specifically on the context of economic, social, political, and scientific
constraints that affect global food security. Available as an e-book.

Immigration and Immigrants

Bibliography

282 **National immigration forum.** http://www.immigrationforum.org/.
National Immigration Forum. Washington: National Immigration
Forum. Updated frequently.

Publications listed on the National Immigration Forum website are a
treasure trove of fact sheets, news briefs, analysis briefs, and full-length
reports on all aspects of immigration in the United States. Care is taken
to show both conservative and more liberal political perspectives on
immigration. Especially useful for broad and balanced overviews, as
well as for up-to-date information on current and pending legislation
in the U.S. Congress dealing with immigration. Many publications here
are available for free download; some more substantial ones are priced
and can be ordered here, as well as otherwise. Much material is from this
organization, but important resources from other bodies are also listed.
A valuable online bibliography covering current and recent materials on
immigration.

283 **Women in global migration, 1945–2000: A comprehensive
multidisciplinary bibliography.** Eleanore O. Hofstetter. xi, 535 p.
Westport, Conn.: Greenwood Press, 2001. ISBN: 0313318107.

016.304808209045   Z7164.I3H62; JV6347

Covers materials published from 1945–99 that describe, analyze, or otherwise document women immigrants. Includes books, chapters, journal
articles, dissertations, reports, and many other sources from a broad
range of disciplines. A rich resource for this time period before electronic
indexes and full-text sources. Available as an e-book.

Dictionaries and Thesauruses

284   **Dictionary of American immigration history.** Francesco Cordasco. xxv, 784 p. Metuchen, N.J.: Scarecrow Press, 1990. ISBN: 0810822415.

325.7303   JV6450.D53

Terms and events are included in this useful reference volume.

Encyclopedias

285   **American immigration.** Grolier Educational Corporation. 10 v., ill. Danbury, Conn.: Grolier Educational Corporation, 1999. ISBN: 0717292835.

304.873   JV6450.A59

The ten volumes of this thorough reference work for children will provide solid and accurate information to help in their study and understanding of how immigration takes place, and why people migrate to new homes.

286   **Encyclopedia of American immigration.** James Ciment. 4 v. (1576 p.), ill., maps. Armonk, N.Y.: M.E. Sharpe, 2001. ISBN: 0765680289.

304.87303   JV6465.E53

Thematic essays, organized in four parts: (1) immigration history; (2) immigration issues; (3) immigrant groups in America; (4) immigration documents. Entries include photos, maps, and charts. Glossary and bibliography. General, geographic, and legal-judicial subject indexes.

287   **Encyclopedia of diasporas: Immigrant and refugee cultures around the world.** Melvin Ember, Carol R. Ember, Ian A. Skoggard, Human Relations Area Files, Inc. 2 v., map. New York: Springer, 2005. ISBN: 9780306483219.

305.90691203   JV6225.E53

Multidisciplinary encyclopedia examines the overall effect of migration on those who migrate and on the cultures of which they become a part. In the first volume, "Diaspora Overviews" surveys more than 20 ethnic groups that have experienced significant voluntary or forced immigration. "Topics" covers the effect that immigrant cultures have had on their new locales. The second volume is devoted to diaspora communities and contains some 50 portraits of individual diaspora communities. A great new reference work, long overdue, and very welcome. An essential title for research and general collections.

288 **Encyclopedia of immigration and migration in the American West.** Gordon Morris Bakken, Alexandra Kindell. 2 v. (xxix, 848 p.), ill., maps. Thousand Oaks, Calif.: Sage Publications, 2006. ISBN: 1412905508.

304.878003   HB1965.E53

More than 300 entries cover numerous topics on the great migration from the eastern United States towards the Mississippi and west. Length varies from a few paragraphs to some dozen pages. Diversity in western migration is stressed, and the struggles of individuals and groups, such as the Mormons, are a focus. Native Americans are well-represented. Entries include suggestions for further reading and volumes conclude with an overall index. A useful reference set for school and general collections. Available as an e-book.

289 **The encyclopedia of the Indian diaspora.** Brij V. Lal, Peter Reeves, Rajesh Rai. 416 p. Honolulu, Hi: University of Hawaii Press, 2006. ISBN: 824831462.

909.0491411003   DS432.5.E53

Scholarly encyclopedia with signed articles. Contents are divided into two major sections: context and communities. Context contains chapters on the Indian context, age of merchants, age of colonial capital, age of globalization, Indian leadership and the diaspora, life in the diaspora, and voices from the diaspora. Communities include South Asia, Southeast Asia, East Asia, Central Asia, Middle East, Africa and the Indian Ocean, the Caribbean and South America, North America, Europe, Australasia and Oceania. An excellent and unique reference source on migration of Indians overseas. Classified bibliography. Comprehensive index.

Guides

290 **Bridging cultures between home and school: A guide for teachers: with a special focus on immigrant Latino families.** Elise Trumbull. xxi, 172 p., ill. Mahwah, N.J.: L. Erlbaum Associates, 2001. ISBN: 0805835199.

370.1170973   LC1099.3.B74

Teachers always face challenges in bringing the children in their class-rooms into a common framework of shared culture so that teaching and learning can go on. When children come from immigrant families, it is especially important to facilitate this acculturation in appropriate ways. Useful handbook presents practical suggestions, which are especially appropriate for children in Hispanic immigrant families. Available as an e-book.

291 **Immigrants and aliens: A guide to sources on UK immigration and citizenship.** Roger Kershaw, Mark Pearsall, Great Britain. xiii, 130 p., ill., port. Kew, [London, U.K.]: [Great Britain], Public Records Office, 2000. ISBN: 1873162944.

304.8410072   JV7620.K47

As home base for the historic territory of the British Empire, Great Britain today has become in some ways as much a melting pot of cultures and immigrants as the United States. The current situation, especially in relation to immigration law and the potential for immigrants to become citizens, is covered in this focused guide to British resources. Includes bibliographical references and index.

292 **State of the world's refugees: Human displacement in the new millennium.** [U.N. High Commissioner for Refugees (UNHCR)]. New York; [Oxford]: Oxford University Press. ISBN: 0199290954.

State of the world's refugees has an irregular publication pattern. This 5th ed. (2006) is subtitled *Human displacement in the new millennium* and follows the previous 2000 ed. subtitled, *Fifty years of humanitarian action.* The theme of the new edition is ominous—internal displacement seldom has any positive aspects and usually accompanies serious losses in the country (natural disasters, war, political unrest). This solid reference series surveys important issues in immigration and describes their effects. Illustrated, with maps and tables.

Also available online at http://www.unhcr.org/cgi-bin/texis/vtx/template?page=publ&src=static/sowr2006/toceng.htm.

293 **Understanding your refugee and immigrant students: An educational, cultural, and linguistic guide.** Jeffra Flaitz. 306 p., ill. Ann Arbor, [Mich.]: University of Michigan Press, 2006. ISBN: 9780472030989.

LB43.F53

When teachers work with students who have come from entirely different cultures, special considerations are necessary to smooth the learning process and help the students feel a part of the larger culture. Country profiles include statistics, a historical synopsis, and an overview of official national education policy. Includes bibliographical references.

294 Welcome to the United States: A guide for new immigrants.
U.S. Citizenship and Immigration Services. vi, 102 p., ill., maps. Washington: U.S. Department of Homeland Security, Citizenship and Immigration Services, 2005. ISBN: 0160723949.

304.873   JV6455.5

Official guide from the federal government that provides an orientation to American life and customs for newcomers. There are some three-quarters of a million new permanent residents in the United States each year. Also includes basic information on how the U.S. government works.

Also available in electronic form at http://www.uscis.gov/files/nativedocuments/M-618.pdf.

Handbooks

295 Handbook for preparing a resettlement action plan. International Finance Corporation. xii, 79 p., ill. (some color). Washington: International Finance Corporation, 2002. ISBN: 0821351532.

HV640.H35

Staff of the World Bank and the International Finance Corporation collaborated on this handbook, which outlines how a resettlement plan can be formulated in various cultures, with varying resources and by different kinds of governments, to help displaced persons make new homes.

296 Illegal immigration: A reference handbook. Michael C. LeMay. xviii, 341 p., ill. Santa Barbara, Calif.: ABC-CLIO, 2007. ISBN: 1598840398.

325.73   JV6483.L46

Examines questions surrounding the presence of millions of illegal immigrant workers in the United States from a wide range of viewpoints. Every immigration law since 1965 is covered, important court cases are discussed, and various approaches to issues such as labor, services, and citizenship are considered in detail. Brief biographies are provided for those central to issues of illegal immigration. Includes chronology and graphs to show trends. Provides directory of organizations working in the area of illegal immigration, as well as government agencies. Bibliographical references and index. Available as an e-book.

297   **Immigration controls, the family, and the welfare state: A handbook of law, theory, politics, and practice for local authority, voluntary sector and welfare state workers and legal advisors.** Steve Cohen. 367 p. London; Philadelphia: Jessica Kingsley Publishers, 2001. ISBN: 1853027235.
362.8400941   HV4013.G7C65

This British handbook relates the comprehensive 1999 Immigration and Asylum Act to the application of various aspects of social work in public welfare in the United Kingdom. Refugee status is covered, and many case studies are included. Bibliographical references and index. Available as an e-book.

298   **Immigration employment compliance handbook.** Austin T. Fragomen, Steven C. Bell. ill. [New York]: Clark Boardman, 1987–.
344.730162; 347.302162   KF4829.Z9I43

This thorough legal guide from West covers the most up-to-date requirements that employers need to understand and follow in dealing with guest workers. Frequently updated, the most recent is the 2007-8 ed. Addresses issues such as employer I-9 and other IRCA obligations, fines and penalties which may arise from the judicial system, possible immigration-related discrimination, and employee eligibility verification. Also includes some 80 sample forms. Overall purpose is to ensure that employers stay legal with guest workers.

299   **Immigration policy handbook.** National Immigration Forum (U.S.). ill. Washington: National Immigration Forum, 2000–.
                                                                      JV6001.I525

A comprehensive handbook covering all aspects of immigration in the United States according to current law, regulations, and practices. The National Immigration Forum in Washington, D.C., tracks immigration policy for the United States and publishes an update to this guide every few years. The tagline on the NIF website states their mission as: "To embrace and uphold America's tradition as a Nation of Immigrants." At the same time, this organization is careful of accuracy in its publications and other statements, and works to maintain the broad credibility it has achieved in the 25 years of its existence.

300 **Migrant education: A reference handbook.** Judith A. Gouwens. xvii, 228 p. Santa Barbara, [Calif.]: ABC-CLIO, 2001. ISBN: 1576075559.

371.82624   LC5151.G68

What are the special considerations necessary so that children of immigrants can learn in and become a real part of American schools? This handbook provides a history of migrant education in the United States and describes special programs for migrant children today. Special programs that are especially effective are covered in detail. Suggestions are then offered as to best practices in immigrant education. Concludes with a listing of organizations concerned with immigrant education. Bibliographical references and index. Available as an e-book.

Marriage and the Family

Artistic Works

301 **The American family on television: A chronology of 121 shows, 1948–2004.** Marla Brooks. xi, 285 p., ill. Jefferson, N.C.: McFarland, 2005. ISBN: 078642074X.

791.456552   PN1992.8.F33B76

Covering 50 years of family life on television—the quintessential popular culture medium—this reference book traces the evolving expectations and value sets of family life in America. June Cleaver in *Leave it to Beaver* was an idealized stay-at-home mom in the 1950s after World War II was won. Light family sitcoms, *The Cosby show*, for instance, first portrayed to a larger audience upper middle class professional families who happened to be African American. And then there is *Will and Grace*, which isn't really a family, or is it? This is an important guide to the changing American family. Bibliographical references and index.

Bibliography

302 **Annotated bibliography on the Arab family = Bibliyughrafiya hawl al-'ailah al-'Arabiyah.** United Nations, Economic and Social Commission for Western Asia. vi, 136 p. New York: United Nations, 2002.

HQ663.3

The structure, role, and function of the family in Arab countries is referenced in materials identified in this work. U.N. document symbol is E/ESCWA/SD-WOM/2000/2, and work is dated Dec. 11, 2001. Sources in English, French, or Arabic.

Available online at http://www.escwa.un.org/information/publications/edit/upload/sd-wom-00-2.pdf.

303 **Black American families, 1965–1984: A classified, selectively annotated bibliography.** Walter Recharde Allen, Richard A. English, Jo Anne Hall. xxxi, 480 p. New York: Greenwood Press, 1986. ISBN: 0313256136.
016.306808996073   Z1361.N39B5; E185.86

Covers black families for the 20 years before the advent of full text and electronic sources. Annotations are helpful in navigating materials. Good source.

304 **Work-family research: An annotated bibliography.** Teri Ann Lilly, Marcie Pitt-Catsouphes, Bradley K. Googins, Wallace E. Carroll School of Management. xviii, 315 p. Westport, Conn.: Greenwood Press, 1997. ISBN: 0313303223.
016.306360973   Z7165.U5W65; HD4904.25

Publications in the fields of labor and family studies are not often found in the same place, even in electronic index and full-text sources. This bibliography, organized into thematic sections, provides alphabetic entries that identify books and chapters in books, journal articles, as well as reports and other material of miscellaneous types.

Encyclopedias

305 **The encyclopedia of adoption.** 3rd ed. Christine A. Adamec, Laurie C. Miller. xxxvi, 394 p. New York: Facts On File, 2007. ISBN: 081606329X.
362.7340973   HV875.55.A28

Third edition offers concise but sweeping one volume coverage of the rapidly evolving world of adoption. Begins with a brief history of adoption, followed by some 400 entries that cover all aspects of adoption. Topics include international adoptions and legal issues, including laws governing adoption by gays and lesbians. Extensive statistical materials and listings of both private and state adoption agencies. Includes bibliographical references with entries, and index. A solid and useful reference tool in an area where there are few of this kind.

306   The family in America: An encyclopedia. Joseph M. Hawes, Elizabeth F. Shores, Steven Mintz. 2 v., ill. Santa Barbara, Calif.: ABC-CLIO, 2001. ISBN: 1576072320.

306.85097303   HQ536.H365

The two volumes of this survey encyclopedia relate the history of the United States to various events and concerns of the family in a thorough and sweeping coverage of both. For example, topics range from minority families, customs, rites of passage, and holidays, to legal issues including court cases. Addresses current issues such as the image of the family in popular culture today. Includes bibliographical references and index. Available as an e-book.

307   International encyclopedia of marriage and family. 2nd ed. James J. Ponzetti. 4 v. (1838 p.), ill. New York: Macmillan Reference USA, 2003. ISBN: 0028656725.

306.803   HQ9.E52

Remarkably wide-ranging, with substantial, signed entries that cover marriage and family structure in some 50 countries. Includes 12 entries on various racial or ethnic groups, and another 11 entries on religions or beliefs. Cross-references throughout. Each entry concludes with an extensive bibliography for further research. Excellent overall index in the final volume. Illustrated with clear black-and-white captioned photos. While there is a focus on industrialized nations, there is also good coverage of marriage and family in countries in the developing world. Even if this were not part of a field with only a small number of solid resources, this would still be a thorough and well-executed reference set, and is highly recommended for general and research collections. Available as an e-book.

This revised edition of the 1995 *Encyclopedia of marriage and the family* retains only a few of the 400 entries from that edition, as it more than doubles the content found there, along with moving to an international focus.

308   Marriage, family, and relationships: A cross-cultural encyclopedia. Gwen J. Broude. xiv, 372 p., ill. Santa Barbara, Calif.: ABC-CLIO, 1994. ISBN: 0874367360.

306.803   GN480.B76

While not up-to-date even when it was published, this title offers entries on marriage and the family strongly based in sociobiology. Not a primary source in any collection, but still useful when combined with other sources. Includes bibliographical references and index.

Guides

309 **Adoption: The essential guide to adopting quickly and safely.**
Randall Hicks. New York: Perigee, 2007. ISBN: 9780399533686.
362.7340973   HV875.55.H53

The author's two decades of experience as a topflight adoption attorney inform the information provided in this thorough handbook, covering all aspects of the adoption process for a popular audience. Fourteen types of adoption are outlined. Advice on selecting an appropriate attorney is given, along with coverage of various aspects of agency and private adoption. Warning signs for risky adoptions are described and legal issues are noted throughout. Especially useful is a state-by-state review of adoption practices. Recommended for general collections.

310 **The adoption answer book.** Brette McWhorter Sember. x, 261
p., forms. Naperville, Ill.: Sphinx Publishing, 2007. ISBN:
1572486074.
362.7340973   HV875.55.S45

This practical guide to adoption is thorough and useful, and while hugely popular in its approach, also solid and sound. Covers ground not often a focus of adoption writing, including second-parent adoption, parent-initiated adoption, kinship adoption, and embryo donation/adoption. Also covers gay and lesbian adoption, surrogacy, and includes a focus on raising an adopted child. Includes sample letters of inquiry and sample adoption agreements, along with an index and extensive bibliographical references to both print and electronic resources. A well-written reference volume that should be in general collections.

311 **The American Bar Association guide to marriage, divorce and**
families. American Bar Association. xvi, 239 p., ill. New York:
Random House, 2006. ISBN: 037572138X.
346.73015   KF505.A87

A sound and useful handbook for the lay person from the American Bar Association. Recently revised, handbook covers premarital agreements, what constitutes valid and invalid marriages, same-sex marriages, civil unions and domestic partnerships, finances, children, and separation, annulment, and divorce. Also covers child support, custody arrangements, and domestic violence. Suggestions are offered for how to use information and insights gleaned from this volume. A must-have reference volume in general collections.

312   **Child abuse sourcebook: Basic consumer health information about the physical, sexual, and emotional abuse of children, with additional facts about neglect, munchausen syndrome by proxy (MSBP), shaken baby syndrome, and controversial issues related to child abuse, such as withholding medical care, corporal punishment, and child maltreatment in youth sports, and featuring facts about child protective services, foster care.**
Dawn D. Matthews. xiii, 620 p. Detroit: Omnigraphics, 2004. ISBN: 0780807057.

362.76   HV6626.52.C557

Provides thorough coverage of the various forms of child abuse and related issues. This is a powerful standard reference for those who have the responsibility to prevent or to report child abuse, and for everyone who may suspect child abuse.

What constitutes child abuse? What can be done about it? This source-book is a good starting point for discerning and understanding what you suspect may be happening. A good reference for parents and other care-givers who have questions about the issues that surround child discipline. Highly recommended for general collections.

313   **Gay and lesbian rights: A guide for GLBT singles, couples and families.** 2nd ed. Brette McWhorter Sember. xvi, 285 p. Naperville, Ill.: Sphinx Publishing, 2006. ISBN: 1572485507.

342.73087   KF4754.5.S455

Positive, solid, and thorough legal handbook. Entries provide detailed cov-erage of the legal considerations that gay, lesbian, bisexual, and transgen-der persons need to keep in mind to protect themselves and their family members. Protections for GLBTs include hate crime laws, and the illegality of discrimination at various levels. Laws and practices in each relevant individual state are spelled out, and the situation abroad is covered as well. A useful concluding feature is a section of frequently asked questions, suggestions for talking with your kids about being gay, and a listing of individual state departments of vital records. Carefully detailed, practical, and sound. Bibliographical references and index.

314   Gay parenting: Complete guide for same-sex families. Shana Priwer, Cynthia Phillips. vi, 233 p. Far Hills, N.J.: New Horizon Press, 2006. ISBN: 0882822713.

649.1086640973   HQ75.28.U6P75

Guide discusses the legal protections necessary for the safety of both children and their gay or lesbian parents. Deals with adoption, fostering, and surrogacy, as well as the special considerations for transgender parents, and how gay parents can best nurture their children at each stage of their lives. A practical and useful guide. Bibliographical references and index.

315   Together again: A creative guide to successful multigenerational living. Sharon Graham Niederhaus, John L. Graham. xviii, 299 p., ill. Lanham, Md.: M. Evans, 2007. ISBN: 9781590771228.

646.78   HQ519.N54

Skyrocketing costs for housing for the next generation and for senior care for the older generation, are creating an environment where at least two, and sometimes three, adult generations share the same home. This practical guide offers cautionary advice and suggests positive steps that can be taken by those entering into such relationships to make them work better. Addresses physical changes in a home that will enable privacy for all concerned, and those that will make a home more accessible for seniors. Finances and legal matters are also discussed. Bibliographical references and index.

Handbooks

316   Adoption: A reference handbook. 2nd ed. Barbara A. Moe. Santa Barbara, Calif.: ABC-CLIO, 2007. ISBN: 9781598840292.

362.7340973   HV875.55.M645

Beginning with an essay that presents an overview of adoption today, this handbook includes a chronology of important dates leading to the present state of adoption, as well as biographies of key figures in the progression of adoption. Includes facts, figures, and a summary presentation of important U.S. federal laws, policies, and court cases concerning adoption. A mini-directory of organizations and government agencies rounds out the volume. Includes index and extensive bibliographical references to both electronic and print resources. Available as an e-book.

317 **American families: A research guide and historical handbook.**
Joseph M. Hawes, Elizabeth I. Nybakken. viii, 435 p. New York:
Greenwood Press, 1991. ISBN: 0313262330.
306.850973   HQ535.A585

Begins with an overview of changes in the study of the family in recent
times. Addresses the family as a changing concept during various time
periods: the pre-industrial family from 1600–1850, the new middle class
family from 1815–1930, families in the Great Depression from 1930–40,
families in World War II, the Baby Boom from 1940–55, and postwar
families from 1955 to the time of this title's publication in 1991. Topical
chapters cover women and families, African American families, Native
American families, and immigrant families. Bibliographical references and
index.

318 **Childminder's handbook.** Allison Lee. x, 212 p., ill. London; New
York: Continuum International Publishing Group, 2007. ISBN:
0826490247.
362.712068   HQ778.7.G7L44

This English handbook provides practical guidance for those thinking
about or engaged in providing day care for children, or "childminders" in
British parlance. Covers the home as a location for day care, along with
the potential impact on one's own family, business, safety, and health
issues. English definitions for laws and regulations make this especially
relevant for that geography. The no-nonsense and comprehensive discussion of issues relevant to creating a day care business is so well done
that this is a useful title for general collections in the United States.
Includes index.

319 **Complete guide to gay and lesbian weddings: Civil partnerships
and all you need to know.** Jo Webber, Matt Miles. 160 p. Bennetts
Close Slough SL1, [U.K.]: Foulsham, The Publishing House, 2006.
ISBN: 0572032749.

British publication presents a thorough and detailed plan for creating
weddings for gay and lesbian couples that are festive, comfortable, and
meaningful. Also deals with legal matters of entering into civil partnerships in the United Kingdom. Other than the legalities, this handbook
would also be of interest to American gay and lesbian couples planning a
wedding. Recommended for both general collections for popular use and
for research collections.

SOCIAL CONDITIONS AND SOCIAL WELFARE

The American publication of much the same name, *Complete guide to gay and lesbian weddings* (320), is also of interest.

320 **The complete guide to gay and lesbian weddings.** K. C. David, Wendy Paton. xix, 220 p., ill. New York: Thomas Dunne Books/St. Martin's Griffin, 2005. ISBN: 0312338791.

395.2208664   HQ1033.D38

A popular handbook for creating a same-sex ceremony that is classic, elegant, and legal. Practical detailed advice ranges from how to hire a caterer, to sample menus for the reception, to finding gay-friendly clergy or others to officiate. A serious but fun and practical planning guide. Includes index. More information is found on the website hosted by the same author at www.gayweddings.com.

Note also the British publication of much the same name: *The complete guide to gay and lesbian weddings: Civil partnerships and all you need to know* (319).

321 **Gay marriage.** Lauri S. Friedman. 143 p., ill. (chiefly color). Detroit: Greenhaven Press/Thomson Gale, 2006. ISBN: 0737732229.

306.8480973   HQ1034.U5G39

With another edition already announced for 2008, and a previous one in 2005, this handbook provides comprehensive coverage of both legal and societal issues for gay marriage. Since the situation is changing rapidly, this is one area where the most up-to-date and solid reference materials are needed in collections of all types.

322 **Handbook of adoption: Implications for researchers, practitioners, and families.** Rafael Art Javier, David Brodzinsky. xvi, 563 p., ill. Thousand Oaks, [Calif.]: SAGE Publications, 2007. ISBN: 1412927501.

362.734   HV875.H36

Thorough coverage of all aspects of adoption in 33 chapters of this multidisciplinary handbook. Domestic and international adoptions, identity issues in adoption, and transracial adoption are among the topics covered. A solid reference work for professionals, scholars, and students working with any aspect of adoption today. Also for families involved with or interested in adoption. Includes statistics, tables, indexes, and extensive bibliographical entries.

323 **Handbook of contemporary families: Considering the past, contemplating the future.** Marilyn Coleman, Lawrence H. Ganong. xiii, 622 p. Thousand Oaks, Calif.: Sage Publications, 2004. ISBN: 0761927131.

305.850973   HQ536.H3185

What have in the past been termed alternate lifestyles are today often simply part of the mix that makes up families and society. Gender and race are not the defining issues they once were. Multigenerational households, and households of unrelated families, are a modern correlation of the extended families of aunts and cousins from the past. What makes this title a useful reference volume, in addition to the signed and well-documented essays that make up its content, is the sense of wholeness that comes from considering the past, present, and future together. Includes bibliographical references and indexes.

324 **Handbook of domestic violence intervention strategies: Policies, programs, and legal remedies.** Albert R. Roberts. xxiv, 530 p., ill. Oxford; New York: Oxford University Press, 2002. ISBN: 0195151704.

362.829270973   HV6626.2.H36

The 23 chapters of this thorough and groundbreaking handbook provide comprehensive coverage of the legal and programmatic tools that can be used to help victims of domestic violence. These are interventions that are available to help the tens of thousands of women in the United States who suffer battering and other physical and mental domestic violence each year, including stalking. A serious and in-depth examination of how domestic violence of all types is seen under the law, and how women in these situations can be helped. Includes bibliographical references and indexes. Highly recommended for both research and general collections. Available as an e-book.

325 **Handbook of dynamics in parent-child relations.** Leon Kuczynski. xv, 488 p., ill. Thousand Oaks, Calif.: Sage Publications, 2003. ISBN: 0761923640.

306.874   HQ755.85.H355

Twenty signed chapters examine how children are reared and how their socialization is developed in family contexts according to recently evolving research. Parents and children are viewed as agents in family dynamics. Includes bibliographical references and indexes.

326 **Handbook of families and poverty.** D. Russell Crane, Tim B. Heaton. Thousand Oaks, Calif.: Sage Publications, 2008. ISBN: 9781412950428.

362.5560973   HC110.P6.H36

Various disciplines offer differing frameworks for understanding families in poverty. The strategies they offer for helping the poor differ and often complement each other. In this broad-ranging handbook, signed essays reflect perspectives from sociology, psychology, social work, family studies, and child development. Also includes viewpoints reflecting business practices and public policy. Addresses issues of help for poor families outside the public welfare system. Bibliographical references and index.

327 **Handbook of family communication.** Anita L. Vangelisti. xx, 767 p. Mahwah, N.J.: L. Erlbaum Associates, 2004. ISBN: 080584130X.

306.87   HQ519.H36

How do members of a family convey to each other what they intend to say and do? How does communication really take place? Comprehensive handbook covers current theories and research on issues of family communication throughout the life course. Includes bibliographical references and indexes. Available as an e-book.

328 **Handbook of family diversity.** David H. Demo, Katherine R. Allen, Mark A. Fine. xviii, 460 p., ill. New York: Oxford University Press, 2000. ISBN: 0195120388.

306.85   HQ518.H1538

A beautifully crafted reference work that opens with a consideration of the factors that can define diversity within a family or a community. Well-written signed chapters examine the evolving picture of diversity in families from a broad range of disciplines. Personal narratives are added to the scholarly analysis to give further definition to the issues being discussed. Diversity includes racial and ethnic groups, poverty and economics, and gender, including gays and lesbians, and so on. Includes bibliographical references and index.

329 **Handbook of world families.** Bert N. Adams, Jan Trost. xii, 649 p., ill. Thousand Oaks, Calif.: Sage Publications, 2005. ISBN: 0761927638.

                                                               HQ515.H3356

Authors from 25 countries in six world regions contributed the thoughtful essays in this thorough handbook. What is family in different cultures? How local, national, or global are the concepts and practices relating to family? Both theoretical and research perspectives are presented. As we move towards a globalized humankind, the basic societal structure of the family can help in our understanding of each other and our world. This title nicely bridges theory and application and is both solidly grounded and highly readable. A necessary title for research collections, as well as general collections, especially those serving multicultural or special ethnic populations. Includes bibliographical references and indexes.

330   Handbook on dementia caregiving: Evidence-based interventions in family caregiving. Richard Schulz. xiii, 330 p., ill. New York: Springer, 2000. ISBN: 0826113125.

362.19683   RC521.H355

Caring for a parent or other close relative suffering from dementia is one of the most challenging tasks a family can face. As physical health improves and lifespans increase, the loss of mental capacity becomes one of the realities of aging. How can the family cope? What does it mean to be responsible as a family? Facts and strategies are detailed. A useful handbook for general collections. Includes bibliographical references and index.

331   Helping in child protective services: A competency-based casework handbook. 2nd ed. Charmaine Brittain, Deborah Esquibel Hunt. xix, 556 p., ill. Oxford; New York: Oxford University Press, 2004. ISBN: 0195161890.

362.71   HV741.H45

Practical handbook and desk reference on casework investigation, covering step-by-step procedures in combination with discussion of issues and contextual factors. Prepared under the auspices of American Humane. Available as an e-book. Glossary, index.

332   The Praeger handbook of adoption. Kathy S. Stolley, Vern L. Bullough. 2 v. Westport, Conn.: Praeger Publishers, 2006. ISBN: 0313333351.

362.734   HV875.P694

More an encyclopedia than a handbook, covers all aspects of adoption in signed essays, including adoption in different cultures, time periods, and in a variety of circumstances. Perspective is multidisciplinary and multi-cultural. Bibliographies, appendixes, and indexes. Photographs. Includes bibliographical references and indexes.

Population Planning

Atlases and General Overview

333 **Atlas of global development: A visual guide to the world's greatest challenges.** World Bank. 144 p., color ill., color maps. Glasgow, [Scotland, U.K.]; Washington: Collins; World Bank, 2007. ISBN: 9780821368565.

HD82

This annual publication of the World Bank, now produced in a handsome and informative edition by the Collins company, provides a visual statement of where the environmental and economic resources are in the world, as well as the population centers. Includes economic categories for countries, such as those classified by the U.N. as developing, least developed, and so on.

334 **The gay and lesbian atlas.** Gary J. Gates, Jason Ost. x, 232 p., ill. Washington: Urban Institute Press, 2004. ISBN: 0877667217.
306.7660973   HQ76.3.U5G355

This highly useful atlas comes in two sections. The first, and narrative part, reviews the reasons for the study of gay and lesbian location patterns, and then discusses sources for the data underlying this work. Estimates are given for the size of the gay and lesbian population in the United States. Analyzes where gay and lesbian couples live, as well as other demographic characteristics. The second part contains the maps. Bibliographical references and index.

335 **The global citizen's handbook: Facing our world's crises and challenges.** HarperCollins. 1 atlas (144 p.), color ill., color maps. New York; Washington: Collins; World Bank, 2007. ISBN: 9780061243424.
338.900223   G1046.G1W53

A successor to the more plainly-titled, *World Bank atlas,* this work presents population, social, economic, and development information for the entire world in graphic form through its extensive collection of thematic maps. Includes bibliographical references and index.

336 **Planet in peril: An atlas of current threats to people and the environment.** GRID-Arendal. 38 p., color ill., color maps. Arendal, Norway; Paris: UNEP/GRID-Arendal; Le Monde diplomatique, 2006. ISBN: 8277010389.

363.7   GE25.P53

This English translation of the French *Atlas 2006*, produced by *Le Monde diplomatique*, presents in a compelling graphic format, with its thematic maps, the relationship between population concentrations and global ecosystems and natural resource stocks. Deals with climate change, shortage of water, overuse of natural resources, and an expanded catalog of the negative impact of humankind on the earth. Some balance is possible and is provided by depictions of renewable energy and sustainable production. Bibliographical references.

Bibliography

337 **Pro-choice/pro-life issues in the 1990s: An annotated, selected bibliography.** Richard Fitzsimmons, Joan P. Diana. xi, 284 p. Westport, Conn.: Greenwood Press, 1996. ISBN: 0313293554.

016.363460973   Z6671.2.A2F49; HQ767.5.U5

The debate over abortion rights continues to be an emotionally charged issue in the social sciences. This bibliography offers annotated references to serious discussion and analysis on both sides.

Encyclopedias

338 **Encyclopedia of abortion in the United States.** Louis J. Palmer. vii, 420 p., ill., maps. Jefferson, N.C.: McFarland, 2002. ISBN: 0786413867.

363.46097303   HQ767.5.U5P35

Comprehensive coverage of legal, political, religious, and medical issues relating to abortion in the United States today. Includes a summary of all United States Supreme Court opinions on abortion up until the year 2002. Also covers abortion laws for individual states. Provides directory of abortion organizations in the United States. Especially useful are the carefully reasoned and documented essays on political topics such as protests, and medical topics such as cloning and stem cell research. Bibliographical references and index.

339 **Encyclopedia of population.** Paul George Demeny, Geoffrey McNicoll. 2 v., ill. New York: Macmillan Reference USA, 2003. ISBN: 0028656776.

304.603   HB871.E538

A broad-ranging encyclopedia that covers population and related life course and lifestyle issues. Over 300 signed entries range in length from a few sentences to a thousand words. Contains some 60 biographical entries that cover the lives of those who have made significant contributions to the field of population studies. Includes a chronology of important events in population studies, bibliographical references, and an index. Available as an e-book.

Handbooks

340 **Handbook of population.** Dudley L. Poston, Michael Micklin. New York: Springer, 2006. ISBN: 9780387257020.

Handbook is a worthy update and successor to the 1959 classic, *The study of population*, ed. by Hauser and Duncan. This new guide covers in broad and comprehensive terms the development of theory and practice in the field of population studies in the intervening half-century. Deals with both theoretical constructs and field research, and presents a variety of useful methods for analyzing numbers and observations. A summary of the field of demography, and an overall guide to how population is studied today. Bibliographical references and indexes. Available as an e-book.

341 **World population: A reference handbook.** 2nd ed. Geoffrey Gilbert. xvi, 298 p., ill. Santa Barbara, Calif.: ABC-CLIO, 2005. ISBN: 1851099271.

304.6   HB871.G47

Beginning with a historical survey, this thorough and well-documented handbook continues with a chronology, biographies of notable figures in population work, statistical tables and graphs, and a list of organizations that deal with population issues. Also covers population growth over time, projections for the future, and key legal decisions. Available as an e-book.

Periodicals and Dissertations

342 **The state of world population.** United Nations Fund for Population Activities. ill. New York: United Nations Fund for Population Activities. ISSN: 1020-5195.

304.605   HB848.S73

Annual publication from the United Nations Fund for Population Activities that sums up critical issues and provides summary statistics on key global population issues. Each issue concentrates on a different theme. In 2007, it was *Unleashing the potential of urban growth*, with the Youth Supplement, a separate publication, titled *Growing up urban*. In 2006, the focus was on *A passage to hope: Women and international migration*, while the Youth Supplement was titled *Moving young*.

Available on the Web in PDF at http://www.unfpa.org/publications/index.cfm.

Poverty and the Poor

Atlases and General Overview

343 **An atlas of poverty in America: One nation, pulling apart, 1960–2003.** Amy Glasmeier. xix, 97 p., color ill., color maps. New York: Routledge, 2006. ISBN: 0415953359.
339.46097309045   HC110.P6G543; G1201.E625G5

Remarkable material resources in America exist side-by-side with the presence of large numbers of poor people. What can be learned about concentrations of the poor? Would introducing a different economic factor—highways, public transportation, businesses with jobs—have an impact? This atlas provides some visual answers and opens the way for policy and other innovations that could help alleviate poverty. Color illustrations and maps. Bibliographical references and index.

Encyclopedias

344 **Encyclopedia of world poverty.** Mehmet Odekon. 3 v., ill., maps. Thousand Oaks, Calif.: SAGE Publications, 2006. ISBN: 1412918073.
362.503   HV12.E54

Far-ranging work presents, in three volumes, perspectives on and analysis of poverty on a global scale from a myriad of disciplines. Begins with a detailed chronology from antiquity forward. Main section contains more than 800 signed entries, which range in length from a few paragraphs to some half dozen pages. Covers the ways poverty is defined and measured in various contexts, as well as the effects of poverty on special groups, including women, children, and the elderly. Includes historical context, along with political and economic factors in specific countries and settings. Provides biographies of individuals who have made significant contributions to the study or alleviation of poverty. Aid organizations are covered, along with statistical data that may not be readily available elsewhere. Includes cross-references, bibliographies, and index. Also available in electronic format.

Guides

345   **Asian Development Bank.** http://www.adb.org/. [Asian Development Bank]. Manila, Philippines: Asian Development Bank. Updated frequently.

Asian Development Bank (ADB) is a multilateral development institution owned by 67 members, 48 from the Asia-Pacific region and 19 from other areas. Its aim is to help its member countries improve the welfare of the region's people, especially the nearly two billion who live on less than two dollars U.S. each day. Asia-Pacific remains home to two-thirds of the poor in the world. Annually, ADB lends about $6 billion dollars U.S. and supports technical assistance of some $180 million U.S. With headquarters in Manila, it also has 26 other offices around the world.

Of special note are the open publications, many on this website, by ADB of applications and other documentation for many projects it supports. Most international aid projects supported by other bodies are done largely or altogether out of view. It is extremely useful to be able to study such documentation when trying to understand work which may be undertaken to alleviate poverty, especially within an international perspective.

346   **NGOs and the Millennium Development goals: Citizen action to reduce poverty.** Jennifer M. Brinkerhoff, Stephen C. Smith, Hildy Teegen. New York: Palgrave Macmillan, 2007. ISBN: 140397974X.
362.557091724   HC60.N499

Non-governmental organizations—advocacy groups for peace, the environment, human rights, and so on—are called NGOs in U.N. parlance. They have emerged in the last two decades as powerful forces for helping the U.N. achieve real results inside the nations which make up its membership, by alleviating poverty and, by extension, reducing hunger and homelessness as part of the U.N.'s Millennium Development goals. Biblio-graphical references and index.

Handbooks

347 **Handbook of families and poverty.** D. Russell Crane, Tim B. Heaton. Thousand Oaks, Calif.: Sage Publications, 2008. ISBN: 9781412950428.
362.5560973   HC110.P6.H36

Various disciplines offer differing frameworks for understanding families in poverty. The strategies they offer for helping the poor differ and often complement each other. In this broad-ranging handbook, signed essays reflect perspectives from sociology, psychology, social work, family studies, and child development. Also includes viewpoints reflecting business prac-tices and public policy. Addresses issues of help for poor families outside the public welfare system. Bibliographical references and index.

348 **Meeting the needs of students and families from poverty: A handbook for school and mental health professionals.** Tania Thomas, Donald Presswood. Baltimore: Paul H. Brookes, 2007. ISBN: 9781557668677.
371.826942   LC4065.T56

Students who live in poverty can present special challenges, and have special needs, that must be recognized if they are to achieve their best in school. Handbook provides perspectives from various disciplines such as history, society, politics, policy, psychology, and so on, to present a well-rounded picture of concerns and strategies. Bibliographical references and index.

Internet Resources

349 **World income inequality database.** http://www.wider.unu. edu/research/Database/en_GB/database/. World Institute for Development Policy Research. Helsinki, Finland: World Institute for Development Policy Research, 2007; 1998.

"The UNU-WIDER World Income Inequality Database (WIID) collects and stores information on income inequality for developed, developing, and transition countries."—*Website* Beginning in 1998, this database has provided solid and well-referenced detailed data on poverty ("Income Inequality") on a worldwide basis, covering over 150 countries or areas. With a strong economic and statistical base, this is not a quick reference tool, but rather one for serious research into the situation of poverty in the world. Data is not otherwise readily available, if at all. Available as a downloadable ZIP file.

Politics, Economics, and Organizations

Bibliography

350 **Sociology, anthropology, and development: An annotated bibliography of World Bank publications, 1975–1993.** Michael M. Cernea, April L. Adams, Ismail Serageldin. xiii, 301 p. Washington: World Bank, 1994. ISBN: 082132781X.
016.301   Z7164.S68C47; HM41

The World Bank has drawn on many disciplines to inform and strengthen its work in development over the world. This bibliography identifies sources from several fields that informed its work for the time period before full-text and multidisciplinary databases became available, and so this title has lasting reference value. Includes indexes. Available as an e-book.

351 **The sociology of religion: An organizational bibliography.** Anthony J. Blasi, Michael W. Cuneo. xxix, 459 p. New York: Garland, 1990. ISBN: 0824025849.
016.3066   Z7831.B54

Entries for 3,207 books, articles, and dissertations published through 1988 (some 1989 imprints are included), arranged under names of religions, denominations, and small religious bodies and movements. Most have brief annotations. Materials are in Western languages, for the most part English, and largely reflect North American scholarship. Provides convenient access to a substantial body of research. Author and subject indexes.

The authors' *Issues in the sociology of religion: A bibliography* (Garland, 1990) is a companion volume covering literature published through 1984. Entries are listed under issues within three broad categories: structure, processes, and disciplinary conceptualizations. Author and alphabetical contents index. The amount of overlap between the two volumes is unclear; different arrangement and subject access within each volume make each useful.

Dictionaries

352   Historical dictionary of human rights and humanitarian organizations. 2nd ed. Robert F. Gorman, Edward S. Mihalkanin. lxxi, 403 p., [8] p. of plates, ill. Lanham, Md.: Scarecrow Press, 2007. ISBN: 0810855488.

323.025   JC571.G655

Beginning with a useful list of abbreviations in an area where there are many, this volume provides a chronology of important events in human rights history in the 20th century. Introductory essays define human rights as the concept has evolved in the last century. Dictionary contains several hundred entries on organizations ranging from large multinationals, such as the United Nations, with large paid staffs, to rather small and largely volunteer bodies. Coverage includes the where, why, and how of organizations, as well as relevant information on events, people, conferences, and movements. Extensive bibliographical references.

353   Historical dictionary of the United Nations. Jacques Fomerand, A. LeRoy Bennett. cix, 571 p. Lanham, Md.: Scarecrow Press, 2007. ISBN: 9780810854949.

341.2303   JZ4984.5.B395

Beginning with a list of abbreviations and a chronology of important events in the more than half-century of the U.N.'s existence, the core of this thorough reference work is made up of some 900 entries that discuss the work of the U.N., the structure of its central organization, its myriad agencies scattered across the globe, its peacekeeping and humanitarian missions, and the people who have been central to its work, including secretaries general. An especially useful focus is on the U.N.'s primary mandate to prevent war and to mitigate its effects where it cannot be prevented. Concluding section contains the full text of key documents. Includes extensive bibliographical references.

Directories

354   Directory of religious organizations in the United States of America. James V. Geisendorfer, McGrath Publishing Company.

553 p. [Wilmington, N.C.]: McGrath Publishing Company, 1977. ISBN: 0843406097.

291.6502573   BL2530.U6D57

The organizational structures of religious bodies in the United States are discussed and explained in this thorough directory. Beginning with essays that provide a variety of definitions of religion, legal and regulatory issues affecting religious organizations are covered in some detail. Issues include taxation, employment practices, sexual misconduct of leaders, provision of health care for employees, and education. Includes bibliographical references and index.

Encyclopedias

355 Encyclopedia of associations. Gale Research. Detroit: Gale Research, 1987. ISSN: 0894-3869.

061.3   Z5055.U4; AS22.E53

In 1954, Frederick Ruffner, a sales representative, was looking to find the name and address of an organization and was shocked to learn that no such directory existed at that time. He then self-published an encyclopedia of associations and founded Gale Publishing, which soon became one of the largest reference book publishing companies in U.S. history.

The encyclopedia of associations is still the preeminent source for information on nonprofit U.S. membership organizations of national scope. Each entry includes organization name, address, phone number, primary official's name and title; fax number, when available; founding date, purpose, activities, and dues; national and internat. conferences; and more. Alphabetical name and keyword index.

Companion volumes: *Encyclopedia of associations: Regional, state, and local organizations.* (Gale Research, 1987–) and *Encyclopedia of associations: International organizations* (Gale Research, 1989–).

Also available as both a CD-ROM and online as Associations Unlimited (www.gale.cengage.com).

Aggregated Gale reference sources are available at Gale Virtual Reference Library (Gale Cengage Learning, 2002–).

356 Encyclopedia of the United Nations and international agreements. 3rd ed. Edmund Jan Osman'czyk, Anthony Mango. 4 v. New York: Routledge, 2003. ISBN: 0415939208.

341.2303   KZ4968.O84

The history and function of the United Nations as a global organization that is still shifting, evolving, and seeking enough funding for service (but somehow still going strong after 60 years) is summed up in the insightful entries in this thorough encyclopedia. Entries are usually not long, but do provide a real breadth and depth of information. In addition, provides texts of some major international agreements. Includes bibliographical references and index.

357 International encyclopedia of economic sociology. Jens Beckert, Milan Zafirovski. xxv, 773 p. London; New York: Routledge, 2006. ISBN: 0415286735.

306.3   HM548; HM35

Significant encyclopedia in a burgeoning new field includes some 250 signed entries. Examines how economics and society are interrelated. Entries are cross-referenced and include succinct bibliographies. Overall index.

358 International encyclopedia of organization studies. Stewart Clegg, James Russell Bailey. Thousand Oaks, [Calif.]: Sage Publications, 2008. ISBN: 9781412915151.

302.3503   HD31.I564

This four volume set, numbering more than 1600 p., is a welcome and defining addition to the relatively new discipline of organizational sociology. Other types of social groups—families, neighborhoods, and workplaces—have long been studied, but organizations themselves offer different and discernible structures, with somewhat standardized sets of internal organization, and ways in which people relate to those groups and hierarchies. The influence of the surrounding culture is explored, along with core relationships with economics and other disciplines. Entries reflect a strong multidisciplinary focus, frequently with an international perspective. Includes cross-references, bibliographical references, and index.

Guides

359 Guide for participants in peace, stability, and relief operations. Robert Perito. Washington: United States Institute of Peace Press, 2007. ISBN: 9781601279.

341.584   JZ6374.G85

Guide discusses expected and effective norms and behaviors for a broad range of organizations as they work in humanitarian and relief efforts and achieve stability in many different situations. Such work has to be undertaken in light of the nature of the particular emergency and in the context of the culture of the society where it takes place. Best practices for working in these organizations must be central and balanced in light of their philosophy and mission. A telling reference work for understanding the nature and function of international, non-governmental organizations, U.S. governmental civilian agencies, and the U.S. military. Includes bibliographical references and index.

Handbooks

360   Handbook of community movements and local organizations.
Ram A. Cnaan, Carl Milofsky. ix, 436 p., ill., maps. New York; London: Springer, 2007. ISBN: 0387329323.

307.33   HM766.H36

Sociologists have most often studied community life in terms of groups formed by familial, geographic, or workplace associations. Organizations that have been considered at all have been those with formal and paid staffs, yet organizations with largely unpaid and voluntary memberships exert substantial influence in society and on national and international policy. Emerging theories of civil society are now beginning to incorporate the voluntary aspect. This handbook draws on that experience, which is beginning to define this emerging discipline within organizational sociology, itself a recently-defined field. The contributors to this handbook are a stellar group in this new field, and they have created a group of accessible and readable essays. Bibliographical references and index.

361   The handbook of economic sociology. 2nd ed. Neil J. Smelser, Richard Swedberg. ix, 736 p., ill., map. Princeton, N.J.; New York: Princeton University Press; Russell Sage Foundation, 2005. ISBN: 0691121257.

306.3   HM548.H25

The publication of the 1st ed. of this handbook in 1994 sent out the call to sociology to inform and further economic theory and applications in a post-Cold War and increasingly globalized world. In this 2nd ed., 30 contributed essays document the development and maturation of the field in the intervening decade. The first section addresses general concerns, ranging from economic anthropology to emotions and the economy. In the second part on the economic core, economic history and the new globalization are examined, along with the sociology of economic institutions and the sociology of companies and industries. The final section provides an economic frame of reference for understanding various social systems, including law, education, religion, and the environment. Overall index.

362 The handbook of political sociology: States, civil societies, and globalization. Thomas Janoski. xxi, 815 p. New York: Cambridge, 2005. ISBN: 0521819903.

306.2   JA76.H383

Organized into five sections, the 32 signed essays from the leading lights in the field make up a handbook that defines the complex and dynamic field of political sociology in both classic and contemporary terms. A section of nine chapters on theories begins the work, followed by sections on civil society, formation of the state, state policy, and globalization. Each chapter could serve as a treatise on political sociology; taken together, they define and provide a comprehensive overview of what matters in this field. Includes bibliographical references and indexes. Available as an e-book.

363 Handbook of sustainable development. Giles Atkinson, Simon Dietz, Eric Neumayer. Northampton, Mass.: Edward Elgar, 2007. ISBN: 9781843765776.

Explores the relationship among economics, social needs, and the environment, including the urban setting, trade, poverty, and related topics. What does it mean to be economically responsible, and to be so in a way that does not critically damage the future? Includes bibliographical references and index. Available as an e-book.

364 Handbook of the economics of giving, altruism and reciprocity. Serge-Christophe Kolm, J. Mercier Ythier. v. 1, ill. Amsterdam, [Netherlands]; London: Elsevier, 2006–. ISBN: 0444506977.

HB523.H366

Giving (termed "nonmarket voluntary transfers") is examined from economic and societal perspectives in this careful handbook. Historical foundations of the field are presented, as well as perspectives on giving from various disciplines. The second volume provides a comprehensive set of applications for family giving, and charity and charitable institutions. International aid is considered, as is the welfare state. Includes bibliographical references and indexes. Available as an e-book.

365   **How the Army runs: A senior leader reference handbook.** 26th ed.
       Army War College (U.S.). xxiv, 553 p., ill. (some folded), maps,
       charts. Carlisle, Pa.: U.S. Army War College, 2007.

                                                                    UB210

In this 25th ed. of the U.S. Army's leadership and command handbook,
current theory and practice on the management of one of the largest
organizations in the world is discussed. Issued every two years, handbook
traces evolving theories of both field command and overall administration. While not held in many non-military libraries in paper format, this
title is available on the Internet at http://www.carlisle.army.mil/usawc/
dclm/html/linkedtextchapters.htm.

366   **The United Nations system: A reference handbook.** Chadwick F.
       Alger. xvi, 375 p. Santa Barbara, Calif.: ABC-CLIO, 2006. ISBN:
       1851098054.

341.23   JZ4986.A44

The size and geographic extent of the United Nations organization, along
with the complexity and magnitude of its missions, have spawned a complex worldwide system which well warrants its own thorough guidebook.
Includes historical summary and chronology, identifies units and agencies,
reprints key documents. Includes bibliographical references and index.
Available as an e-book.

Statistics

367   **Statistics sources.** Paul Wasserman, Gale Research Company.
       Detroit: Gale Research, 1962–. ISSN: 0585-198X.

016.31   Z7551.S83; HA1

A finding aid to statistical resources, arranged in dictionary format with
topics and countries in alphabetical order. Sources for the U.S. are cited
directly under topical headings, whereas sources for other countries are
entered under the name of the country with topical subdivisions.

Social Psychology

Bibliography

368   **African social psychology: A review and annotated bibliography.**
       Michael Armer. xii, 321 p. New York: Africana, 1974; 1975.

016.3011096   Z7165.A4A75

More than 30 years after publication, this bibliography remains useful for providing references to traditional social structures in Africa. Combined with newer and more general works in social psychology, this bibliography enables researchers and practitioners to include traditional and more global aspects of the culture in their work.

369 **Role portrayal and stereotyping on television: An annotated bibliography of studies relating to women, minorities, aging, sexual behavior, health, and handicaps.** Nancy Signorielli, Elizabeth Milke, Carol Katzman, Corporation for Public Broadcasting. xix, 214 p. Westport, Conn.: Greenwood Press, 1985. ISBN: 0313248559.

016.3022345   Z7711.S53; PN1992.6

Stereotypes of many kinds were common on American television up until the early 1980s. This annotated bibliography provides access to materials that give a guided tour of that landscape. Includes indexes.

370 **The sociology of emotions: An annotated bibliography.** Beverley Cuthbertson-Johnson, David D. Franks, Michael Dornan. xxviii, 222 p. New York: Garland, 1994. ISBN: 08240232188.

016.3025   Z7204.E5C87; HM291

Since the mid-1970s, when the sociology of emotions emerged as a strong new subdiscipline in the field, emotions have developed as an important factor in social psychology. This bibliography gathers into a convenient listing scholarship and research from the formative period of the field. Still useful more than a decade after original publication, and nicely updated by the bibliographies in newer works such as *Handbook of the sociology of emotions* (383).

Dictionaries and Thesauruses

371 **The dictionary of personality and social psychology.** 1st MIT Press ed. Rom Harré, Roger Lamb. xi, 402 p. Cambridge, Mass.: MIT Press, 1986. ISBN: 0262580780.

155.2   BF698.D527

Derived from the authors' *The encyclopedic dictionary of psychology* (8), with many entries and reference lists updated to provide tighter focus on the main theories and issues of personality and social psychology. Extensive cross-references are provided, as is a modest subject index.

Encyclopedias

372 **The Blackwell encyclopedia of social psychology.** A. S. R. Manstead, Miles Hewstone, Susan T. Fiske. xvi, 694 p. Oxford, U.K.; Cambridge, Mass.: Blackwell, 1995. ISBN: 0631181466.
302.03   HM251.B476

More than 300 topical entries can be used easily by students, teachers, and researchers of social psychology alike. Focusing on particular phenomenon, concepts, and theories, signed entries by international authorities vary from brief 50-word definitions to lengthy 3,000-plus-word essays with bibliographical references. Includes a subject index. Available as an e-book.

373 **Encyclopedia of human development.** Neil J. Salkind, Lewis Margolis, Kimberly DeRuyck. 3 v., ill. Thousand Oaks, Calif.: Sage Publications, 2006. ISBN: 1412904757.
155.03   HM626.E53

Alphabetic entries in the three volumes of this broad-based encyclopedia range over the life course, from how an infant develops identity and learns behaviors to the vicissitudes of old age. Human development is comprehensively defined as referring to the entire individual, including physical, psychological, and social aspects. More than 650 signed entries vary in length from a few hundred to more than 5,000 words. Topics in human development are drawn from multiple related disciplines, including psychology, education, anthropology, and biology. Biographical entries are provided for those who have made important contributions to the field. Brief bibliographical references and an index. Available as an e-book.

374 **Encyclopedia of relationships across the lifespan.** Jeffrey S. Turner. xii, 495 p. Westport, Conn.: Greenwood Press, 1996. ISBN: 031329576X.
302.03   HM132.T83

In addition to the relationship of the individual and various concentric social groups, lifespan studies adds the element of the aging process and looks at how society deals with different ages. This landmark encyclopedia covers lifespan issues from the perspective of their effect on personal development and progression. Bibliographical references and index. Available as an e-book.

375   **Encyclopedia of social psychology.** Roy F. Baumeister, Kathleen D.
       Vohs. 2 v., 1248 p. Thousand Oaks, Calif.: Sage Publications, 2007.
       ISBN: 9781412916707.

302.03   HM1007.E53

More than 600 signed entries cover a comprehensive range of topics in
social psychology, especially useful in this burgeoning field newly enriched
by contributions from related disciplines. Entries are clearly phrased and the
place of individual concepts in the overall field is shown. Covers the history
of the discipline, while methods central to research in social psychology
are described in detail. Central themes in the field, such as the meaning
of a sense of self, are presented in some detail, while special relationships
of concepts, such as personal psychology and health, are also included.
Key concepts from a social perspective include culture, groups, influence,
interpersonal relationships, and prejudice. Topics more strongly focused on
psychology include action control, attitude, emotions, evolution, judgment
and decision making, personality, and social cognition. Types of behaviors
that are separately treated include antisocial, problem, and prosocial.

Handbooks

376   **The Cambridge handbook of personal relationships.** Anita L.
       Vangelisti, Daniel Perlman. xxii, 891 p., ill. Cambridge, [U.K.];
       New York: Cambridge University Press, 2006. ISBN: 0521826179.

302.1   HM1106.C36

Theories and observations of interpersonal relationships are thoroughly
drawn out in this handbook, which treats the topic in an exhaustive fashion. Solid and scholarly, provides a serious research framework, derived
from numerous disciplines, for the consideration of how relationships can
be measured and understood. Personal details—divorce, adolescence, and
so on—are identified briefly among the formal constructs which make up
most of the considerable length and breadth of this volume. Bibliographical references and indexes.

377   **The Cambridge handbook of sociocultural psychology.** Jaan
       Valsiner, Alberto Rosa. xvii, 729 p., ill. New York: Cambridge
       University Press, 2007. ISBN: 0521854105.

306.01   HM1033.C34

Sociocultural psychology is relatively new, emerging since the 1980s as a
frontier discipline which draws together and integrates perspectives from

the natural sciences, social sciences, and the humanities to offer a unified concept of how the environment affects perceptions of reality. Scholars from 15 countries contributed the essays in this handbook. Volume begins with solid groundwork in theory and methods, which enables better understanding of later concepts and constructs. Of special note are part four, which discusses "Symbolic Resources for the Constitution of Experience," and part five, which discusses "From Society to the Person through Culture." Highly theoretical, but with solid examples from fieldwork, this handbook offers interesting directions for further study and research. Bibliographical references and index. Available as an e-book.

378 **Handbook of Asian American psychology.** 2nd ed. Frederick T. L. Leong. x, 515 p., ill. Thousand Oaks, Calif.: Sage Publications, 2007. ISBN: 1412941334.

155.8495073   E184.A75H36

Multicultural issues are well covered in this 2nd ed. of a handbook first published in 1998. It has been substantially revised to include new research and theory that have entered the field since that time. Lifespan issues, multiracial and multiple identity matters, awareness of the weight of stereotypes, along with consideration of matters relating to the elderly and to immigrants. Coverage is balanced between theoretical and conceptual, and methodology is addressed.

379 **Handbook of social comparison: Theory and research.** Jerry M. Suls, Ladd Wheeler. x, 504 p., ill. New York: Kluwer Academic/ Plenum Publishers, 2000. ISBN: 0306463415.

302   HM1041.H35

Social comparison is a basic process in the discipline of social psychology and can apply to judgments of things, processes, and events, as well as to development of the self and an identity in society in relation to others. This basic handbook explains the process through which such comparisons are made, what they mean, and why the field of social psychology has continued to explore, modify, and extend the subdiscipline of social comparison for the last half-century. Includes bibliographical references and index.

380 **Handbook of social psychology.** John Delamater. New York: Springer, 2006. ISBN: 9780387325156.

Provides thorough coverage of classic theory in social psychology, dealing with how the individual and social groups relate to and affect each other. Also presents new research and recently developed constructs, and integrates those into the overall survey of the field. Begins with an examination of how the individual comes to perceive both self and the world. Also explains how theory and research have developed a framework for understanding the relationships and interactions between individuals and society as they are present in groups contained in larger groups, and those in even larger groups. Bibliographical references and index. Available as an e-book.

381   The handbook of social psychology. 4th ed. Daniel Todd Gilbert, Susan T. Fiske, Gardner Lindzey. 2 v., ill. Boston: McGraw-Hill, 1998. ISBN: 0195213769.

302   HM251.H224

Updated to reflect changes in the field since its original publication. New topics include emotions, self, and automaticity, and edition is structured to show the levels of analysis used by psychologists.

382   Handbook of social support and the family. Gregory R. Pierce, Barbara R. Sarason, Irwin G. Sarason. xv, 573 p. New York: Plenum Press, 1996. ISBN: 0306452324.

649.1   HQ515.H335

Positioned within a series that focuses on stress and coping, this essential handbook on social support in the family deals with concepts and methodologies in four chapters. The relationship of parents and children, as well as spouses, over the entire lifespan are discussed in nine chapters. The final eight chapters discuss family stress from both normative and non-normative situations. Bibliographical references and indexes. Still the standard handbook for this aspect of family studies.

383   Handbook of the sociology of emotions. Jan E. Stets, Jonathan H. Turner. xiii, 657 p. New York: Springer, 2006. ISBN: 9780387307138.

302.1   HM1033.H37

A comprehensive handbook that thoroughly documents the emergence of emotions as a primary study in sociology and social psychology in the last 30 years. Many contributors are key figures in the field. The first section focuses on the range of emotions studied, their neurological basis, and the place of gender in emotional response. The second section provides an overview of major sociological theories of emotion, including power and status, rituals, identity and self, and so on. Section three looks at theory and research on specific emotions, while the fourth section examines how the sociology of emotions has influenced other parts of sociology, as well as other fields. Available as an e-book.

384   The new handbook of language and social psychology. W. P. Robinson, Howard Giles. xx, 668 p. Chichester, England, [U.K.]; New York: J. Wiley, 2001. ISBN: 0471490962.

302.2019   P106.N447

This updated edition of the standard handbook on language and social psychology brings in the considerable research and theoretical advances of the decade since the 1st ed. in 1990. Provides extensive coverage on how language is used to communicate the individual and the place that person claims in society. Computer-based communication is also explored. A key resource in sociolinguistics. Bibliographical references and indexes.

385   The SAGE handbook of conflict communication: Integrating theory, research, and practice. John G. Oetzel, Stella Ting-Toomey. xvi, 792 p., ill. Thousand Oaks, Calif.: Sage Publications, 2006. ISBN: 0761930450.

303.6   HM1126.S24

Two dozen signed essays explore conflict and what it means for communication in a variety of interpersonal situations. Handbook begins with definitions and a welcome survey of quantitative methods, often overlooked or presented only minimally in other social psychology handbooks. The interplay of conflict and communication ranges across diverse topics, including dating and marriage, work life, racial and ethnic conflict, and difficulties in organizations. Special consideration is given to cultures in particular countries, some developing. Noteworthy are chapters on the rapidly emerging fields of crisis and hostage negotiation, and conflict resolution in international and intercultural situations. Bibliographical references and indexes.

386   The Sage handbook of methods in social psychology. Carol Sansone, Carolyn C. Morf, A. T. Panter. xxvii, 528 p., ill. Thousand Oaks, [Calif.]: Sage Publications, 2004. ISBN: 076192535X.

302.01   HM1019.S24

Basic handbook of the methodological framework for social psychology is made up of signed chapters in three sections. First section examines the research process and suggests ways to focus on the goals to be accomplished; second section outlines structures and strategies for design and analysis, with statistical analysis at a basic level. Third section looks at ethical considerations and cross-disciplinary enrichments that can be achieved. Includes bibliographical references and indexes.

387 **The Sage handbook of social psychology.** Michael A. Hogg, Joel Cooper. xxi, 525 p. London; Thousand Oaks, Calif.: Sage, 2003. ISBN: 0761966366.

302 HM1033.S24

Handbook contains 23 signed chapters, beginning with a history of social psychology stretching back over a century. A chapter is devoted to accepted methodology and another deals with "Honoring Culture Scientifically" while working in the field. Sections that follow are devoted to progressive organizational hierarchies; they deal with individual processes, interpersonal processes, processes within groups, and intergroup processes and society. Within each of these sections, the psychology of the individual is related to social processes and structures. Key concepts are identified and clear language is used throughout. Bibliographical references and index.

A Concise Student Edition was published in 2007.

388 **Social psychology: Handbook of basic principles.** 2nd ed. Arie W. Kruglanski, E. Tory Higgins. xiii, 1010 p., ill. New York: Guilford Press, 2007. ISBN: 1572309180.

302 HM1033.S637

Handbook manages to cover thoroughly all the traditional ground in social psychology, but does so with a fresh voice that makes the concepts and theories accessible. Entries move across organizationally hierarchical structures, from individual to groups and society, a standard and sound way to survey concepts in the field. A special strength is coverage of multilingual and multicultural issues. Bibliographical references and indexes. Available as an e-book.

Social Work

Bibliography

389 **Gerontological social work: An annotated bibliography.** Iris A. Parham. ix, 207 p. Westport, Conn.: Greenwood Press, 1993. ISBN: 0313285381.

016.3626 Z7164.O4G44; HV1461

In the early 1990s, geriatric social work was developing when medical advances and societal expectations meant that being old no longer implied that meaningful life was over. This bibliography documents the literature from the various disciplines that came together to create a new and positive framework for social work with the elderly. Includes indexes.

390   Lesbian, gay, bisexual, and transgender issues in social work: A comprehensive bibliography with annotations. James I. Martin, Ski Hunter. v, 51 p. Alexandria, Va.: Council on Social Work Education, 2001. ISBN: 0872930831.

016.3628   HV1449

Bibliography provides a broad range of references that give useful perspectives on social work with specific minority sexual populations. Annotations provide guidance to content so that particular references can be chosen to answer particular needs. Index.

Dictionaries and Thesauruses

391   The social work dictionary. 5th ed. Robert L. Barker. Washington: NASW Press, 2003. ISBN: 087101355X.

361.303   HV12.B37

Since the 1st ed. in 1987, and now in its 5th ed. from 2003, this is the standard listing of social work terms. Contains more than 9,000 entries, including terms, concepts, organizations, and persons, both present and historical.

Encyclopedias

392   Encyclopedia of social work. 20th ed. Terry Mizrahi, Larry E. Davis, National Association of Social Workers. 4 v. : ill. Washington: NASW Press, 2008. ISBN: 9780195306613.

361.303   HV12

Social work is one of the longest established and most complex disciplines within the field of sociology. Society, law, crime, community, custom, family, race, gender, age, children, and other concepts central to social work practice, have evolved very quickly. The National Association of Social Workers (NASW) meets the need for comprehensive encyclopedic coverage of social work practice for those within and outside the field.

NASW's flagship publication began as the *Social work year book* in 1929. The title changed in 1965 to *Encyclopedia of social work*, with several

Supplements focused on updates in social work. Includes bibliographical references and index.

Guides

393   **Advocacy skills for health and social care professionals.** Neil Bateman. 185 p. London; Philadelphia: J. Kingsley, 2000. ISBN: 1853028657.

361.3   HV40.B329

One of the most delicate and important tasks that a social worker can undertake is to advocate for a patient or client when they cannot advocate for themselves. This handbook examines what advocacy is, when it should be employed, ethics for its use, how it works, and the legal considerations involved. Includes bibliographical references and indexes.

394   **Cultural competence for social workers: A guide for alcohol and other drug abuse prevention professionals working with ethnic/ racial communities.** Joanne Philleo, Frances Larry Brisbane, Leonard G. Epstein, Center for Substance Abuse Prevention (U.S.). xiv, 218 p. [Rockville, Md.]: U.S. Department of Health and Human Services, Public Health Service, Substance Abuse and Mental Health Services Administration, Center for Substance Abuse Prevention, [1995].

HV5824.E85C85

Provides a conceptual framework and offers practical suggestions for working with various ethnic groups. Particular consideration is given to work with major individual groups: African Americans, Hispanics, Native Americans, and Asian Americans. The concept of cultural competence is offered as the ability to deal with the cultural aspects of treatment for drug and alcohol abuse.

395   **The family functioning scale: A guide to research and practice.** Ludwig L. Geismar, Michael Camasso. xxi, 194 p., ill. New York: Springer, 1993. ISBN: 0826179401.

362.828   HV697.G447

The family functioning scale (FFS) in various permutations is a powerful social work tool to provide a standardized measurement of the overall functionality of a family and of the relationships within a family. FFS can serve in particular to identify areas of serious problems, including situations of child, elder, or spousal abuse. Classic handbook describes the role and function of FFS. Includes bibliographical references and index.

396 **Social work with the first nations: A comprehensive bibliography with annotations.** Joyce Z. White. v., 73 p. Alexandria, Va.: Council on Social Work Education, 2001. ISBN: 0872930858.
362.84

Handbook goes into detail about expectations and dynamics of Native Americans, also termed First Nations, and traditionally called American Indians. Social workers who work with client families of Native Americans benefit by having a strong cultural reference to best serve their needs. A useful work in the field.

Handbooks

397 **Handbook for child protection practice.** Howard Dubowitz, Diane DePanfilis. xxii, 681 p., ill. Thousand Oaks, [Calif.]: Sage Publications, 2000. ISBN: 076191370X.
362.760973   HV6626.52.H36

What constitutes child abuse and how can it be prevented? What are the signs to look for, and how can the social worker be effective in this environment? Handbook covers the entire range of social work practice that can create a protective and healing environment in a situation of child abuse. Bibliographical references and index.

398 **Handbook for working with children and youth: Pathways to resilience across cultures and contexts.** Michael Ungar. xxxix, 511 p., ill. Thousand Oaks, [Calif.]: Sage Publications, 2005. ISBN: 1412904056.
362.7   BF723.R46H357

This thorough and well-documented collection of signed essays, from the perspective of a myriad of disciplines, explores the personal characteristics and cultural factors that further resilience, which is defined as survival despite difficult circumstances. Theories, methodology, and interventions are placed in cultural and psychological context. Explores the roles for social workers, caregivers, and others who can help foster resilience, as well as the cultural context each can bring to the work.

Covers diverse national and international settings. Bibliographical references and indexes.

399   Handbook of clinical social work supervision. 3rd ed. Carlton E. Munson. xxi, 635 p., ill. Binghamton, N.Y.: Haworth Social Work Practice, 2002. ISBN: 0789010771.

361.320683   HV40.54.M86

Third edition of the classic handbook for supervision of social work in clinical settings updates previous editions and offers a new approach to partnership between supervisor and social workers. New technologies and managed care have changed. Includes many case studies to make practical the principles advanced.

400   Handbook of health social work. Sarah Gehlert, Teri Arthur Browne. xx, 747 p., ill. Hoboken, N.J.: Wiley, 2006. ISBN: 0471714313.

362.10425   HV687.A2H36

The development of professional practice in health social work is the foundation of this large handbook which ranges across myriad populations and health concerns. Discusses the role of the social worker as a member of a medical team. Of special note is coverage of ethical concerns, the role of the community, and the role of spirituality and sexuality in health social work. Covers the issues and concerns in working with specific diseases, conditions, and circumstances, including palliative and end-of-life care. Bibliographical references and indexes.

401   Handbook of social work in health and aging. Barbara Berkman, Sarah D'Ambruoso. New York: Oxford University Press, 2006. ISBN: 0195173724.

362.10425   HV1451.H34

Nearly 100 signed essays provide up-to-date and comprehensive coverage of social work practice in situations of special health conditions and with the elderly. Beginning essays discuss particular issues of aging, from age-related cardiovascular disease, to HIV, to mental health problems, to risk of suicide. Essays also discuss different special populations, including prisoners, gays, grandparents, and various individual ethnic and racial groups. Final section of the handbook discusses applied methodology, as well as surveys of social work field practice with an older population and their caregivers. Bibliographical references and index. Available as an e-book.

402   Handbook of social work practice with vulnerable and resilient populations. 2nd ed. Alex Gitterman. xviii, 910 p. New York: Columbia University Press, 2001. ISBN: 023111396X.

361.32   HV91.H265

More than two dozen signed essays discuss the issues of social work practice with people who have eating problems, are going through a divorce, are homeless, as well as with immigrants and refugees, gays and lesbians, and so on. Bibliographical references and indexes. Available as an e-book.

403   Handbook of social work with groups. Charles D. Garvin, Lorraine M. Gutiérrez, Maeda J. Galinsky. 527 p., ill. New York: Guilford Press, 2006. ISBN: 9781593854003.

HV45.H26

Signed essays cover the theory, methods, and practice of social work with groups. Addresses group dynamics as a way to further the goals of social work practice. Especially useful for coverage of group work with particular populations. Includes bibliographical references and indexes. Available as an e-book.

404   Immigration controls, the family, and the welfare state: A handbook of law, theory, politics, and practice for local authority, voluntary sector and welfare state workers and legal advisors. Steve Cohen. 367 p. London; Philadelphia: Jessica Kingsley Publishers, 2001. ISBN: 1853027235.

362.8400941   HV4013.G7C65

This British handbook relates the comprehensive 1999 Immigration and Asylum Act to the application of various aspects of social work in public welfare in the United Kingdom. Refugee status is covered, and many case studies are included. Bibliographical references and index. Available as an e-book.

405   Social work practice with lesbian, gay, bisexual, and transgender people. 2nd ed. Gerald P. Mallon. New York: Haworth Press, 2007. ISBN: 9780789033574.

362.8   HV1449.F68

Thorough handbook is a revised edition of the classic practice handbook for social work with GLBTQ persons, *Foundations of social work practice with lesbian and gay persons,* Haworth, 1998. Provides detailed guidelines based on practice advocated by the National Association of Social Workers (NASW) and the Council on Social Work Education (CSWE). Includes a solid foundation for any good social work program and deals with a broad range of particular issues for GLBTQ persons, with chapters on:

- LGBT persons of color, heterosexism, racism, and sexism
- Roots of conflicts in allegiances and pressures for unity via homogeneity
- Internalized homophobia, heterocentrism, and gay identity
- Clinical assessment for families where sexual orientation is an issue
- LGBT parenting

Includes bibliographical references; a detailed appendix of symbols, definitions, and terms; and an index.

Indexes; Abstract Journals

406 PsycINFO. American Psychological Association. Washington: American Psychological Association, [n.d.]. ISSN: 0033-2887. http://www.apa.org/psycinfo/.
150.5   BF1.P65
The most comprehensive index to the literature of psychology, indexing more than 1,200 English-language journals and reports and providing descriptive, nonevaluative abstracts. Formerly published in print as *Psychological abstracts* (ceased with 2006). Coverage has varied widely over the history of this title, extending back to 1872 in part. Abstracts are arranged by subject categories following the *Thesaurus of psychological index terms* (30). Coverage of books and dissertations, dropped in 1980, was resumed in 1992. Coverage of foreign-language materials was dropped in 1988. The database replaces associated indexes such as *Cumulative author index to Psychological abstracts* (Washington: American Psychological Association, 1959/63–1981/83) and *Author index to Psychological index, 1894–1935, and Psychological abstracts,* 1927–1958 (Boston: G. K. Hall, 1960–).

407 Social work abstracts. National Association of Social Workers. Washington: National Association of Social Workers, 1965–. ISSN:

1070-5317. http://www.naswpress.org/publications/journals/swab
.html.

361.005   HV1.S6455

Comprehensively indexes some 450 journals covering a broad range of
the social work field on an international basis. A current awareness tool
for practitioners, students, and scholars in a complex field that can shift
quickly. Topics include theory, practice, service areas, social issues, and
social problems. Produced by the National Association of Social Workers.

Electronic resource coverage begins with 1977; the paper version goes
back to 1961; updated quarterly.

Title for paper varies:

- *Abstracts for social workers,* 1961–77
- *Social work research and abstracts,* 1977–93
- *Social work abstracts,* 1994–present

Periodicals and Dissertations

408   **Children and schools.** National Association of Social Workers.
      Washington: National Association of Social Workers, 2000–.
      ISSN: 1532-8759.

371   LB3013.4.S62

This quarterly journal reports on the latest developments and perspectives
in school social work. Schools present special circumstances and challenges for social workers. The following have to be taken into account: the
structure of a school, its staff and teachers, the legal framework involved
with school and child, the parents or guardians of the children, and the
child who must deal with all these elements.

Internet Resources

409   **Social science research network.** http://www.ssrn.com/. Social
      Science Electronic Publishing, Inc. [Rochester, N.Y.]: Social Science
      Electronic, 1990–.

                                                              H62

Composed of a number of specialized research networks in the social sciences encouraging communication among readers, authors, and other
subscribers concerning their own and others' research. Topics include
accounting, economics, entrepreneurship, financial economics, health

economics, information systems and eBusiness, legal scholarship, management (including negotiation and marketing), political science, social and environmental impact, social insurance, and the humanities. The eLibrary consists of an abstract database containing abstracts of scholarly working papers and forthcoming papers, and an electronic paper collection of downloadable full-text documents in PDF format. Journals, publishers, and other cooperating institutions provide working papers. Access to the database and collection is free; some services may require registration or fees.

Urban and Regional Studies

Atlases and General Overview

410   **Atlas of shrinking cities = Atlas der schrumpfenden Städte.** Philipp Oswalt, Tim Rieniets, Kulturstuftung des Bundes (German Federal Cultural Foundation). 160 p., ill., maps. Ostfildern, [Germany]: Hatje Cantz, 2006. ISBN: 3775717145.

307.26   HB1951

A modern phenomenon is the significant loss of population in many of the world's cities, termed "shrinking cities." Often accompanied by economic downturn and the degradation of housing, industrial, and other businesses, as well as supporting infrastructure, populations are lost offshore or sprawl into formerly rural landscapes, which creates ecological harm. Atlas provides some 30 world maps, 50 charts and diagrams, and documents in fair detail the shrinking of some 40 cities.

411   **Fifty major cities of the Bible: From Dan to Beersheba.** John C. H. Laughlin. xviii, 246 p., ill., maps. London; New York: Routledge, 2006. ISBN: 0415223148.

220.91   DS111.1.L38

Cities of the ancient world, as recorded in the Bible, were often a critical oasis of civilization and order in an otherwise unsettled world. Ancient city patterns raise interesting modern questions about how cities can be organized and lived in. Bibliographical references and index. Available as an e-book.

Bibliography

412   **The black family in urban areas in the United States: A bibliography of published works on the black family in urban**

areas in the United States. 2nd ed. Lenwood G. Davis. 84 p.
Monticello, Ill.: Council of Planning Librarians, 1975.
016.309208; 016.301421   Z5942.C68; E185.86

The extended family of generations, kin, and close friends—in the next
house, or in the same or nearby community—was a key element of family life among African Americans in the United States, stretching back
across the days of the African diaspora. As African Americans and others
moved into cities, smaller family units often became isolated, while others
remade vital bonds with those who made up their new urban communities. Ties that were undone and remade provide a useful perspective on
the formation and value of family among African Americans at this time.
Later works do not capture this phenomenon or this era. This title should
be kept in the reference collections of research libraries serious about the
study of African Americans, and of the family in a broader context.

413   Blacks in an urban environment: A selected annotated
      bibliography of reference sources. Gail A. Schlachter, Donna Belli.
      45 p. Monticello, Ill.: Council of Planning Librarians, 1975.
016.309208; 016.9730496073   Z5942.C68; Z1361.N39E185

In 1975, America was still largely a segregated society, in the South by law, and
in the North by neighborhood. Understanding what it meant to be African
American, and living in the cities of America during this time, is thoroughly
outlined in the sources identified in this bibliography. Later materials do not
deal with this time period. Important title for research collections.

Encyclopedias

414   Cities of the Middle East and North Africa: A historical
      encyclopedia. Michael Dumper, Bruce E. Stanley, Janet L. Abu-
      Lughod. xxvii, 439 p., ill., maps. Santa Barbara, Calif.: ABC-CLIO,
      2007. ISBN: 1576079198.
307.760956   HT147.5.C574

Useful volume discusses and compares the rich cultural treasures of cities
and towns of the Middle East and North Africa. Maps, glossary, and index.
Available as an e-book.

415   Encyclopedia of American urban history. David R. Goldfield.
      Thousand Oaks, Calif.: Sage, 2007. ISBN: 0761928847.
307.7640973   HT123.E49

Urban history is broadly defined here, bringing in current issues such as gender and ethnicity. Alphabetical arrangement of entries covers subjects and individuals. Articles are signed and include bibliographies as well as sometimes extensive references for further reading. Synoptic "reader's guide" provides access to thematically related entries. Indexed.

416 Encyclopedia of the city. Roger W. Caves. xxx, 564 p. Abingdon, Oxon, [Oxfordshire, U.K.]; New York: Routledge, 2005. ISBN: 0415252253.

307.7603 HT108.5.E63

Compact encyclopedia of the built environment from around the world covers a wide range of urban topics from numerous disciplines. American and European concepts are covered. Biographies are provided for individuals especially significant for working with the urban setting. Entries are brief, a page or two in length at the longest, and are signed. Discusses theory of urban use and reuse, environment, and architectural and philosophical matters dealing with cities and towns. Bibliographical references and index. Available as an e-book.

417 Encyclopedia of urban cultures: Cities and cultures around the world. Melvin Ember, Carol R. Ember. 4 v., ill., maps. Danbury, Conn.: Grolier, 2002. ISBN: 0717256987.

307.7603 HT108.5.E53

Thorough coverage, in four volumes, of urban cultures on a global basis. Presents 16 topical essays, and some 240 entries on major cities or metropolitan areas from around the world. Entries include location, population, tourist attractions, languages, history, and a detailed discussion of the origins and current situation of cultural makeup and identity. Bibliographical references and index.

418 Encyclopedia of world cities. Immanuel Ness. 2 v., ill. Armonk, N.Y.: M.E. Sharpe, 1999. ISBN: 0765680173.

307.7603 HT108.5.N47

A basic encyclopedia covering 132 cities around the globe. Among the elements covered for each are location, size, history, form of government, economics, and transportation, in entries of some six pages in length. Maps and statistics are given. A useful reference set, accessible to younger readers and those seeking quick and ready coverage. Includes bibliographical references and index. Available as an e-book.

Guides

419 **Street talk: Da official guide to hip-hop and urban slanguage.**
Randy Kearse. Fort Lee, N.J.: Barricade Books, 2006. ISBN:
156980320X.
427.97308996   PE3727.N4K43

Culture is communicated through language in a primary way. This dictionary and handbook on street talk and urban language creates a framework for understanding what is said in the urban environment, especially among the young, and for speaking in ways that allow better two-way understanding. Music, often the coin of urban culture, uses this language heavily. This dictionary can decode otherwise obscure lyrics.

Handbooks

420 **Handbook of urban health: Populations, methods, and practice.**
Sandro Galea, David Vlahov. xiii, 599 p., ill. New York: Springer,
2005. ISBN: 0387239944.
362.1042   RA566.7.H36

Public health is a basic concern in the urban environment. Potential problems include the closeness of the population, possible lack or failure in provision of clean water and sanitation, and gaps in the delivery of safe foodstuff. Handbook describes these and other possible problem areas and looks at ways to prevent their occurrence. Physical health of the population is also considered. Bibliography and index. Available as an e-book.

421 **Urban sprawl: A comprehensive reference guide.** David C. Soule,
Neal Peirce. xxii, 570 p., ill., maps. Westport, Conn.: Greenwood
Press, 2006. ISBN: 0313320381.
307.760973   HT384.U5U75

Handbook examines in detail the situation of urban sprawl today, including environmental protection, regional planning to curb its continued growth, and revitalization of urban centers. Extensive bibliography and index.

Indexes; Abstract Journals

422 **Index to current urban documents.** http://www.urbdocs.com.
Greenwood Electronic Media. Westport, Conn.: Greenwood
Publishing Group, 2000.

Indexes publications of many large U.S. and Canadian cities; access to PDF files of publications indexed. Searchable by city, state, topic, or keyword; browseable by city or topic. Information prior to 1995 is accessible via the print *Index to current urban documents* (Greenwood, 1972–) and the associated microfiche collection.

Violence

Bibliography

423   International armed conflict since 1945: A bibliographic handbook of wars and military interventions. Herbert K. Tillema. vii, 360 p. Boulder, [Colo.]: Westview Press, 1991. ISBN: 0813383110.
016.90982   Z6204.T53; D843

Gathers together a listing of the wars and military conflicts otherwise often difficult to identify; covers conflicts from the end of World War II until about 1990. Fills in the time period before the Armed Conflict Database (448) begins coverage.

424   Political violence in the United States, 1875–1974: A bibliography. Jarol B. Manheim, Melanie Wallace. xi, 116 p. New York: Garland, 1975. ISBN: 0824010930.
016.3016330973   Z7165.U5M27; HN90.V5

The century ending in 1974 was remarkable for the extent of political violence in the United States, ranging from presidential assassinations to labor riots to anarchist destruction of private property. For its coverage of this time, and also as a foundation covering the years before most modern indexes began, this bibliography has permanent reference value.

Chronologies

425   Political violence and terrorism in modern America: A chronology. Christopher Hewitt. xix, 199 p. Westport, Conn.: Praeger Security International, 2005. ISBN: 0313334188.
303.62097309045   HN90.V5H49

American terrorism is chronicled in a thorough listing of the 3,100 bombings, shootings, kidnappings, and robberies in the United States from 1954 through 2005, that were enacted to achieve social or political ends. Listing for each incident includes the date, type, group or person responsible, location, and other details. Bibliography and index.

426   **Racial and religious violence in America: A chronology.** Michael Newton, Judy Ann Newton. xiv, 728 p. New York: Garland, 1991. ISBN: 0824048482.

303.6   HN90.V5R33

Useful chronology that details violent acts committed on the basis of race and religion throughout U.S. history. Includes bibliographical references and index.

Dictionaries and Thesauruses

427   **Dictionary of terrorism.** John Richard Thackrah. London; New York: Routledge, 2004. ISBN: 0415298202.

303.62503   HV6431.T56

A brief conceptual map provides an idea of the activities, concepts, counterterrorism terms, events, future, groups, ideas, and individuals that are covered in this book. The glossary gives translations of commonly used non-English terms in the context of terrorism. The dictionary itself provides extensive explanations of terms, people, groups, and movements. Includes a brief chronology of major terrorist events and bibliography. General index. Available as an e-book.

428   **Talking terrorism: A dictionary of the loaded language of political violence.** Philip Herbst. xvii, 220 p. Westport, Conn.: Greenwood Press, 2003. ISBN: 0313324867.

303.603   HV6431.H455

More a collection of articles on particular words than a true dictionary, this volume contains 150 main entries with an average length of about one page per entry, with broader topics (like "Revolution" or "Zionism") receiving multipage treatment. Entries cover definitions and etymology and focus on the social and political contexts of usage. There are also numerous cross-reference entries. General bibliography; name-subject index. Also available as an e-book.

Directories

429   Guerrilla and terrorist organisations: A world directory and
bibliography. Peter Janke, Richard Sim. xxviii, 531 p., maps. New
York: Macmillan, 1983. ISBN: 0029161509.

322.42025   JC328.6.J36

In 1983, guerrilla organizations were the principal agents of what has
come to be called terrorism, and were usually found in remote regions and
unstable developing economies, so they were often not documented. This
early and comprehensive coverage on a global basis of guerrilla and terrorist organizations is especially valuable to provide both factual information
and listings of what was being written about them at the time. Includes
index.

Encyclopedias

430   Assassinations and executions: An encyclopedia of political
violence, 1900 through 2000. Rev. ed. Harris M. Lentz. xii, 291 p.
Jefferson, N.C.: McFarland, 2002. ISBN: 0786413883.

909.81   HV6278.L45

Encyclopedia documents a century of crimes that targeted and murdered
political and public figures. Some 1,200 entries, arranged chronologically,
vary in length from a few sentences to a page. Failed attempts are included.
Prologue provides a brief account of earlier assassinations throughout history, from Julius Caesar through 1899.

The 1st ed. of this title covers the period from 1865 through 1986,
while this edition focuses on events from 1900 through 2000. Essays in
each edition document both famous and little-known killings of prisoners
and political figures. Information contained in the encyclopedia is difficult
to find otherwise. Bibliography and index.

431   Encyclopedia of domestic violence. Nicky Ali Jackson. New York:
Routledge, 2007. ISBN: 0415969689.

362.829203   HV6626.E534

Signed articles cover domestic violence for the entire lifespan, from childhood to old age. More traditional areas include battered women, child
abuse, and dating violence. Also covers understudied areas such as ritual
abuse-torture within families, domestic violence against those with disabilities, and domestic violence in military families. Examines role of

culture in domestic violence and describes therapies used in combating it. Also covers legal aspects and current research. Cross-references, bibliographies, and index. Available as an e-book.

432 Encyclopedia of juvenile violence. Laura L. Finley. xxiii, 336 p. Westport, Conn.: Greenwood Press, 2007. ISBN: 0313336822.
364.36097303   HV9104.E59

Examines juvenile violence at the criminal level through 270 signed articles with detailed bibliographies. Historical coverage includes the changing view of the child criminal over time. Incidence of juvenile violence is measured over time and in various cultures. Examines treatment of children and youth in the legal system, as well as media coverage of children and juveniles as criminals. Children as victims and as perpetrators are examined fully, and key topics in juvenile justice are covered, including gangs, guns, gender, and the urban setting. Includes bibliographical references and index.

433 Encyclopedia of rape. Merril D. Smith. xxvii, 301 p. Westport, Conn.: Greenwood Press, 2004. ISBN: 0313326878.
362.88303   HV6558.E53

Some 186 signed entries cover in detail the history of sexual violence in the United States, and globally, and put it into a cultural framework. A useful chronology begins the volume; terminology is given clear definitions throughout. Describes treatment of rape in the courts currently and historically, as well as individual drugs associated with date rape. Traces evolving advocacy and protection for victims in much of the current world. Provides extensive bibliographies of print materials, as well as Internet sites and films. Alphabetic and subject indexes. Available as an e-book.

434 Violence in America: An encyclopedia. Ronald Gottesman, Richard Maxwell Brown. 3 v., ill. New York: Scribner, 1999. ISBN: 0684804875.
303.6097303   HN90.V5V5474

A landmark reference work that provides a remarkably comprehensive and well-researched survey of violence in the United States from 1622 through 1999. Nearly 600 signed entries cover various ways to think about violence: types of violence, depiction of violence in the arts, and violence as manifested in sports. A number of biographies are included, from Wyatt

Earp to Lizzie Borden, as well as lesser-known but very violent individuals. Describes violence in cities and includes entries on the United States in wars. Illustrations, charts, statistics, and extensive bibliographies.

Guides

435   **International terrorism agreements: Documents and commentary.** Donald J. Musch. iii, 457 p. Dobbs Ferry, N.Y.: Oceana Publications, 2004. ISBN: 0379215357.

K5256.A35M87

Brings together in one volume the full text of some two dozen international agreements designed to combat terrorism. These agreements are often otherwise difficult to identify, or even find in individual legal references and databases. Also provides useful commentary. Concludes with a chronology of terrorist acts for the years from 1961 to 2003. Includes bibliographical references.

436   **Sexual violence, the reality for women.** London Rape Crisis Centre. x, 144 p. London: Women's Press, 1984. ISBN: 0704339102.
362.88   HV6569.G7S48

This slight volume from the London Rape Crisis Centre provides detailed strategies for women to deal with the mental and emotional aftershocks of sexual violence. Also provides insight into ways that law enforcement deals with such crimes.

Handbooks

437   **Bullying, victimization, and peer harassment: A handbook of prevention and intervention.** Joseph E. Zins, Maurice J. Elias, Charles A. Maher. xix, 428 p., ill. New York: Haworth Press, 2007. ISBN: 0789022184.
371.782   LB3013.3.B83

Examines school violence narrowly defined as bullying and harassment by other students. Within this focus, covers in detail emerging research, theory, prevention, intervention, and professional practice. Special emphasis is also given to peer sexual harassment and dating-related aggression. Covers high school and middle school issues, as well as multi-ethnic groups from Europe and Canada, and the United States. Goes beyond traditional views to explain aggression in schools and among students. Cutting-edge intervention programs are described. Includes bibliographical references and index.

438   The Cambridge handbook of violent behavior and aggression.
Daniel J. Flannery, Alexander T. Vazsonyi, Irwin D. Waldman. New York: Cambridge University Press, 2007. ISBN: 9780521845670.
303.601   HM1116.C36

Aggressive and violent behavior is covered comprehensively from biological and cultural perspectives. Genetics is examined as a filter for understanding causes of violent behavior. International and cross-cultural definitions and explanations are presented. Examines current research on both qualitative and quantitative measures of violent behavior; discusses violence at the personal, family, community, national, and international levels. Discusses outcomes and countermeasures for violent behavior. Bibliographical references and index. Available as an e-book.

439   Domestic violence: A reference handbook. 2nd ed. Margi Laird McCue. Santa Barbara, Calif.: ABC-CLIO, 2007. ISBN: 9781851097791.
362.8292   HV6626.2M43

In this thoroughly revised 2nd ed., family violence is considered in historical context in the United States. Current legal and social issues are presented in a survey of strategies for prevention. Describes services available for victims of domestic violence. Bibliographical references, including Internet resources, and index. Available as an e-book.

440   Handbook of children, culture, and violence. Nancy E. Dowd, Dorothy G. Singer, Robin Fretwell Wilson. l, 483 p., ill. Thousand Oaks, Calif.: Sage Publications, 2006. ISBN: 1412913691.
362.76   HQ784.V55H34

A comprehensive, interdisciplinary examination of violence against, by, and around children in a myriad of formats, especially in American culture. Examples include sexual predators in the home and from outside, other forms of abuse, forced service as child soldiers, bullying in schools, school shootings, pornography on the Internet, violence on television and in video games, and both drug and gang activities in neighborhoods and schools. Looks at broader policy and technology questions, including V-chips for television sets and regulation of video games. Bibliographical references and indexes.

441   Handbook of peace and conflict studies. Charles Webel, Johan
          Galtung. London; New York: Routledge, 2007. ISBN: 0415396654.
303.66   JZ5538.H36

Beginning with philosophical foundations of peacemaking, 24 signed
articles describe in detail the peaceful resolution of conflict and prevention
of violence from a variety of perspectives. Topics include nuclear disarma-
ment, conflict mismanagement, the spirit of war and the spirit of peace,
north-south conflicts, the role of religion, and the language of peacemaking. Future directions are suggested for teaching peacemaking and conflict
resolution. International perspective. Entries have substantial individual
bibliographies. Index. Available as an e-book.

**442   The handbook of school violence and school safety: From
          research to practice.** Shane R. Jimerson, Michael J. Furlong. xxiv,
          688 p., ill. Mahwah, N.J.: Lawrence Erlbaum Associates, 2006.
          ISBN: 0805852239.
371.782   LB3013.3.H346

Encyclopedic coverage of school violence in 78 signed articles goes beyond
description to suggest causation and offer remedies. Detailed and well-
documented articles cover a wide range of school violence, beginning
with antisocial and aggressive behaviors among youth. Essays describe
legal aspects of school violence and how the school environment can be
structured and remedied, where needed, to remove or reduce elements
that promote or allow violence.

Emphasis is on detailed coverage of particular problems, so that bullying is covered in six articles, anger management is the topic of two more,
and safe schools takes up another six. Threat assessment, weapons in the
hands of students, and dealing with shootings at schools are all addressed.
A number of theories of school violence prevention are described, with
case studies for schools where they have been used. Covers international
and rural situations, as well as responses to school violence. Bibliographical references and indexes.

443   Handbook of violence. Lisa A. Rapp-Paglicci, Albert R. Roberts,
          John S. Wodarski. xx, 460 p. New York: Wiley, 2002. ISBN:
          0471414670.
303.6   HM1116.H36

A thorough and comprehensive survey of violence in the modern world.
What is the effect on children and adolescents of living in a violent home

in terms of their own future violent behavior? How does violence in the community promote future violence? How can gangs be understood and countermeasures enacted? What is required to reach girls to combat violence and delinquency? How does workplace violence occur and how can it be prevented? These questions are considered in detail and response strategies are suggested. Bibliographies and index. Available as an e-book.

444 **The handbook of women, stress, and trauma.** Kathleen A. Kendall-Tackett. xv, 278 p., ill. New York: Brunner-Routledge, 2005. ISBN: 0415947421.

616.85210082   RC451.4.W6H365

Violence against women in numerous forms is detailed in this highly-focused work, with 12 chapters that describe the effect violence has on the psychological and physical health of women and girls. Age-specific dangers are spelled out, as well as sexual and intimate partner violence. Covers violence in special populations: women of color, those with disabilities, lesbian women. Discusses family and other relationships. Bibliographical references and index. Available as an e-book.

445 **Handbook of workplace violence.** E. Kevin Kelloway, Julian Barling, Joseph J. Hurrell. 696 p., ill. Thousand Oaks, [Calif.]: SAGE, 2006. ISBN: 0761930620.

363.32   HF5549.5.E43H36

Provides a mainstream view of workplace violence and its prevention and remedies. A short introductory section of three essays offers several theories on the overall dynamics of violence in the workplace. The middle, and longest, section covers in detail a number of forms that workplace violence can take: emotional abuse, bullying, sexual harassment, and violence among those who work in nursing, schools, labor unions, police service, and the military in times of war. The final section covers various remedies and responses employers and victims can make to prevent or to deal with incidents of workplace violence. Twenty-six signed essays include bibliographies. Index.

446 **Perspectives on violence.** Frederick K. Blucher. 193 p., ill. New York: Nova Science Publishers, 2003. ISBN: 1590334779.

303.60973   HN90.V5.P47

A handbook of violence in circumstances where it is usually not reported, studied, or otherwise acknowledged by authorities or scholars. Includes interpersonal violence, battered men, violence among disabled persons, including those who are blind, deaf, or hard of hearing, suicide among children who have witnessed violence in their families, comic book violence, bullying among female prisoners, and television violence. Useful and different perspectives. Bibliographical references and index.

447   Rape and sexual assault III: A research handbook. Ann Wolbert Burgess. xxi, 318 p. New York: Garland, 1991. ISBN: 0824071816. 362.8830973   HV6561.R369

Thorough and detailed handbook covers many aspects of the circumstance of rape in the United States. Deals with responses to rape on the part of victims, their families and friends, and medical and legal authorities. Prevention of rape is emphasized, rape-murder is detailed, and special cases such as incest and pedophilia are discussed. Covers the role of pornography and mass media in relation to rape. Bibliographies and index.

Indexes; Abstract Journals

448   Armed conflict database. http://acd.iiss.org/armedconflict/. IISS Defence Analysis Department. [London; Washington]: International Institute for Strategic Studies.
                                                                                               U21.2

A landmark resource, and in some ways unique, this database provides global coverage for current and ongoing violent conflict in the world, whether among nations or by rogue groups. Especially useful for an up-to-date directory of non-state parties, including terrorist organizations, giving location, numbers, and history. Provides geographic presentation of armed conflict. Covers both internal and international conflicts, as well as incidents of terrorism. Refugees, returnees, and internally displaced persons are counted, described, and placed in geographic context. Details are also provided for weapons used and their flows. Fatalities and the costs of war in both human and economic terms are provided. Historical background and timelines.

Note that an additional subscription is needed to access the full text of many reports, a worthwhile add-on. Note also that a number of conflicts that predate the coverage of this database can be found in the 1991 print publication, *International armed conflict since 1945: A bibliographic handbook of wars and military interventions* (423).

Quotations

449   The words of Desmond Tutu. Desmond Tutu, Naomi Tutu. 109 p., ill. New York: Newmarket Press, 1989. ISBN: 1557040389.
283.68   BX5700.6.Z8T875

Desmond Tutu raised a powerful voice for peace in the violent South Africa of apartheid. In this volume, his daughter has chosen a hundred selections from his sermons, other writings, and speeches. Topics include Faith and Responsibility; Apartheid, Violence, and Nonviolence; Family, Community: Black and White; and Toward a New South Africa. Also includes the text of his Nobel Peace Prize acceptance speech. Includes bibliographical references.

Statistics

450   Warfare and armed conflicts: A statistical reference to casualty and other figures, 1500–2000. 2nd ed. Micheal Clodfelter. xvi, 840 p. Jefferson, N.C.: McFarland, 2001. ISBN: 0786412046.
904.7   D214.C54

1st ed., 1992.

"The major aim of this work is to present a record of casualties of modern warfare in the last five centuries."—*Introd.* Expands the time period of previous edition by over 100 years with the inclusion of statistics from conflicts in the 16th century. Provides historical context for statistics presented, as well as their significance. Author attempted to include statistics on every war for which statistics exist. Entries are arranged chronologically within regional subdivisions. Bibliography. Index.

4 > RACE AND ETHNICITY

General Works

Artistic Works

451   Encyclopedia of multiculturalism. Susan Auerbach. 6 v. (xiii, 1812 p.), ill., maps. New York: Marshall Cavendish, 1994. ISBN: 1854356704.
306.4460973   E184.A1E58

An unusual reference set, being highly visual, with more than half of its pages taken up with graphic materials, including photographs, maps, tables, and out-takes from document pages. A broad and sweeping definition of multicultural is used to draw in entries, reaching across religious groups, economic groups, racial and ethnic groups, feminism, and so on. Includes an extensive group of biographies. The 1998 supplement includes people and events of the intervening time, as well as an updated chronology, subject list, and general index, which cover both original and new materials. Although almost a decade has elapsed since the publication of this work, and much has been published about related ethnic and cultural topics, no other reference work has appeared to fully replace it.

Bibliography

452   **Substance abuse among ethnic minorities in America: A critical annotated bibliography.** Howard M. Rebach. 469 p. New York: Garland, 1992. ISBN: 0815300662.
016.3622908693   Z7164.D78S8; HV5825

This lengthy annotated bibliography offers a rich compilation of references for the study of alcohol and drug abuse among the various ethnic minorities in the United States. Cultural factors from ethnic traditions are suggested, and readings explore the relationship of each ethnic minority to the mainstream culture, as an enabling or even causative factor.

Dictionaries and thesauruses

453   **Dictionary of race, ethnicity and culture.** Guido Bolaffi. xviii, 355 p. London; Thousand Oaks, Calif.: SAGE Publications, 2003. ISBN: 0761968997.
305.8003   GN495.6.D53

A curious, but quite useful, combination of dictionary and encyclopedia. Word definitions are of a weighty length, are signed, and include cross-references and bibliographic entries. There is even an index. Depth, not breadth, is this work's strength.

Directories

454   **Encyclopedic directory of ethnic newspapers and periodicals in the United States.** 2nd ed. Lubomyr Roman Wynar, Anna T. Wynar. 248 p. Littleton, Colo.: Libraries Unlimited, 1976. ISBN: 0872871541.
070.48402573   Z6953.5.A1W94; PN4882

Covers 63 ethnic groups that have continued to publish in their native languages. Groups are of European, Asian, West Asian, and Latin American extraction. Excluded are African American, Native American, or other ethnic groups (e.g., Irish Americans) whose papers are primarily in English. Begins with a bibliographical essay on the ethnic press in the United States, including statistical tables and discussion of bibliographical control. Entries are arranged by ethnic group with address, editor, date started, sponsor, language, circulation, frequency and price, and a note describing content. Both native-language and English-language papers are listed. An appendix gives a statistical analysis of newspapers for each ethnic group. Concludes with a title index. First ed., 1972.

Complementary works: Wynar's *Guide to the American ethnic press: Slavic and East European newspapers and periodicals* (Kent, Ohio: Center for the Study of Ethnic Publications, School of Library Science, Kent State University, 1986) and Sally M. Miller, ed., *The ethnic press in the United States: A historical analysis and handbook* (New York: Greenwood Press, 1987), which consists of bibliographic essays on the history of the press in 27 American ethnic groups.

Encyclopedias

455 **Civil rights in the United States.** Waldo E. Martin, Patricia Sullivan. 2 v., ill. New York: Macmillan Reference USA, 2000. ISBN: 0028647653.

323.097303   E184.A1C47

The 730 signed entries on civil rights in America include an appropriate focus on the civil rights struggles of African Americans, and also "other people of color as well as other marginalized groups such as women, lesbians and gays, immigrants and the 'differently-abled.'"—*Pref.* Overall coverage, content, and format of entries, clear illustrations, and careful indexing are excellent. A stellar reference work on legal progress in the United States for the protection of the rights of ethnic minorities, as well as other groups.

456 **The encyclopedia of ethnic groups in Hollywood.** James Robert Parish, T. Allan Taylor. xiii, 722 p., ill. New York: Facts on File, 2003. ISBN: 0816046042.

791.436520693   PN1995.9.M56M85

Entries for movies, television programs, personalities, genres (situation comedy, sci-fi, etc.), and issues related to minority portrayals and opportunities are organized into five sections—*African Americans, Asian*

Americans, Hispanic Americans, Jewish Americans, and *Native Americans.*
Cross-references, detailed index, and bibliography.

457 Encyclopedia of minorities in American politics. Jeffrey D.
Schultz, Helen Thomas. 2 v. (774 p.), ill., ports. Phoenix, Ariz.:
Oryx Press, 2000. ISBN: 1573561290.
305.80097303   E184.A1E574

Some 2,000 alphabetic entries in this two volume work examine the place
of four of America's largest minority groups in the political process:
African Americans, Asian Americans, Hispanic Americans, and Native
Americans. Key persons, events, organizations, and movements are covered in some detail. Lengthy sections detail the struggles for full political
participation. Includes key elements from the legal framework, including
important cases and decisions such as those creating affirmative action.
Provides full text of important documents. Includes bibliographical references and indexes.

458 Encyclopedia of modern ethnic conflicts. Joseph R. Rudolph.
xxvi, 375 p., ill., maps. Westport, Conn.: Greenwood Press, 2003.
ISBN: 0313313814.
305.8003   GN496.E56

Ethnic conflicts often make news in part because of the large number of
people involved. But even a small conflict can be significant in its effect
on global affairs from an extended and relational meaning. This volume
traces the import of 38 key ethnic conflicts through in-depth case studies set in careful context in signed essays. Full descriptions include the
cultural and historical context which precipitated the event, how it was
managed by authorities, and what its significance and lasting effects
were. There are also a chronology, cross-references, and a bibliography
for each entry. Volume begins with maps which place the conflict in
global spatial context. Includes bibliographical references and index.
Available as an e-book.

459 Encyclopedia of race and ethnic studies. Ernest Cashmore. xx,
491 p. London; New York: Routledge, 2004. ISBN: 0415286743.
305.8003   GN495.6.C37

A one-volume encyclopedia on race and ethnic studies which expands on
the author's *Dictionary of race and ethnic relations* 4th ed., 1997. Broad-
based in theory and concept, building from an Anglophile center, many

entries are written by the editor, while others are contributed and signed. In an evolving field, concepts, terms, definitions, and events from the world change rapidly, and are well-represented here as of its publication date. Both historical context and current events are included. Extensive list of Internet resources. Cross-references, bibliographical references, and index. Available as an e-book.

460   Encyclopedia of racism in the United States. Pyong Gap Min. 3 v., ill. Westport, Conn.: Greenwood Press, 2005. ISBN: 0313326886.
305.80097303   E184.A1E773

Building its 447 signed entries and 26 primary documents around racism defined as "racial victimization for all racial and ethnic minority groups," coverage is encyclopedic and formed around concepts, theories, events, and both social and legal constructs. Racism is broadly defined, and hidden racism is explored. Three volumes of alphabetic entries conclude with a section of primary documents and original writings. Cross-references, bibliographical references, and index.

461   Encyclopedia of the stateless nations: Ethnic and national groups around the world. James Minahan. 4 v. (xxii, 2241 p.), ill., maps. Westport, Conn.: Greenwood Press, 2002. ISBN: 0313316171.
909.82903   D860.M56

This four-volume reference work, a follow-up work to *Nations without states* (Praeger, 1996), tells a remarkable story of some 350 groups which have a national identity but not a national state which they consider their own. Inclusion is based on three factors: self-identity as a distinctive group; distinctive national outward trappings, especially a flag; and the formation of a nationalist type of organization focusing on self-determination. Some groups are fairly innocuous (Southerners and New Englanders in the United States, for example), others are of recurring concern in world affairs (including Kurds and Basques). Provenance of information is often not clear, and may be drawn variously from published reports, government sources, and from the organizations themselves. Since many of these groups are little known outside their own regions, and yet can move suddenly and dramatically onto the world stage, as reflected in the evening news, this is valuable coverage both from its encyclopedic nature and from the difficulty in finding this information otherwise. Includes bibliographical references and index. Available as an e-book.

462   **Encyclopedia of the world's minorities.** Carl Skutsch, Martin
       Ryle. 3 v. (xxxi, 1413 p.). New York: Routledge, 2005. ISBN:
       157958392X.
305.8003   GN495.4.E63
Substantial, well-written, and well-documented. The 562 signed entries
are arranged alphabetically and range in length from about 1,000 to 5,000
words. Entries fall into four principal categories: 251 are on individual
minority groups, including location, population, languages spoken, and
religious affiliation; while 173 cover the ethnic groups of individual
nations, their history, social conditions, and the present ethnic climate and
circumstance in that nation. Another 75 entries cover topical concerns in
minority affairs, while there are also an impressive 62 biographical entries.
Includes cross-references, bibliographical references, and index.

463   **Gale encyclopedia of multicultural America.** 2nd ed. Robert
       Dassanowsky, Jeffrey Lehman, Rudolph J. Vecoli. 3 v. (xxxii, 1974
       p.), ill. Detroit: Gale Group, 2000. ISBN: 0787639869.
305.80097303   E184.A1G14
A solid reference set in three volumes providing a scholarly take on
multiculturalism. Signed essays describe at length some 150 individual
ethnic groups in America, including African Americans, Mexican
Americans, and tribal groups within Native Americans. Historical background, languages, culture, religion, family, and current situation as to
cultural identity and assimilation are provided in detail for each group.
Available as an e-book.

Guides

464   **Ethnic groups and population changes in twentieth-century
       Central-Eastern Europe: History, data, and analysis.** Piotr
       Eberhardt. xxxii, 559 p., ill., maps. Armonk, N.Y.: M.E. Sharpe,
       2003. ISBN: 0765606658.
305.800947   HB3582.7.A3.E2313
Brings together dozens of statistical sources to compile figures on ethnic
groups in the various parts of Central and Eastern Europe for the 20th
century. Extremely useful for historical figures on numbers of ethnic
groups living in disputed regions, areas of massive deportations, and
countries devastated by World War II. More than 200 tables and graphs of
the ethnic structure of various countries and regions from 1900 through

the mid-1990s. Particularly useful for those studying Jewish history in Eastern Europe or ethnic history in the Balkans. Not useful for the Roma/ Gypsy population of the region because of a lack of reliable data. Index of ethnic groups/nationalities and geographic names.

465 World Christian encyclopedia: A comparative survey of churches and religions in the modern world. 2nd ed. David B. Barrett, George Thomas Kurian, Todd M. Johnson. 2 v., ill., color maps. Oxford; New York: Oxford University Press, 2001. ISBN: 0195079639.

230.003   BR157.W67

1st ed., 1982.

A topical and comparative encyclopedia of many aspects of Christianity offering country-by-country surveys, numerous statistical tables, chronologies, and directory information. The authors and their international network of collaborators, contributors, and local editors have organized and interpreted vast amounts of information from surveys compiled by churches worldwide. Includes atlas, dictionary, bibliography, indexes.

Barrett and Johnson's *World Christian trends, AD 30–AD 2200* is a companion volume that interprets and analyzes the data in *World Christian encyclopedia*. Also includes chronology of world evangelization, demographics of martyrdom, glossaries, maps. CD-ROM version packaged with book.

Both works are somewhat challenging to navigate and interpret but offer unique statistical data.

Handbooks

466 The handbook of ethical research with ethnocultural populations and communities. Joseph E. Trimble, Celia B. Fisher. xxix, 366 p. Thousand Oaks, Calif.: Sage Publications, 2006. ISBN: 0761930434.

305.80072   GN495.4.T75

As respect for the self-determination of ethnic populations experiences dramatic growth, guidelines for appropriate field research become more restrictive. This handbook suggests ways that such work can be carried out without being intrusive. Includes bibliographical references and indexes. Highly useful.

467   **National minorities in Europe: Handbook.** Christoph Pan, Sibylle
Pfeil Beate. ill., maps. Wien, [Austria]: Braumüller, 2003–. ISBN:
3700314434.

D1056

Encyclopedic coverage of minority issues in Europe today. The first
long section deals with the historical content, the relationship of states
to minorities, and a group of entries which deal with the languages of
minorities in an exhaustive way. Languages are seen as both a window
onto minority affairs and a mirror of minority culture, perhaps an
especially European take on the culture of minorities. A second lengthy
section covers in-depth the minority situation in each of 36 European
countries, while third and fourth sections deal at length with the requirements and need for minority protection in Europe today. Concluding
appendixes include the full text of a charter, conventions, protocols, and
other key documents dealing with minorities from the overall European
perspective. Much of the material here is not found in other reference
works, and is at best difficult to find. Includes bibliographical references
and indexes.

Indexes; Abstract Journals

468   **Ethnic newswatch.** http://www.proquest.com/products_pq/
descriptions/ethnic_newswatch.shtml. ProQuest Information and
Learning. Ann Arbor, Mich.: ProQuest.

Searchable, full-text collection of over 250 national and regional newspapers, magazines, and journals of the ethnic and minority press. Focus is
on African American, American Indian, Asian American, and U.S. Latino
publications, though periodicals from Jewish, Arab American, Eastern
European, multi-ethnic communities, and other minority groups are also
included. Search capabilities available in both English and Spanish, as well
as the option to search by specific ethnic group. Coverage starts in 1990,
with the companion database, Ethnic Newswatch: A History, extending
coverage back to 1960.

Periodicals and Dissertations

469   **Center for Research Libraries' ethnic press database.** http://
www.crl.edu/content.asp?l1=5&l2=23&l3=44&l4=26. Center for
Research Libraries. [Chicago]: Center for Research Libraries.

Database of more than 2,000 periodicals and newspapers held by the Center and published in Canada and the United States by various ethnic groups. Search by title, ethnic group, language, state/province, or date.

African Americans

Artistic Works

470   **Blacks in black and white: A source book on black films.** 2nd ed. Henry T. Sampson. xii, 735 p., ill. Metuchen, N.J.: Scarecrow Press, 1995. ISBN: 0810826054.

791.4308996073   PN1995.9.N4S2

The black film industry in America began about 1910, and flourished as a world apart where black culture and art were free to be expressed. Both filmmakers and performers are chronicled here; their work in most cases is not otherwise remembered or documented. Of more than a dozen books created around the time of the 1st ed. of this work in 1977, this is the standout that major reviews of that time identified as the title with lasting reference value. Twenty-five years later, and now in a 2nd ed., that judgment still holds. This work opens a remarkable view of that vanished world, gone now those 50 years, and enables us to touch on a wonderful body of black artistic expression.

Atlases and General Overview

471   **The African-American atlas: Black history and culture—an illustrated reference.** Molefi K. Asante, Mark T. Mattson. xi, 251 p., ill. (some color), color maps. New York; London: Macmillan; Prentice Hall International, 1998. ISBN: 0028649842.

973.0496073   E185.A79

Grounded in solid research and richly illustrated, the 14 chapters of this chronological handbook of the African American experience are subtitled with phrases from African American tradition. Beginning with African Origins: "I got my religion from out of the sun"; stretching to The Great Enslavement: "De Udder Worl' is not like dis"; to The Transforming of America: "Before this time another year." The concluding chapter, Dates to Remember, serves as an overall chronology. Provides a solid framework for understanding African American history in the United States.

472   **Atlas of African-American history.** Rev. ed. James Ciment. New
York: Facts On File, 2007. ISBN: 9780816067138.
973.0496073   E185.C55

A newly-revised edition of the classic reference atlas in the field. Summa-
rizes in chronological order major stages in the African diaspora throughout the Western hemisphere. Also relates the African American experience
to the overall history of the times. Chapters include Slavery, the Climb Up
from Slavery, the 19th Century, the Early 20th Century, the Civil Rights
Years, and the Late 20th Century. Atlas in the title refers to numerous
graphical elements throughout, including photos, drawings, charts, boxes,
maps. Rich source for chronologies. Includes bibliographical references
and index.

473   **The atlas of African-American history and politics: From the
slave trade to modern times.** Arwin D. Smallwood, Jeffrey M.
Elliot. xii, 179 p., color maps. Boston: McGraw-Hill, 1998. ISBN:
0070584362.
973.0496073   E185.S574

While it has become generally recognized that history books long excluded
the contributions of many groups, including perhaps most notably African Americans, other reference material did likewise. This powerful atlas
of some 150 originally-drawn maps goes far toward correcting the car-
tographic aspect of this broad omission, and on a worldwide basis. With
compelling graphic enhancements, this is a must-have reference for both
general and research collections.

474   **The Black Studies Center.** http://bsc.chadwyck.com/home/home.
do. [Schomburg Center for Research in Black Culture, New York
Public Library]. Ann Arbor, Mich.: ProQuest, 2005.

Treasure trove of online resources, many full text, created by the Schomburg Center for Research in Black Culture of the New York Public Library.
A vital group of resources to support the study of African American
thought and experience. Includes essays, and articles from journals, newspapers, and other publications. Sections include:

Schomburg studies on the black experience - Interdisciplinary essays.
International index to black periodicals - Both scholarly and popular,
   much full text.
Marshall index - A guide to black periodicals, 1940–46.

Newspapers - Full-text backfile of influential black newspapers: *Chicago defender, Daily defender, New York Amsterdam news.*

Literature index - Covers over 70,000 bibliographic citations for fiction, poetry, and literary reviews published in 110 black periodicals and newspapers between 1827–1940.

Bibliography

475 **African American organizations, 1794–1999: A selected bibliography sourcebook.** Rosalind G. Bauchum. Lanham, Md.: University Press of America, 2001. ISBN: 076182085X.
016.305896073   Z1361.N39B38; E185.5

Covering a broad sweep of years, this annotated bibliography provides a window onto the organizations that enabled and informed (and even saved the lives of) African Americans in the United States for more than two centuries. Some 270 citations, reference books, journal articles, reports, reviews, dissertations, bibliographies, and websites. Organizations include churches, professional and business associations, lodges and labor groups, colleges and universities, and fraternal organizations. Related narrative encyclopedia: *Organizing black America* (523).

476 **African-American newspapers and periodicals: A national bibliography.** James Philip Danky, Maureen E. Hady. xxxv, 740 p. Cambridge, Mass.: Harvard University Press, 1998. ISBN: 0674007883.
015.7303508996073   Z6944.N39A37; PN4882.5

Lists 6,562 periodical and newspaper titles, both current and ceased, by and about African Americans, housed in library collections. Includes publications from foreign countries. Entries are arranged alphabetically by title and include dates of publication, frequency, publisher and editor information, variant titles, standard numbers, and library holdings. Includes subject, feature, editor, publisher, and geographic indexes.

Other sources for African American newspapers: *A reference guide to Afro-American publications and editors, 1827–1946* (Ames [Iowa]: Iowa State Univesity Press, 1993), by Vima Raskin Potter. Based on Warren Henry Brown's *Checklist of Negro newspapers in the United States* (1827–1946), Potter added place of publication, year of publication, undated publication, and editor indexes. *Extant collections of early black newspapers: A research guide to the black press, 1880–1915, with an index to the Boston*

Guardian, 1902–1904 (497), by Georgetta Merritt Campbell, includes historical essays on the African American press, a union list of holdings and microform availability. Arranged by state, city, and title.

477   **An annotated bibliography of Mary McLeod Bethune's Chicago defender columns, 1948–1955.** Carolyn LaDelle Bennett, Mary McLeod Bethune. xiii, 126 p., [4] p. of plates, ill. Lewiston, N.Y.: Edwin Mellen Press, 2001. ISBN: 0773475907.
016.37092   Z1361.N39B47; E185.86

Mary McLeod Bethune raised one of the strongest and most unifying voices for African American inclusion in mainstream American life at the dawn of the modern civil rights era. This guide leads to specific samples of her writings, where once again she tells all of us what the situation of African Americans was at the time, and why it had to be changed.

478   **Antislavery newspapers and periodicals.** John W. Blassingame, Mae Henderson, Jessica M. Dunn. 5 v., ill. Boston: G.K. Hall, 1980– 1984. ISBN: 0816181632.
016.0713   Z1249.S6A57; E449

The titles indexed here are so important that their full text is widely available today, some 150 years after their publication, and in several formats: microfilm, in databases such as Proquest's American Periodicals Series (www.proquest.com/products_pq/descriptions), and even in modern print facsimile. The scholarly analysis that is provided in the annotated entries in this five-volume secondary reference is a powerful tool in understanding the radical, even revolutionary, nature of what was being said.

Through the first 65 years of the 19th century, slavery was still legal in nearly all of the world, and had been an accepted, if decried, part of economic and political reality since the dawn of history. The letters referenced here, an immediate form of communication in the world in which they were published, went far toward creating what was arguably a necessary, and perhaps even sufficient, condition for Abraham Lincoln to issue the first Emancipation Proclamation in Sep. 1862, beginning an end to slavery in the United States (which was abolished with the ratification of the 13th Amendment to the U.S. Constitution in Dec. 1865).

This reference provides a highly useful context for, and identification of, the body of abolitionist letters that played such a strong role in ending this heinous institution in the United States.

479   **Bibliographic checklist of African American newspapers.**
Barbara K. Henritze. xxviii, 206 p. Baltimore: Genealogical, 1995.
ISBN: 0806314575.

071.3   Z6944.N39H46; PN4882.5

The 5,539 titles included are organized by state, then by city. Information
for each item includes publication frequency, years of publication, and
the source(s) in which the particular title was identified. Following the
list of sources is a bibliography that includes the sources, other publications relevant to African American publishing, and a title index. Entries
are brief and identify only that the publications existed, with no location or holdings information included. Still a valuable starting point for
researchers attempting to identify relevant titles. For additional information on African American newspapers, see Danky's comprehensive
African-American newspapers and periodicals: A national bibliography
(476).

480   **Bibliographic guide to black studies.** Schomburg Collection of
Negro Literature and History. Boston: G.K. Hall. ISSN: 0360-2710.

016.9730496073   Z1361.N39S373a; E185

Still an important reference work; publ. 1975–97. Annual volumes contain
bibliographic descriptions for a wide range of publications cataloged during each year by the New York Public Library, including books, pamphlets,
sound recordings, microfilm publications, and serials from the Schomburg Center for Research in Black Culture.

481   **A bibliographical guide to black studies programs in the United
States: An annotated bibliography.** Lenwood G. Davis, George H.
Hill, Janie Miller Harris. xvii, 120 p. Westport, Conn.: Greenwood
Press, 1985. ISBN: 0313233284.

016.9730496073   Z1361.N39D353; E184.7

Still an important reference work. Contains 725 annotated entries, alphabetically arranged in four chapters: 79 major books and pamphlets providing a history and overview of the topic; 72 general works, including titles
on the development of black studies at large, traditionally white universities; 68 dissertations; and 500 articles published in scholarly and general
interest periodicals. Author index.

Later listing found in 2005 *Encyclopedia of black studies* (519). Available as an e-book.

482   **A bibliography of the Negro in Africa and America.** Monroe
Nathan Work. xxi, 698 p. Mansfield Center, Conn.: Martino
Publishing, 2006; c1928. ISBN: 1578980798.
016.973.0496073   Z1361.N39W8; E185

In-depth bibliography on African Americans in the Americas covers not
only the United States, but also the Caribbean and Latin America, from
the earliest times up until 1928. These materials are otherwise almost
universally difficult or impossible to identify. The classified arrangement
is a strength, grouping like materials together, and an author index enables
navigation through the volume. An essential advanced reference tool, evi-
denced by continual reprinting, most recently in 2006.

483   **Black access: A bibliography of Afro-American bibliographies.**
Richard Newman. xxviii, 249 p. Westport, Conn.: Greenwood
Press, 1984. ISBN: 0313232822.
016.0169730496073   Z1361.N39N578; E185

Created in 1984 when the first comprehensive bibliographies of various
aspects of the African American experience had begun to flourish. This
bibliography of bibliographies, the ultimate reference type, provides in a
single gathering a window onto the early landscape of black consciousness and pride as the black community became mainstream in America.
Includes indexes. Worth retaining in the permanent reference collection.

484   **The Black aged in the United States: A selectively annotated
bibliography.** 2nd ed. Lenwood G. Davis. xiv, 277 p. New York:
Greenwood Press, 1989. ISBN: 0313259313.
016.3052608996073   Z1361.N39D354; E185.86

More than 600 entries identify books, journal articles, dissertations, theses,
and government documents dealing with aging among African Americans
up until the date of this publication in 1989. Historical notes recount aging
issues among enslaved African Americans. Directory of homes for elderly
black persons is given for the years 1860 to 1988. A part of African American history that is difficult, if not impossible, to find elsewhere.

485   **Black alcohol abuse and alcoholism: An annotated bibliography.**
Thomas D. Watts, Roosevelt Wright. xix, 265 p. New York: Praeger,
1986. ISBN: 0030057132.
016.36229208996073   Z7721.W37; HV5292

For the time period before online indexes began full coverage, this print resource is still valuable for leading researchers to documentation on alcoholism among African Americans. The cultural context provided is a valuable addition to present-day electronic resources. The narrow focus strengthens the breadth of coverage of alcoholism.

486   **Black American families, 1965–1984: A classified, selectively annotated bibliography.** Walter Recharde Allen, Richard A. English, Jo Anne Hall. xxxi, 480 p. New York: Greenwood Press, 1986. ISBN: 0313256136.
016.306808996073   Z1361.N39B5; E185.86

Covers black families for the 20 years before the advent of full text and electronic sources. Annotations are helpful in navigating materials. Good source.

487   **Black Americans in autobiography: An annotated bibliography of autobiographies and autobiographical books written since the Civil War.** Rev. and expanded ed. Russell C. Brignano. xi, 193 p. Durham, N.C.: Duke University Press, 1984. ISBN: 0822305593.
016.9730496073022B   Z1361.N39B67; E185.96

Four lists, all but the last annotated: full autobiographies, works from a variety of genres describing only a portion of an author's life, works which Brignano could not obtain, and post-1945 reprints of Civil War and pre–Civil War autobiographies. Occupation/activity, organization, geographic, chronological, and title indexes.

488   **The black family in urban areas in the United States: A bibliography of published works on the black family in urban areas in the United States.** 2nd ed. Lenwood G. Davis. 84 p. Monticello, Ill.: Council of Planning Librarians, 1975.
016.309208; 016.301421   Z5942.C68; E185.86

The extended family of generations, kin, and close friends—in the next house, or in the same or nearby community—was a key element of family life among African Americans in the United States, stretching back across the days of the African diaspora. As African Americans and others moved into cities, smaller family units often became isolated, while others remade vital bonds with those who made up their new urban communities. Ties that were undone and remade provide a useful perspective on the formation and value of family among African Americans at this time. Later works do not capture this phenomenon or this era. This title should be kept in the reference collections of research libraries serious about the study of African Americans, and of the family in a broader context.

489   **Black immigration and ethnicity in the United States: An annotated bibliography.** [Center for Afroamerican and African Studies], University of Michigan. xi, 170 p. Westport, Conn.: Greenwood Press, 1985. ISBN: 0313243662.
016.305896073   Z1361.N39B553; E185

Provides 1,049 annotated entries alphabetically arranged in six sections: (1) Bibliographies and general surveys of literature, (2) General literature on immigration and ethnicity, (3) U.S. immigration legislation and policies, (4) Aspects of black immigration, (5) Studies of black immigrant groups, (6) Selected works on black immigration to Canada and Great Britain. Includes books, articles, dissertations, and government publications. Author and subject indexes.

490   **Black slavery in the Americas: An interdisciplinary bibliography, 1865–1980.** John David Smith, Stanley L. Engerman. 2 v. (xix, 1847 p.). Westport, Conn.: Greenwood Press, 1982. ISBN: 0313231184.
016.3063620973   Z7164.S6S63; HT1049

Classed bibliography of 15,667 citations in 25 chapters (both topical and geographical), with many subdivisions. Limited to English language materials: books, articles, theses and dissertations, review articles. Covers all aspects of slavery, except that political aspects (including antislavery and abolition movements) are largely omitted. Author and subject indexes.

491   **Black studies: A select catalog of National Archives microfilm publications.** Rev. ed. [National Archives Trust Fund Board, National Archives and Records Administration]. Washington: National Archives Trust Fund Board, National Archives and Records Administration, 2007. ISBN: 1880875276.
016.9730496073   Z1361.N39U63; E185

Long out of print, this catalog remains a valuable resource to help identify materials in the U.S. National Archives for research on African American issues and topics.

492   **Blacks and media: A selected, annotated bibliography, 1962–**
       1982. J. William Snorgrass, Gloria T. Woody. xiv, 150 p. Tallahassee,
       Fla.: University Press of Florida, 1985. ISBN: 0813008107.
016.0015108996073   Z5633.A37S56; P94.5.A37

Covers 20 years of media representation of African Americans. Beginning
with racist stereotypes, moves toward a more idealized existence, still with
stereotypes, but in a more positive way. Documents this changing landscape as it moves toward a view of African Americans as people, like any
other.

493   **Blacks in an urban environment: A selected annotated**
       bibliography of reference sources. Gail A. Schlachter, Donna Belli.
       45 p. Monticello, Ill.: Council of Planning Librarians, 1975.
016.309208; 016.9730496073   Z5942.C68; Z1361.N39E185

In 1975, America was still largely a segregated society, in the South by law,
and in the North by neighborhood. Understanding what it meant to be
African American, and living in the cities of America during this time, is
thoroughly outlined in the sources identified in this bibliography. Later
materials do not deal with this time period. Important title for research
collections.

494   **Black-white racial attitudes: An annotated bibliography.**
       Constance E. Obudho. xii, 180 p. Westport, Conn.: Greenwood
       Press, 1976. ISBN: 0837185823.
016.3014510420973   Z1361.N39O28; E185.61

The year 1976 was an important one in terms of racial attitudes in America.
Effects of the 1964 Civil Rights Act were beginning to be felt in the ways
that Americans thought, felt, and interacted. This annotated bibliography
takes a broad look at what it meant to be black or white in America at that
time. Few sources, electronic or otherwise, have captured that same world.
Important for collections in research libraries.

495   **Black/white relations in American history: An annotated**
       bibliography. Leslie Vincent Tischauser. xiv, 189 p. Lanham,
       Md.; Pasadena, Calif.: Scarecrow Press; Salem Press, 1998. ISBN:
       0810833891.
016.305800973   Z1361.N39T57; E185.61

Documents 50 years of black and white relations in America in more than
700 works, from 1944 until about 1998. Covers the monumental shifts in

racial empowerment after World War II and up to and through the civil rights movement of the 1960s and following—a turbulent and highly energized time when society was reinventing itself for the betterment of all. Indexes allow access to these important materials.

496 Dictionary catalog of the Schomburg Collection: Supplement 1974, (1962–1974). Schomburg Collection of Negro Literature and History, [New York Public Library]. 580 p. Boston: G. K. Hall, 1976. ISBN: 0816100624.

019.1097471   Z1361.N39N55; E185

First published in nine volumes in 1962 as the *Dictionary catalog of the Schomburg Collection of Negro Literature and History,* with later supplements up until 1974, this was a landmark reference set which showed in exact detail the richness and variety of materials held at the New York Public Library for the study of the African American experience. Still an important source because it provides a focused look at what was available at that time, and is still useful today.

497 Extant collections of early black newspapers: A research guide to the black press, 1880–1915, with an index to the Boston guardian, 1902–1904. Georgetta Merritt Campbell. xxvi, 401 p. Troy, N.Y.: Whitston, 1981. ISBN: 0878751971.

011.35   Z6944.N39C35; PN4882.5

Begins with an historical essay on the African American press that includes a brief bibliography and a list of sources used in compilation. A union list follows, arranged by state, city, and title, giving holdings and microform availability. The *Guardian* index occupies p. 216–385. The work concludes with an afterword on the historical context of the African American press and a note outlining bibliographic coverage of African American newspapers in the 20th century prior to 1981. Campbell's work is the culmination of previous efforts to locate, collect, and preserve African American newspapers, beginning with Armistead Scott Pride's *Negro newspapers on microfilm: A selected list* (Washington: Library of Congress, Photoduplication Service, 1953), a forerunner in providing a register of 19th-century African American papers. Campbell consolidates Pride's listings, adding many collections and locations.

Other sources for African American newspapers: *Survey of black newspapers in America* ([Kennebunkport, Maine]: [Mercer House Press], 1979), by Henry La Brie III; *Black press handbook: Sesquicentennial 1827–1977* (Washington: National Newspaper Publishers Association, 1977).

498   G. K. Hall interdisciplinary bibliographic guide to black studies.
[Schomburg Center for Research in Black Culture]. Detroit: Gale
Group, 1999–2003.
016.9730496073   Z1361.N39S373a; E185

Updates the *G. K. Hall Dictionary catalog of the Schomburg Collection of
Negro Literature and History* of the New York Public Library, which for
many years was the gold standard for quality and completeness of coverage for materials on black history and culture. These annual supplements
cover 1999-2003. This title is continued by the Schomburg's electronic
Black Studies on Disc (541), which reaches back to 1988.

499   Health of Black Americans from post reconstruction to
integration, 1871–1960: An annotated bibliography of
contemporary sources. Mitchell F. Rice, Woodrow Jones. xxiii, 206
p. New York: Greenwood Press, 1990. ISBN: 0313263140.
016.362108996073   RA448.5.N4.R52

No. 26 of *Bibliographies and indexes in Afro-American and African studies*
series.
        A comprehensive annotated bibliography of the literature on "the con-
dition of blacks [including] ... patterns of mortality, morbidity and utiliza-
tion behaviors of blacks from slavery to the mid-20th century" that aims to
provide "a fuller understanding of the history of health care inequities in the
U.S."—*Introd.* In three chapters: 1871–1919, 1920–50, 1951–60. Entries give
full bibliographic information. Subject and author indexes.
        A companion volume by the same compilers, *Black American health:
An annotated bibliography*, treats the literature of the 1970s and 1980s.

500   In black and white: A guide to magazine articles, newspaper
articles, and books concerning more than 15,000, black
individuals and groups. 3rd ed. Mary Mace Spradling. 2 v. (xiii,
1282 p.). Detroit: Gale Research, 1980. ISBN: 0810304384.
920.009296073   Z1361.N39S655; E185.96

3rd ed., 1980; 1985 suppl. Third edition is the last edition.
        Provides a rich source of information on African Americans as they
have appeared in a wide range of print publications up until that time.
Remains a powerful bibliographic tool, firstly, for the time period it covers, because databases available more than 20 years later focus on earlier
or later years than are covered here. Secondly, it is still worthwhile for
the large number of African Americans it covers, some 15,000, in sharp

contrast to the 1,000 to 2,000 people found in most modern databases. A source that should be retained in reference collections.

501   **A list of references for the history of black Americans in agriculture, 1619–1974.** Joel Schor, Cecil Harvey, [Agricultural History Center, University of California, Davis]. v, 116 p. Davis, [Calif.]: Agricultural History Center, University of California, Davis, 1975.

016.3316396073   Z7164.L1S33; HD1525

Although dated, this thorough bibliography is a window onto African American contributions to agriculture as the economic base of the United States. Despite slavery, the dignity, ingenuity, and hard work on the part of millions of African Americans in large measure created the food and fiber basis for life in the United States in colonial and federal times, and beyond.

Chronologies

502   **African American breakthroughs: 500 years of black firsts.** Jay P. Pederson, Jessie Carney Smith. xvii, 280 p., ill. New York: U X L, 1995. ISBN: 0810394960.

973.0496073   E185.A2523

African Americans have been responsible for many inventions and innovations throughout history. This well-researched volume documents many of them and restores credit where others have claimed it. A useful reference work, offering material which is difficult, if not impossible, to find otherwise. Section on "Voices" provides some 35 full or excerpted speeches and other important statements of African Americans.

503   **African American chronology: Chronologies of the American mosaic.** Kwando Mbiassi Kinshasa. viii, 189 p., ill. Westport, Conn.: Greenwood Press, 2006. ISBN: 0313337977.

973.049607300202   E185.K48

This new chronology offers a fresh perspective on African American life, achievements, and struggles. Includes bibliographical references and index.

504   **Black chronology: From 4 B.C. to the abolition of the slave trade.** Rev. ed. Ellen Irene Diggs. xii, 312 p. Boston: G.K. Hall, 1983. ISBN: 0816185433.

960.0202   DT17.D5

This 1983 revised edition of the landmark 1970 edition gathers additional materials not previously known to the author. Timelines place into context the African experience over a sweeping time period of some 6,000 years. Includes bibliographic references and index. This is a useful title for advanced reference work.

505 The black New Yorkers: The Schomburg illustrated chronology.
Howard Dodson, Christopher Moore, Roberta Yancy, Schomburg Center for Research in Black Culture. ix, 470 p., ill., map. New York: John Wiley, 2000. ISBN: 0471297143.
974.700496073   F128.9.N4D63

Richly illustrated. Details nearly 400 years of African American history and culture in New York City and New York State. Beginning with free Afro-Caribbean trader Jan Rodriguez in 1613, each time period, through 1999, is treated in detail. Biography especially strong. "Fascinating story of great achievement and struggle in a dynamic global context."—*Introd.*

506 The chronological history of the Negro in America. Peter M. Bergman, Mort N. Bergman. 698 p. New York: Harper and Row, [1969].
973.097496   E185.B46

Painstaking research makes the extensive documentation for black achievement, and struggles, provided in this landmark reference work still relevant today, some 40 years after its publication in 1969. Worth keeping on the reference shelf as a primary source.

Organized into topical sections:

- 1492–1618: Slavery. The Beginning
- 1619–1792: Under British Rule
- 1793–1864: From the Cotton Gin to the Emancipation Proclamation
- 1865–1877: Reconstruction
- 1878–1908: "Separate But Equal." The Darkest Period
- 1909–1932: The Genesis of the NAACP
- 1933–1954: From the New Deal to Brown v. Board of Education
- 1955–1968: "With All Deliberate Speed"

507 Chronology of African American history: From 1492 to the present. 2nd ed. Alton Hornsby. xlix, 720 p., ill. Detroit: Gale Research, 1997. ISBN: 0810385732.
973.049607300202   E185.H64

A solid and reliable chronology reaching back to the beginnings to trace the remarkable contributions, and challenges, of African Americans throughout American history. Often otherwise undocumented, this carefully researched volume credits African Americans with much that they did, and are often not recognized for doing. Materials presented here are often difficult, if not impossible, to find otherwise, unless one digs through primary sources. Highly useful in both general and research collections.

508   My soul is a witness: A chronology of the civil rights era in the United States, 1954–1965. Bettye Collier-Thomas, V. P. Franklin. xvii, 268 p., ill. New York: Henry Holt, 2000. ISBN: 0805047697.
973.049607300202   E185.61.C697

Twelve years might seem an unusually narrow focus for a book-length chronology, but the turbulent times examined in detail in this 268 p. volume marked a true sea change in American law and society as African Americans were finally recognized as full citizens.

509   Timelines of African-American history: 500 years of black achievement. Thomas Dale Cowan, Jack Maguire, Richard Newman. 368 p. New York: Berkley Publishing Group, 1994. ISBN: 0399521275.
973.049673   E185.C86

With roots in the well-researched *Chronological history of the Negro in America* (506) (1969), this nicely organized listing of black achievements brings terminology and perspectives up-to-date and makes them more readily available to students, scholars, and the general public. Includes bibliographical references and index.

Dictionaries and Thesauruses

510   Dictionary of Afro-American slavery. Randall M. Miller, John David Smith. xix, 892 p. Westport, Conn.: Praeger, 1997. ISBN: 0275957993.
973.0496073   E441.D53

Short-entry encyclopedia of 297 signed articles and accompanying bibliographies that cover the "diverse aspects of the slavery experience in North America."—*Introd.* Designed to be a comprehensive reference source for issues in African American slavery, and to provide a synthesis of scholarship on this topic. Includes chronology and subject index.

Directories

511 **Black Americans in Congress, 1870–1989.** Bruce A. Ragsdale, Joel D. Treese, [Office of the Historian of the House of Representatives]. xii, 164 p., ill. Washington: U. S. Government Printing Office, 1990.

328.730922B   E185.96.R25

Published as a U.S. Government Document in 1990, this biographical reference provides long-overdue recognition to African Americans who have served in the U.S. Congress for more than a century, from 1870 until 1989. Created by the Office of the Historian of the House of Representatives, and nicely illustrated, this is a welcome addition to the biography shelf.

512 **Who's who among African Americans.** Gale Research Inc. New York: Gale Research, 1996–. ISSN: 1081-1400.

920.073   E185.96.W52

From the first ed. for 1975–76 through the 20th ed. publ. in 2007, this well-done Gale title continues to be the standard reference for notable African Americans. Current ed. on a rolling basis is also available online through LexisNexis. Acquiring and keeping in an accessible location—not remote storage—is the classic example of why print publ.—on a year by year basis—are essential for biographical research on persons, living and dead.

About 10,000 entries in the 1st ed., increased to more than 20,000 in the 19th ed. (2006). Terminal obituaries section and geographic and occupational indexes. Information largely collected by questionnaires to the biographees. Indexed in Biography and Genealogy Master Index (Gale, 2001–). Full text (12th ed., 1998, to 19th ed., 2006) in Biography Resource Center (Gale Group, 2002–).

An earlier work, *Who's who in colored America* (1st ed., 1927, to 7th ed., 1950) includes geographical and vocational listings. Full text in African American Biographical Database (Proquest Information and Learning Company, 2001–).

Encyclopedias

513 **African Americans at war: An encyclopedia.** Jonathan Sutherland. 2 v. (xxi, 819 p.), ill. Santa Barbara, Calif.: ABC-CLIO, 2004. ISBN: 1576077462.

355.0092396073   U52.S88

In well-researched essays, thorough encyclopedia documents the remarkable achievements of African Americans in military combat. Recent scholarship, and also emerging recognition of the contributions of African Americans to society, have contributed to the emergence of this useful new reference work. Available as an e-book.

514 **Africana: The encyclopedia of the African and African American experience.** 2nd ed. Anthony Appiah, Henry Louis Gates. 5 v., ill. (some color), color maps. Oxford; New York: Oxford University Press, 2005. ISBN: 0195170555.

960.03   DT14.A37435

Classic and definitive work on Africa and the African diaspora throughout the world. Over 3,000 entries by some 200 contributors are well-researched and well-referenced. Biographies have great depth and strength. Coverage of historical times, stretching back into antiquity, and the modern world of science, exploration, politics, literature, and the arts, provide a rich framework for understanding the African experience. Provides unique insight into contributions Africans have made in diverse corners of the world, from Cuba to the Far East. Bibliographies and index. A magnificent resource which well fulfills the vision of W.E.B. Du Bois of a true encyclopedia that reflects the breadth, depth, and range of Africa in world history and culture.

RACE AND ETHNICITY

515 **The encyclopedia of African American military history.** William Weir, Molefi Asante, Lloyd Newton. 365 p., ill. Amherst, N.Y.: Prometheus Books, 2004. ISBN: 1591021693.

355.008996073   UB418.A47W45

One of the fruits of racism in America has been the lack of solid reference works on the remarkable contributions of African American soldiers in every military campaign the United States has engaged in, from colonial times to the present. Some 300 beautifully researched entries in this comprehensive new encyclopedia go a long way toward correcting this situation. Well-written, with a keen eye for historical accuracy, this encyclopedia provides detail on individual soldiers and military leaders, battles, campaigns, wars, military policy, and legislation affecting blacks in the military. Replete with illustrations, this is an outstanding reference work highly recommended for both general and research collections.

516   **Encyclopedia of African American society.** Gerald David Jaynes.
       2 v. (xxx, 1058 p.), ill. Thousand Oaks, Calif.: Sage Publications,
       2005. ISBN: 0761927646.
305.896072003   E185.E546

Basic encyclopedia of African American life in the United States. Arranged
alphabetically by topic, 700 entries are from one to a few pages in length;
some are signed. Covers historic eras and facts, as well as modern black
culture through a broad range of topics on issues, ideas, and events. Biographical entries and references are a strength. Exhaustive bibliography
and detailed index. Available as an e-book.

517   **Encyclopedia of African-American culture and history.** Jack
       Salzman, David L. Smith, Cornel West. 5 v., ill. New York: Macmillan
       Library Reference, 1996. ISBN: 0028973453.
973.0496073003   E185.E54

A powerful reference work detailing some 300 years of African American
life in the United States. Struggles of the civil rights movement, including
strong biographical coverage, and progress toward full political participation are a focus. Includes a highly useful section of information by individual U.S. state. Useful updates were made in 2001.
      This is a different reference work in many ways from the 2001 edition
of Palmer's *Encyclopedia of African-American culture and history* (518),
which has a more international focus. Both the earlier work and its update,
and the later work, should be retained in major reference collections.

518   **Encyclopedia of African-American culture and history: The
       black experience in the Americas.** 2nd ed. Colin A. Palmer. 6 v.
       (lxxxvi, 2746 p.), ill. Detroit: Macmillan Reference USA, 2006.
       ISBN: 0028658167.
973.0496073003   E185.E54

A more global and less United States-focused exploration of the African
American experience than in the 1st ed., without information by U.S. state.
Culture broadly defined provides much new information on persons,
events, and trends. Some 500 black-and-white photographs. Concludes
with a collection of around 35 primary documents, section of "Statistics
and Lists," and an overall index. Available as an e-book.
      The first edition in 1996 of this encyclopedia, along with some
updates made in its 2001 revision, remain valuable for the detailed
accounting each provides of the African American experience in the

United States. The focus of the 2006 ed. is changed significantly so that in many ways it is a different title. Both should be retained in a reference collection.

519 **Encyclopedia of black studies.** Molefi K. Asante, Ama Mazama. xxxii, 531 p., ill. Thousand Oaks, Calif.: SAGE Publications, 2005. ISBN: 076192762X.
973.0496073003   E185.E554

Provides an Afrocentric view of the world, which can be a useful counterpoint to the usual Eurocentric view of most Western scholarship. Includes 250 entries by outstanding scholars that give a thorough grounding in the field's concepts and theories. Entries usually include a bibliography. Appendix of black studies programs in the United States and of journals in the field. Index and bibliography. Available as an e-book.

Earlier information is found in *A bibliographical guide to black studies programs in the United States* (Greenwood Press, 1985).

520 **Encyclopedia of the great black migration.** Steven A. Reich. 3 v., ill. Westport, Conn.: Greenwood Press, 2006. ISBN: 0313329826.
307.2408996073075   E185.6.E54

A thorough and well-balanced accounting of the movement of millions of African Americans from the rural South to the industrialized North and West in the decades after the Civil War and of the return of African Americans to the New South of recent years. Special strengths include coverage of work opportunities, labor movements and other economic factors, shifts in society, and the focus on home and family among African Americans. The first two volumes comprise some 400 signed essays in alphabetic encyclopedic format. The third volume is made up of primary documents, writings, and accounts of the experience of African Americans migrating across the United States. An important major reference work that includes bibliographic references and indexes.

521 **Encyclopedia of the underground railroad.** J. Blaine Hudson. vii, 308 p., ill., maps. Jefferson, N.C.: McFarland, 2006. ISBN: 0786424591.
973.711503   E450.H855

The Underground Railroad was a network of helpers and safe houses stretching from the slaveholding regions of the American South, north to

Canada and freedom. Its existence and operation were in violation of U.S. federal law, and bounty hunters looked for escaping African Americans and those helping them. Records and documentation were highly dangerous, and so often slight records, recollections, and tales are the foundation of the historical record of this time. This encyclopedia is a remarkable gathering of information which documents the society of the time, and the movement to freedom of individuals.

522   **Facts on File encyclopedia of black women in America.** Darlene
       Clark Hine, Kathleen Thompson, Facts on File, Inc. 11 v., ill. New
       York: Facts on File, Inc., 1997. ISBN: 0816034257.
920.7208996073   E185.96.F2

The 11 v. of this comprehensive and sweeping encyclopedia document the lives, careers, and culture of African American women. Historical perspective sheds light on their experience, contributions, challenges, and griefs during the 18th and 19th centuries in the first volume titled, "The early years, 1619–1899." Following volumes each focus on a specific theme: literature; dance, sports, visual arts; business and professions; music; education; religion and community; law and government; theatre, arts, and entertainment; social activism; and finally science, health, and medicine. Challenges are discussed, but success is celebrated, and great role models are well-documented for the young of today. Includes bibliographical references and index. Information presented is often difficult or impossible to find otherwise. Well-written throughout. A must-have resource for both research and general collections.

523   **Organizing black America: An encyclopedia of African American**
       associations. Nina Mjagkij. xxix, 768 p., ill. New York: Garland,
       2001. ISBN: 0815323093.
369.396073003   E185.5.O74

Both present and historical organizations for African Americans in the United States are covered in 576 signed entries by 184 scholars. Length varies from a paragraph to several pages, and concludes with a bibliography. Entries trace origins, goals, founders, membership, staff, activities, achievements, failures, and, where no longer active, demise of the association. Interracial organizations and those working to further the interests of African Americans are included. Major cities have entries that describe their local civil, literary, and aid societies for African Americans. Some illustrations; index. Available as an e-book.

524 **The Underground Railroad: An encyclopedia of people, places, and operations.** Mary Ellen Snodgrass. Armonk, N.Y.: M.E. Sharpe, 2008. ISBN: 9780765680938.
973.7115   E450.S65

This 2008 encyclopedia draws together information on a broad range of topics documenting the secret escape routes, places of safety, and methods used by enslaved African Americans escaping from the Southern states.

Guides

525 **African-American holidays, festivals, and celebrations: The history, customs, and symbols associated with both traditional and contemporary religious and secular events observed by Americans of African descent.** Kathlyn Gay, Jean Currie Church, Jessie Carney Smith. Detroit: Omnigraphics, 2007. ISBN: 9780780807792.
394.26973   GT4803.A2G39

Authoritative and unique. Entries include historical background, current observance, contacts, websites, and bibliographies. Appendixes: chronology, calendar, geographical location. Photographs. Combined keyword and name index.

526 **Afro-Americana, 1553–1906: Author catalog of the Library Company of Philadelphia and the Historical Society of Pennsylvania.** Historical Society of Pennsylvania. xiii, 714 p. Boston: G. K. Hall, 1973. ISBN: 081610896X.
016.973   Z1361.N39P48

Philadelphia was a seat of both culture and unprecedented political power in America from the earliest times through the end of the 19th century, and beyond. It was perhaps the major hub where escaping African Americans could cross the Delaware to the safe havens of South Jersey or make their way onto the main line of the Underground Railroad along the eastern banks of the Delaware River, and north to Canada and safety.

Philadelphia was also a city where free African Americans could ply their trades, build personal capital, and lead what were normal lives of the time for almost anyone. The manuscript and library collections reflect that centrality of time and place, and should be seriously considered for researchers working on African American history and culture for the period.

527 **Catalogue of the Charles L. Blockson Afro-American collection, a unit of the Temple University Libraries.** Charles L. Blockson. 770 p., ill. Philadelphia: Temple University Press, 1990. ISBN: 0877227497.

026.0008996073074811   Z1361.N39T29; E185

One of the most important collections of primary source materials on Africans, African Americans, and the African American experience is found in the more than 30,000 items of the Charles Blockson Afro-American Collection at Temple University in Philadelphia.

Drawn from around the world, and beautifully organized, the Blockson Collection includes rare works from the 16th century to the present, special groups of materials, including the Paul Robeson Collection, and a number of important first editions. Important graphic materials in the John Mosley Photograph Collection include some 500,000 photographs, prints, and negatives of "notable black entertainers, Negro Baseball League players, Penn Relays, social and political personalities and the general social life of Pennsylvania."—*Charles Blockson Afro-American Collection Website*

See http://library.temple.edu/collections/blockson/.

528 **The complete Kwanzaa: Celebrating our cultural harvest.** D. Winbush Riley. xi, 387 p., ill. New York: HarperCollins, 1995. ISBN: 0060172150.

394.261   GT4403.R56

Forty years after its creation as an American "First Fruits" celebration rooted in classic African culture, Kwanzaa has arguably achieved mainstream status as an American holiday among African Americans and others who wish to celebrate African American heritage. Celebrated for seven days, from Dec. 26 through Jan. 1, Kwanzaa is a time for joy, as well as reflection.

This thorough handbook explains the origins and significance of Kwanzaa and its seven principles of life and light: Principle 1: Umoja: Unity—Principle 2: Kujichagulia: Self-Determination—Principle 3: Ujima: Collective Work and Responsibility—Principle 4: Ujamaa: Cooperative Economics—Principle 5: Nia: Purpose—Principle 6: Kuumba: Creativity—Principle 7: Imani: Faith. An important statement of a relatively new holiday in American culture.

529 **For every season: The complete guide to African American celebrations, traditional to contemporary.** Barbara Eklof. xxi, 376 p., ill. New York: HarperCollins, 1997. ISBN: 0060178183.

394.7608996073   GT4803.A2

This comprehensive (and joyful) guide to celebrations among African Americans ranges from those celebrations brought in with the African diaspora, to those arising from slavery times, to modern day evolutions, including Kwanzaa. Demonstrates how celebrations help build community and strengthen black identity.

530   Guide to African American and African primary sources at Harvard University. Barbara A. Burg, Richard Newman, Elizabeth E. Sandager. ix, 217 p. Phoenix, Ariz.: Oryx Press, 2000. ISBN: 1573563390.

016.96   Z3509.B87; DT3

A guide that identifies individual titles and areas of strength in the African American and African holdings in the remarkably rich manuscript and other primary source materials at Harvard University. Belies the false, but common, assumption that "everything is on the Internet." This print reference serves as a portal to incredibly rich resources at one of the strongest African American collections in the world. Available as an e-book.

531   Guide to the processed collections in the manuscript division of the Moorland-Spingarn Research Center. Moorland-Spingarn Research Center, Howard University. 65 p. Washington: Moorland-Spingarn Research Center, Howard University, 2000.

Z6621.M66

This catalog lists primary source manuscripts and other major collections entrusted to the library of Howard University. As one of the first universities for African Americans, Howard has created a body of unique resources that document significant elements of black history and culture in America, based on donations for preservation and safekeeping by generations of African Americans. Catalogs like this one enable a broader range of scholars to know about these collections.

532   The Harvard guide to African-American history. Evelyn Brooks Higginbotham, Leon F. Litwack, Darlene Clark Hine. xxxvi, 923 p. Cambridge, Mass.: Harvard University Press, 2001. ISBN: 0674002768.

973.0496073   E185.H326

The definitive annotated bibliography for African American history and culture. Chronological listing provides easy identification of materials for particular time periods. Includes reference to books, journal articles, and reports. Also of special value are listings of manuscript repositories and collections. A solid reference work, highly recommended for research and general collections.

533   Interdisciplinary bibliographic guide to black studies.
Schomburg Collection of Negro Literature and History. 1 v. New York: G.K. Hall, 1998.

Z1361.N39S373a

Covers 1998.

Guide reaches across a broad range of fields to draw in relevant materials to support programs in black studies. Includes a wide range of interdisciplinary sources.

Title changed to *G. K. Hall interdisciplinary bibliographic guide to black studies* for years 1999–2003.

Handbooks

534   The African American holiday of Kwanzaa: A celebration of family, community and culture. Maulana Karenga. 116 p., ill. Los Angeles: University of Sankore Press, 1988. ISBN: 0943412099.
394.268   GT4403.K37

One of the early, full-length handbooks for the celebration of Kwanzaa. Remains a solid reference for its origins, observance, and traditions. Makes detailed reference to the African roots, as well as the strengthening of the American community, which are essential to its celebration. Includes bibliographical references.

535   The Black handbook: The people, history, and politics of Africa and the African diaspora. E. L. Bute, H. J. P. Harmer. vii, 392 p. London; Washington: Cassell, 1997. ISBN: 0304335428.
960   DT20.B86

Brief entries in alphabetical order cover major people, historical events, and politics. Not limited to the African continent; coverage includes emancipation and civil rights in the United States.

536   Blacks Against Drunk Driving: A culture-based handbook to promote traffic safety awareness and action, DOT Report No. HS 809 032. National Black Alcoholism and Addictions Council. iv, 35 p., ill. (some color). Washington: U.S. Department of

Transportation, National Highway Traffic Safety Administration, 2000.

Thorough handbook provides cultural context for preventing driving under the influence among African Americans. Elements that can lead to drunk driving are discussed, and ways to identify and prevent its occurrence are suggested.

537 The blacks in America, 1492–1977: A chronology and fact book. 4th ed. Irving J. Sloan. x, 169 p. Dobbs Ferry, N.Y.: Oceana Publications, 1977. ISBN: 0379005247.

973.0496073   E185.S57

This fourth, and last, edition of a print guide to African Americans and African American life was still fairly unique in 1977, and as such, provides a highly useful snapshot of black life at a time when few other works were recording what is found here. Along with its earlier editions (1st and 2nd eds.) under the title, *The American Negro, a chronology and fact book,* it describes African Americans at an earlier time. Presents a chronology of African Americans in the United States, extensive lists of major organizations, as well as publications of and for African Americans. Provides lists of libraries with significant African American holdings. Also gives a statistical abstract of the economic and social status of African Americans.

538 Praeger handbook of Black American health: Policies and issues behind disparities in health. 2nd ed. Ivor Lensworth Livingston. 2 v. (xlvii, 911 p.), ill., maps. Westport, Conn: Praeger, 2004. ISBN: 0313324778.

362.108996073   RA448.5.N4H364

1st ed., 1994.

Contents: v. 1 (pt. I), Cardiovascular and related chronic conditions (ch. 1–6); v. 1 (pt. II), General chronic conditions ch. 7–13; v. 1 (pt. III), Lifestyle, social, and mental outcomes (ch. 14–26); v. 2 (pt. IV), Sociopolitical, environmental, and structural challenges (ch. 27–38); v. 2 (pt. V), Ethics, research, technology, and social policy issues (ch. 39–47).

This rev. and exp. ed. addresses crucial issues in disparities in health status and access to health care for African Americans, with identification of preventive strategies, interventions, and possible solutions (e.g., ch. 47, "Eliminating racial and ethnic disparities in health: A framework for action"). Index. For professionals and students in public health, medicine, health psychology, health policy, medical sociology, nursing, and possibly other areas of research, education, and study. Also available as an e-book.

Craig Haynes' *Ethnic minority: A selected annotated bibliography*, publ. in 1997, remains a good bibliography to start research in health disparities, complemented by "A selected, annotated list of materials that support the development of policies designed to reduce racial and ethnic health disparities," by Joan E. Donatiello, Peter Droese, and Soo H. Kim (*Journal of the Medical Library Association* 92(2): 257–65, Apr. 2004, available online via http://www.pubmedcentral.nih.gov/articlerender .fcgi?artid=385308).

Healthy People 2010 (www.cdc.gov/nchs/hphome.htm), National Institutes of Health (NIH) (www.nih.gov), and the Centers for Disease Control and Prevention (CDC) (www.cdc.gov) have as a goal to support research that advances the elimination of health disparities among ethnic groups and among the various vulnerable and at-risk populations. Other resources exploring and documenting minority health and health disparities with the goal of promoting racial parity include, for example, "National Library of Medicine Strategic Plan for Addressing Health Disparities 2004–2008" (http://www.nlm.nih.gov/pubs/plan/nlm_health_disp_2004 _2008.html), "National Healthcare Disparities Report" (http://www.ahrq .gov/qual/nhdr06/nhdr06.htm), "Native-American Health" via MedlinePlus (http://medlineplus.gov), NLM's "Native Outreach Activities," (http://www .nlm.nih.gov/medlineplus/nativeamericanhealth.html), "Hispanic outreach activities" (http://sis.nlm.nih.gov/outreach/hispanicamerican .html), "Minority Health—Specific Populations Groups" (http://sis.nlm .nih.gov/outreach/minorityhealth.html), and other websites.

539   Racial justice in America: A reference handbook. David B. Mustard. xiii, 271 p. Santa Barbara, Calif.: ABC-CLIO, 2003. ISBN: 1576072142.

305.896073   E185.M95

This remarkable handbook uses focused essays to trace racial justice— and its negative side when race was used as a basis for injustice—in America from the earliest colonial times to the present. First section of the book lays historical groundwork for understanding racial justice in America. The colonial slave trade is covered, as well as the compromises the new nation made to acquire the labor force necessary to establish a strong economic base through slavery. The growth of the Antislavery

Movement is outlined before the Civil War, as well as racial justice during Reconstruction.

The second part of the volume deals with contemporary issues. Matters of racial issues in contemporary society are covered in chapters on criminal justice, education, employment, wages, living conditions, and political participation. Supporting materials conclude the volume to create a sound foundation for understanding issues of racial justice. A chronology, biographical sketches, laws, cases, statistics, quotations, and a directory of organizations are useful adjutants to the narratives of earlier chapters. Bibliographical references are provided throughout and a lengthy bibliography is given at the end. Index. Available as an e-book.

Indexes; Abstract Journals

540   **Black index: Afro-Americana in selected periodicals, 1907–1949.**
Richard Newman. xxxi, 266 p. New York: Garland, 1981. ISBN:
0824095138.
016.9730496073   Z1361.N39N58; E185

Author and subject guide, in dictionary arrangement, to more than 1,000 articles from some 350 periodicals published in the United States, Canada, and Great Britain. Articles are drawn from the *Annual magazine subject index,* 1907–49. New indexing is provided by author and book reviewer, plus expanded subject access. Does not include citations for *Journal of Negro history,* for which a separate index is available. Although the online Retrospective Reader's Guide to Periodical Literature (from the H.W. Wilson Company) provides some of this coverage, this title in paper is still a useful resource, especially since it was augmented by additional content.

541   **Black studies on disc, 1988–present [CD-ROM].** Schomburg
Center for Research in Black Culture, [New York Public Library].
CD-ROMs. [New York?]: G.K. Hall.
                                                                        Z1039.B56

This online catalog of records is drawn from the catalog and indexes of the Schomburg Center for Research in Black Culture of the New York Public Library; it covers the experience and contributions of people of African descent on a global basis. Geographic coverage focuses on the Americas, the Caribbean, and Sub-Saharan Africa. All material formats are included, largely books, serials, microforms, audio and audiovisual resources, photographs, manuscript collections, art, artifacts, and ephemera. Materials acquired and indexed from 1988 to the present are included, with a lag time of two to three years. An online and expanded version of the traditional G.K. Hall catalog of the Schomburg Collection.

542   G. K. Hall index to black periodicals. G. K. Hall. Detroit: Gale
Group, 2000–2005. ISSN: 1539-8307.
974   AI3.O4

Covers African American periodicals beginning with 1950. Indexed with a single alphabetical arrangement interfiling authors, subjects, and cross-references. Includes book, fiction, film, music, and theatrical reviews. The last issue of this print index covered 2004 and included more than 30 scholarly and general-interest publications. The index underwent several title changes: *Index to selected Negro periodicals* (1950–54), *Index to selected periodicals* (1954–65), *Index to periodical articles by and about Negroes* (1966–72), *Index to periodical articles by and about blacks* (1973–83), and *Index to black periodicals* (1984–98).

543   Index to black periodicals. [G.K. Hall]. 15 v. Boston: G.K. Hall,
1988–1999. ISSN: 0899-6253.
974   AI3.O4

Indexes black periodicals, covering 1984–98, which have not been replaced by electronic sources. Succeeded by the *G.K. Hall index to black periodicals,* covering 1999–2004.

544   Index to periodical articles by and about blacks. Hallie Q. Brown
Memorial Library. Boston: G.K. Hall. ISSN: 0161-8245.
974.0496073   AI3.O4

Provided identification for materials published in the African American periodical press from 1973–83. Began to show the fruits of the civil rights movement, as well as many of the frustrations and reflections of the attendant violence, which was the cost of positive change. Succeeded by *Index to black periodicals;* preceded by *Index to periodical articles by and about Negroes.*

545   Index to periodical articles by and about Negroes. Hallie Q.
Brown Memorial Library. Boston: G.K. Hall. ISSN: 0073-5973.
051   AI3.O4

Covering the time period from 1966–72, this index provides a window onto African American publications during the civil rights era. Succeeded by *Index to periodical articles by and about blacks.*

546 The Kaiser index to black resources, 1948–1986. Schomburg
     Center for Research in Black Culture, [New York Public Library]. 5
     v. Brooklyn, N.Y.: Carlson, 1992. ISBN: 0926019600.
016.9730496073   Z1361.N39K34; E185

Consists of 174,000 references to articles, reviews, and obituaries published
in 150 African American scholarly and general interest periodicals, as well
as publications covering the Caribbean. Entries are arranged chronologically (newest items first) in 15,000 subject headings. Subject headings were
derived from those used by the New York Public Library, along with additional headings developed for this publication. Notes, photographs, and
illustrations that accompany articles are indexed. Annotations accompany
some entries. Scattered cross-references. No index.

Manuscripts and Archives

547 **Afro-American sources in Virginia: A guide to manuscripts.**
     Michael Plunkett. xviii, 323 p. Charlottesville, Va.: University Press
     of Virginia, 1990. ISBN: 0813912520.
016.97500496073   Z1361.N39P496; E185.93.V8

Contains 1,038 annotated entries alphabetically arranged in 22 sections,
each covering a single repository. Collections of historical societies and of
college and university libraries are described. Materials cited include plantation and church records, the archives of traditionally black colleges and
universities, diaries, photographs, and the papers of politicians, businesses,
and civil rights groups. Subject index.

   A digital version is posted on the Web at http://www.upress.virginia
.edu/plunkett/mfp.html.

Quotations

548 **African American quotations.** Richard Newman, Julian Bond. xvi,
     504 p. Phoenix, Ariz.: Oryx Press, 1998. ISBN: 1573561185.
081.08996073   PN6081.3.A36

This highly useful gathering of some 2,500 quotations from over 300
years of African American life is drawn from more than 500 individuals.
Arranged in chapters by broad subjects, both general ("Adolescence") and
others focused on African American life ("Black Pride"). Includes indexes
for individuals and their occupations, as well as topics covered. Sources are
not identified. Available as an e-book.

549   **The black Americans: A history in their own words, 1619–1983.**
Milton Meltzer. x, 306 p., ports. New York: T.Y. Crowell, 1984.
ISBN: 0690044194.
973.0496   E185.B55

This nicely-drawn history of the African American experience is made up
of quotations from various sources: speeches, magazine articles, letters,
diaries, eyewitness retellings, and so on. While suitable for middle school
and above, this is still a fresh telling of the black story in America and is
worthwhile for general and even research collections.

550   **The black handbook: 100 and more quotes by Garvey, Lumumba,
and Malcolm X.** Marcus Garvey, Patrice Lumumba, Malcolm X. 34
p. Chicago: Third World Press, 1975. ISBN: 0883780607.
909.0496   E185.97.G3B55

In 1975, black political consciousness was finally emerging into the mainstream of American life. This collection of quotations and maxims documents three of the most powerful voices that created the pathways for that
to happen. Their words remain fresh, relevant, and provocative after 30
years.

551   **Black pearls: Daily meditations, affirmations, and inspirations
for African-Americans.** Eric V. Copage. 1 v. (unpaged). New York:
Quill, W. Morrow, 1993. ISBN: 0688122914.
158.108996073   E185.86.C588

A yearlong daybook of 365 quotations from African Americans. Includes
life skills guides, with inspirational to practical advice. Sources include
African proverbs, media personalities like Oprah Winfrey and Bill Cosby,
and political activists like Dr. Martin Luther King, Jr. and Rosa Parks. Each
day's entry addresses a different topic from an African American perspective. A refreshing form of quotation book useful in general collections.

552   **In our own words: A treasury of quotations from the African-
American community.** Elza Dinwiddie-Boyd. xiii, 409 p. New
York: Avon Books, 1996. ISBN: 0380779102.
081.08996   PN6081.3.I5

A solid book of quotations from African Americans, arranged in topical
chapters and well-referenced. Begins with a chapter on "Courage," ranging
through one on "Kwanzaa and Christmas," to "Perseverance: Our Staple,"
and concluding with a powerful "Ancestor Speaks."

553 **The Martin Luther King, Jr. companion: Quotations from the speeches, essays, and books of Martin Luther King, Jr.** Martin Luther King, Coretta Scott King, Dexter Scott King. xiii, 108 p., ill. New York: St. Martin's Press, [1999]. ISBN: 0312199902.

323.092   E185.97.K5A25

The legendary voice and thought of Dr. Martin Luther King, Jr., comes alive again in this classic volume, with selections made from his writings and speeches by his wife, Coretta Scott King. Both famous and lesser-known speeches are included.

554 **My soul looks back, 'less I forget: A collection of quotations by people of color.** D. Winbush Riley. xii, 498 p. New York: HarperCollinsPublishers, 1993. ISBN: 0062700863.

081.08996073   PN6081.3.M9

Among numerous volumes of quotations by Africans and African Americans, this one stands out because it provides both the source and date of each quotation, as well as solid identification for the speaker. Drawn from the time of Aesop to the present, some 7,000 quotations are grouped in more than 450 topics from "Ability" to "Youth" in an alphabetic arrangement. Materials referenced include books, magazines, literary sources, speeches, media (including radio and television), historical documents, and so on. There is also an extensive section of bibliographical references, indexes by speaker or source, and subject.

RACE AND ETHNICITY

201

555 **A political dictionary of black quotations reflecting the black man's dreams, hopes, visions.** Osei Amoah. 261 p. London; Pawtucket, R.I.: Oyokoanyinaase House, 1989. ISBN: 0951403508.

305.896   E185.61.P66

This British volume gathers together a broad range of quotations from African Americans and other black peoples on political topics.

556 **Songs of wisdom: Quotations from famous African Americans of the twentieth century.** Jay David. ix, 176 p. New York: W. Morrow, 2000. ISBN: 0688164978.

973.0496073   PN6081.3.S66

A treasure trove of quotations from African Americans from the 20th century, ranging from the famous to the obscure. Fourteen chapters provide topical arrangement in standard categories such as arts, childhood, sports, and so on. Additional categories especially suitable for African Americans include civil rights and race relations. Individuals are not identified beyond the name given, and sources are not provided.

557 Till victory is won: Famous black quotations from the NAACP.
Janet Cheatham Bell. xvii, 186 p., ill. New York: Pocket Books, 2002. ISBN: 0743428250.
081.08996073   PN6081.3.T55

From its founding in 1909, the National Association for the Advancement of Colored People (NAACP) has advocated for social justice and racial equality in America. This compilation of quotations from that work brings a clear focus to the depth and range of the struggle. History in the words of those making it.

558 The world of W.E.B. Du Bois: A quotation sourcebook. W. E. B. Du Bois, Meyer Weinberg. viii, 282 p., port. Westport, Conn.: Greenwood Press, 1992. ISBN: 0313286191.
305.89607302   E185.97.D73A25

This volume presents quotations from W.E.B. Du Bois that discuss his ideas about the possibility of racial harmony, bringing reason and order to our thinking about race, and justice and freedom for all. Available as an e-book.

Statistics

559 The African American education data book. Michael T. Nettles, Laura W. Perna. 3 v., ill. Fairfax, Va.: Frederick D. Patterson Research Institute of the College Fund/UNCF, 1997.
371.82996073   LC2717.N47

Contains a wealth of statistical information about African American students in the American educational system. Statistics include, but are not limited to, performance on a variety of standardized tests, employment status relative to education, and level of educational attainment. Includes data on other ethnic/racial groups. Vol. 1 includes higher and adult education; v. 2 covers preschool through high school; and v. 3 focuses on the transition from school to college or school to work.

560 Black Americans. Numbers and Concepts. Boulder, Colo.: Numbers and Concepts, 1990–. ISSN: 1048-6992.
305.8960730021   E185.5.B512

Since 1990, this annual publication has provided statistics on African Americans and African American life in the United States. This statistical breakout is especially useful because the data is otherwise scattered among numerous other publications.

561   Black demographic data, 1790–1860: A sourcebook. Clayton E. Cramer. viii, 165 p., ill. Westport, Conn.: Greenwood Press, 1997. ISBN: 031330243X.

973.0496073   E185.18.C73

Demographic data on African Americans for the period 1790 to 1860 is difficult to ascertain with any degree of certainty. Understanding the social, political, and economic aspects of black life during this period requires accurate figures, difficult or impossible when many were enslaved. This sourcebook goes far toward providing such information.

562   Historical statistics of black America. Jessie Carney Smith, Carrell Horton. 2 v. (lxxxii, 2244 p.). New York: Gale Research, 1995. ISBN: 0810385422.

973.0496073021   E185.H543

The alphabetically arranged essays in this two-volume set cover the history of African Americans in the United States by using as many numbers, figures, and counts as possible. Statistics are well-documented and reliable. An interesting and useful reference work for both research and general collections. Includes bibliographical references and index.

563   Statistical record of black America. Carrell Horton, Jessie Carney Smith, Gale Research. 4 v., ill. Detroit: Gale Research, 1990–1997. ISSN: 1051-8002.

305.8960730021   E185.5.S83

A breadth of statistical detail is provided in this landmark work on African Americans. Counts are provided for all aspects of the lives of black Americans. This information is often difficult or impossible to find in other sources. For historical statistics, see also the companion title, *Historical statistics of black America.*

Internet Resources

564   African American newspapers. http://www.accessible.com/accessible/. Accessible Archives. Malvern, Pa.: Accessible Archives, 1997–.

071   E184.6

Full text of major 19th-century African American newspapers, which present the news of the day from an African American perspective. Also greatly enriched by biographical entries, statistics, essays and editorials by notable and ordinary African Americans, poetry, fiction, and ads. Newspapers include:

The Christian recorder: 1861–Apr. 1862, some later issues through 1902;

The colored American/ Weekly advocate: Jan. 7, 1837–Dec. 25, 1841;

Freedom's journal: Mar. 16, 1827–Mar. 28, 1829;

Frederick Douglass paper: 1851–Dec. 1852, some later issues through 1859;

The national era: Jan. 7, 1847–Dec. 1853, some later issues through Mar. 12, 1860;

The north star: Dec. 3, 1847–Apr. 17, 1851; and

Provincial freeman: 1854–57.

565 **African American research.** http://www.archives.gov/genealogy/heritage/african-american/. National Archives and Records Administration (NARA). College Park, Md.: U.S. National Archives and Records Administration. Updated frequently.

The U.S. National Archives contains a rich store of primary materials relating to the African American experience. This web guide goes far toward identifying major topics covered, and explains how to access particular groups of records in four major areas: Pre-Civil War, Military Records, Post-Civil War Records, and Links to Resources. The last area has some 30 hot links to material descriptions. A valuable resource often overlooked. It is usually necessary to travel to the National Archives to use the materials there.

566 **The African-American mosaic.** http://www.loc.gov/exhibits/african/intro.html. Library of Congress. Washington: Library of Congress, 2000; 1993.

E184.6

This 2000 online guide updates the 1993 Library of Congress print publication of the same name. Created for an exhibit at the Library of Congress, it identifies materials on a broad range of historical topics, including slavery, abolition, and migration. Also looks at the civil rights struggle, as well as modern African American life.

567 **The Atlantic slave trade and slave life in the Americas.** http://
hitchcock.itc.virginia.edu/Slavery/. Jerome S. Handler, Michael L.
Tuite, Virginia Foundation for the Humanities and Public Policy.
Charlottesville, Va.: Virginia Foundation for the Humanities;
Digital Media Lab at the University of Virginia Library. Updated
frequently.

HT975

Some 1,300 images on this website are drawn from a broad range of
sources, with most from the period of slavery. Depicts the circumstances and experience of enslaved Africans who were taken from
Africa, and of their descendants in the slave societies of the New
World.

Site is searchable by keyword and also under the following categories:

- Maps: Africa, New World, Slave Trade
- Pre-Colonial Africa: Society, Polity, Culture
- Capture of Slaves and Coffles in Africa
- European Forts and Trading Posts in Africa
- Slave Ships and the Atlantic Crossing (Middle Passage)
- Slave Sales and Auctions: African Coast and the Americas
- New World Agriculture and Plantation Labor
- Plantation Scenes, Slave Settlements and Houses
- Domestic Servants and Free People of Color
- Miscellaneous Occupations and Economic Activities
- Marketing and Urban Scenes
- Music, Dance, and Recreational Activities
- Family Life, Child Care, Schools
- Religion and Mortuary Practices
- Military Activities and U.S. Civil War
- Physical Punishment, Rebellion, Running Away
- Emancipation and Post-Slavery Life
- Portraits and Illustrations of Individuals

Each image opens first in a smaller format, and then in a larger one.
Sources are carefully noted.

568 **Black thought and culture.** http://www.alexanderstreet2.com/
bltclive. Alexander Street Press. Alexandria, Va.: Alexander Street
Press, 2003–.

E185

A single source for the published works of numerous historically important black leaders. Includes well-known works, and also some 5000 p.
of unique, fugitive, and never-before-published materials. When complete, will provide some "100,000 pages of monographs, essays, articles,
speeches, and interviews written by leaders within the black community
[in the U.S.] from the earliest times to 1975. . . ."—About the Database
Now includes some 1,300 nonfiction items written by over 1,000 prominent African Americans. Includes journal articles, essays, speeches, pamphlets, letters, and other materials. Search by title, subject, or words in
the full text.

569   **Oxford African American studies center.** http://www.oxfordaasc.
      com/. Henry Louis Gates, Oxford University Press. New York:
      Oxford University Press, 2006–.

E185

Gathered together in a single electronic package in this remarkable
resource is a broad and deep range of materials on the African American
experience. Some 7,500 articles from Oxford University Press reference
sources, 100 primary sources, more than 1,200 images, 100 maps, 200
charts and tables, and some 6,000 biographies. Major sources include the
African American national biography, Africana, black women in America,
2nd ed., and the *Encyclopedia of African American history.*

570   **Southern Poverty Law Center.** http://www.splcenter.org/.
      [Southern Poverty Law Center]. Montgomery, Ala.: Southern
      Poverty Law Center. Updated frequently.

From its beginnings in 1971 as a small civil rights law firm, the Southern
Poverty Law Center has created a powerful international presence as a
non-profit organization highly respected for its work to promote toler-
ance through education programs, for its tracking of hate groups, and for
speaking out for those who suffer from discrimination. Online directory
of groups.

Arab Americans

Bibliography

571   **Arab and Muslim Americans of Middle Eastern origin: Social
      and political aspects: A bibliography.** Joan Nordquist. 72 p.

Santa Cruz, Calif.: Reference and Research Services, 2003. ISBN: 1892068362.

Z1361.A73N67; E184.A65

Even at 72 p., this bibliography goes a considerable way towards filling in the gap for materials about Arab Americans in the United States from political and social perspectives.

572 **An Arab-American bibliographic guide.** Philip M. Kayal. 42 p. Belmont, Mass.: Association of Arab-American University Graduates, 1985. ISBN: 0937694665.

016.97304927　　　　　　　　　　Z1361.A73K39; E184.A65

More than two decades after being issued, this publication of the Association of Arab-American University Graduates still offers useful sources for research on the Arab American community in the United States. An updated edition would be most welcome for this thinly-populated area.

573 **The Arab-American experience in the United States and Canada: A classified, annotated bibliography.** Michael W. Suleiman. xix, 604 p. Ann Arbor, Mich.: Pierian Press, 2006. ISBN: 0876503954.

E184.A65; Z1361.A73

A landmark reference book which gathers, for the first time, a sweeping range of references to the Arab American experience in the United States and Canada from the 1840s through 2005. Annotations readily identify which materials are appropriate for retrieval and further study. References are arranged alphabetically in 23 chapters under broad topical headings. Materials included are primarily in English and Arabic. Indexes.

Chronologies

574 **The Arabs in America, 1492–1977: A chronology and fact book.** Beverlee Turner Mehdi. ix, 150 p. Dobbs Ferry, N.Y.: Oceana Publications, 1978. ISBN: 0379005271.

973.04927　　　　　　　　　　　　　E184.A65M44

A useful chronology of the Arab American experience in America from the beginning of European exploration to 1977. Includes notable Arab Americans and events that were influenced by their presence. Through carefully researched factual detail, highlights the contributions of Arab Americans throughout American history. Bibliography and index.

Directories

575 **Arab American media and leadership directory: A guide to assist in communicating with the Arab American community through media contacts, businesses and community leaders.** Ray Hanania. Orland Park, Ill.: Tahit al-Ard Press, 2006–.
305.8927073

Directory for the Chicago area identifies and provides contact information for Arab American business and civic leaders, Arab American organizations, and newspapers and other mass media. Similar directories are available for the areas in and around other major cities, including Washington, D.C.

Encyclopedias

576 **Arab American encyclopedia.** Anan Ameri, Dawn Ramey, Arab Community Center for Economic and Social Services. 1 v. (various pagings), ill. Detroit: U X L, 2000. ISBN: 0787629529.
973.04927   E184.A65A665

A basic, if pedestrian, encyclopedia suitable for schools at grade 5 and above, and for general reference collections. Nineteen subject chapters begin with a timeline and range across historical roots, immigration, education, and culture. Languages and religions are also covered. Topics of special interest for young people are holidays, family structure, and the place of artistic expression. Sidebars emphasize focus of articles. Glossary, bibliography, maps. A teacher's guide is provided.

Guides

577 **Arab American almanac.** Arab-American Historical Foundation. ill. Glendale, Calif.: News Circle, 1984–. ISSN: 0742-9576.
973.04927   E184.A65A45

This almanac serves as an important bridge and introduction between the approx. 3 million Arab Americans in the United States and other parts of U.S. culture. Begun with a 1st ed. in 1974, and updated every few years, the current 5th ed., publ. in 2003, brings up-to-date this self-described "most comprehensive reference book on the Arab-American community in the USA."—*Website* See: http://www.Arab-American-affairs.net/.

Volume begins with a chronology of Arab American contributions to American history and culture, and then describes important American writers who are Arab American or descended from Arab Americans. The next three sections, all directories, are especially useful in a reference setting. The first is a listing of Arab American organizations, the second is for Arab American press and media resources, and the third is for Arab American religious institutions, whether Christian, Druze, or Muslim. Also includes a who's who among Arab Americans, a listing of Arab nation-states, biographies, statistics, language tables.

578   **100 questions and answers about Arab Americans.** Detroit Free Press. Detroit: Detroit Free Press, 2001. http://www.freep.com/legacy/jobspage/arabs/index.htm.

305.8

The *Detroit free press* has created this guide to help journalists more accurately portray Arab Americans. Includes 100 sample questions to elicit information on origins, language, demographics, family life, customs, religion, politics, terminology, and stereotypes associated with Arab Americans.

Handbooks

579   **Arab American yearbook: [The resource and referral guide for and about Arab Americans].** Meredith Corporation. Des Moines, Iowa: Meredith Corporation.

Contains interesting information about, and for, the Arab American community in the United States. Includes a directory of community organizations, one for publications and media in the United States and abroad, and a third for professional business and career contacts. Contains health and statistical information relating to Arab Americans, and a section on financial aid for students. Especially useful are the articles by and about notable Arab Americans.

Periodicals and Dissertations

580   **The Arabic yellow pages: The national directory of Arab-Americans; Dalil al-`Arabi.** [ATW]. ill. Playa Del Rey, Calif.: ATW, 1900s–.

HD2344.5.U6

Also a free website at http://www.arabicyellowpages.us/, *The Arabic yellow pages* provides a comprehensive listing by category of Arab American businesses and organizations in the United States. Site is provided in both English and Arabic.

581   **The news circle.** [Joseph R. Haiek]. ill. Glendale, Calif.: Joseph R. Haiek. ISSN: 0193-1814.

973.04927   E184.A65N49

Intended for both Arab Americans and others interested in Arab American culture and life, this monthly English language magazine is a useful resource for furthering knowledge and understanding of the Arab American community. Includes "news, views, editorials, commentaries, features, profiles, opinion forum, Arab-US business, trade events, politics, Arabic culture and arts, Arab-American society and a calendar of major national events, news analysis, biographies, press/media/books, and advertising."— *Website* See: http://www.Arab-American-affairs.net/.

Asian Americans

Bibliography

582   **Asian American studies: An annotated bibliography and research guide.** Hyung-chan Kim. x, 504 p. New York: Greenwood Press, 1989. ISBN: 0313260265.

016.9730495   Z1361.O7K56; E184.O6

This extensive work provides a solid basis for study and teaching in a wide range of the multicultural and interdisciplinary areas of Asian American studies. Also useful as a reference guide to identify materials in a particular area of interest beyond the classroom. Includes indexes.

583   **The Asian American woman: Social, economic and political conditions: a bibliography.** Joan Nordquist. 72 p. Santa Cruz, Calif.: Reference and Research Services, 1997. ISBN: 0937855944.

016.305895073   Z1361.O7N65; E184.O6

Another in the slight, but workmanlike, reference listings from the Reference and Research Services group. Crossing ethnicity and gender issues, a useful title.

584   **Asians in Latin America and the Caribbean: A bibliography.** Leon Lamgen. 149 p. [Flushing, N.Y.]: Asian/American Center, Queens College, CUNY, 1990.

016.9800495   F1419.A84

There has been so great a focus on the lives of Asians in the United States that the extensive and rich body of materials documenting their experience in Latin America and the Caribbean has gotten little notice. This bibliography provides a window onto a wealth of documentation to explore those issues.

585 **Asians in the United States: Abstracts of the psychological and behavioral literature, 1967–1991.** Frederick T. L. Leong, James R. Whitfield. x, 216 p. Washington: PsycINFO, American Psychological Association, 1992. ISBN: 1557981787.
016.1558495073   E184.O6A87

What does it mean, in terms both of the interior landscape of individual's minds, and also for how they work within and without their own ethnic group, to be Asian in America? This bibliography makes reference to a wide range of useful literature of all types to explore these issues. Includes indexes.

586 **Bibliography of Pacific/Asian American materials in the Library of Congress.** Elena S. H. Yu, Alice K. Murata, Chien Lin, Library of Congress. vii, 254 p. Chicago: Pacific/Asian American Mental Health Research Center, 1982. ISBN: 0934584168.
016.9730495   Z1361.O7Y8; E184.O6

What are the materials held in the U.S. Library of Congress which shed particular light on the thinking and well-being of Americans with Asian and Pacific Rim backgrounds and identities? A useful listing of materials otherwise difficult to identify.

587 **Filipinos in the United States: A print and digital resource guide, a selected and annotated bibliography on the Filipino American experience.** Estela L. Manila. v, 90 p., ill. San Francisco: Asian American Information, 2000. ISBN: 0962110167.

E184.F4

Filipinos have migrated to the United States in recent years for better social conditions and for economic opportunity they cannot find at home. This annotated bibliography identifies references which both document and help in the understanding of their experience in America. Includes bibliographical references and index.

588 **A history reclaimed: An annotated bibliography of Chinese language materials on the Chinese of America.** H. Mark Lai,

Russell Leong, Jean Pang Yip, University of California, Los Angeles. xvi, 152 p. Los Angeles: Resource Development and Publications, Asian American Studies Center, University of California, 1986. ISBN: 0934052085.

016.97304951 Z1361.C4L35; E184.C5

There has been considerable focus on English language materials on Chinese Americans, without taking into account the wealth of articles, books, and other like writings written in Chinese. Some of these materials can be the most useful in providing firsthand accounts from a personal perspective. In addition, for those who read Chinese, the nuances of that language can convey particular meanings to further enrich the understanding of the Chinese American experience. Includes index.

589 **A selected bibliography on the Asians in America.** James I. Wong. v, 135 p. Palo Alto, Calif.: R and E Research Associates, 1981. ISBN: 088247605X.

016.30608995073 Z1361.O7W66; E184.O6

With a focus on Asian Americans in Hawaii, this listing provides references to the Asian American experience away from the American mainland. A perspective not otherwise easily found.

590 **Sikhs in North America: An annotated bibliography.** Darshan Singh Tatla. xxi, 180 p. New York: Greenwood Press, 1991. ISBN: 0313273367.

016.9730882946 Z1361.S47T37; E184.S55

Organized alphabetically by author within general subject areas like migration and settlement, education and employment, family and social change, literature and media, politics and religion. A particular strength is its attention to literature produced by Punjabi writers and ethnic press. A select list of Punjabi writers and their writings, and a list of over 100 periodicals published in North America have been appended to this work.

Encyclopedias

591 **The Asian American encyclopedia.** Franklin Ng, John D. Wilson. 6 v. (xx, 1818, xix p.), ill., maps. New York: Marshall Cavendish, 1995. ISBN: 1854356771.

973.0495003 E184.O6A827

More than 1,000 illustrations, 50 maps, and numerous charts give additional weight to more than 2,000 mostly signed entries in this balanced and
imminently useful reference work in six volumes. Coverage is remarkably
comprehensive, with entries which vary in length from a few lines to several thousand words. Individual coverage is given to the six largest ethnic
groups among Asian Americans: Chinese Americans, Filipino Americans,
Japanese Americans, Asian Indian Americans, Korean Americans, and
Vietnamese Americans. Other individual ethnic groups are also presented
in some detail. History, culture, and language are a focus of coverage. In
addition to bibliographic references, there is a listing of libraries, muse-
ums, research centers, and other facilities where further research can be
carried out. Subject and general index.

592   Asian American reference library. 2nd ed. Helen Zia, Susan B.
Gall, Irene Natividad. 6 v., ill., map, ports. New York: U X L, 2004.
ISBN: 0787675997.
920   E184.O6

This six-volume reference set begins with an almanac containing a variety of information on Asian Americans, including historical notes, special
locations, and contributions. A second part covers biographies of some 75
notable Asian Americans at a length of five to ten pages each, while the third
part is a chronology of events. A fourth section, Voices, contains documents
which report in their own words experiences of Asian Americans. Cumulative index to entire set. A solid and well-researched reference set, suitable for
middle school and high school students, and for general collections. Reference set in same pattern is also available for several other ethnic groups.

Handbooks

593   Handbook of Asian American psychology. 2nd ed. Frederick T.
L. Leong. x, 515 p., ill. Thousand Oaks, Calif.: Sage Publications,
2007. ISBN: 1412941334.
155.8495073   E184.A75H36

Multicultural issues are well covered in this 2nd ed. of a handbook first
published in 1998. It has been substantially revised to include new research
and theory that have entered the field since that time. Lifespan issues,
multiracial and multiple identity matters, awareness of the weight of stereotypes, along with consideration of matters relating to the elderly and
to immigrants. Coverage is balanced between theoretical and conceptual,
and methodology is addressed.

Hispanic Americans

Artistic Works

594   **A biographical handbook of Hispanics and United States film.**
Gary D. Keller, Estela Keller. xi, 322 p., ill. Tempe, Ariz.: Bilingual
Press/Editorial Bilingüe, 1997. ISBN: 0927534568.
791.4308968073   PN1995.9.H47K46

A broad-ranging biographical dictionary on Hispanics in the U.S. film
industry. Contains information on individuals often difficult to locate
otherwise. A useful companion to Keller's 1994 *Hispanics and United States
film: An overview and handbook* (595).

595   **Hispanics and United States film: An overview and handbook.**
Gary D. Keller. 230 p., ill. Tempe, Ariz.: Bilingual Review/Press,
1994. ISBN: 0927534401.
791.4308968   PN1995.9.L37K46

This thorough handbook documents the Hispanic presence in the U.S.
film industry throughout its history. Complemented by Keller's 1997 *Biographical handbook of Hispanics and United States film* (594).

596   **Hispanics in Hollywood: A celebration of 100 years in film and
television.** Luis Reyes, Peter Rubie. xv, 592 p., ill. Hollywood,
Calif.: Lone Eagle Publishing, 2000. ISBN: 1580650252.
791.4308968   PN1995.9.H47R49

Covering films and TV shows featuring Hispanic actors, or Hispanic
themes, this volume is divided into two main sections. One has plot summaries of films or shows themselves, while the second section is made up
of biographies of major players. Contains many black-and-white stills
from films, and also a good system of cross-references among entries. Of
particular note are supplementary essays on the role of Hispanics in the
film and entertainment industry, with much information that is not otherwise available.

Atlases and General Overview

597   **Latino American experience.** http://lae.greenwood.com/.
[Greenwood Publishing Group]. Westport, Conn.: Greenwood
Publishing Group, 2007.

Suitable for advanced middle school and above, as well as to provide highly accessible information to a general audience, this wide-ranging resource of full-text resources focuses on the history and culture of Latinos in the United States. Time period covered is pre-Columbian to the present, reflected in the in-depth timeline. Includes 150 full-text titles, including some reference books, 1,500 images, hundreds of primary sources, and links to 225 important websites. A Classroom Resource Center provides 25 lesson plans and Spanish language activities.

Bibliography

598   Hispanic Americans: Issues and bibliography. Karl A. Lawrence. 192 p., ill. New York: Nova Science Publishers, 2002. ISBN: 159033227X.

305.868073   E184.S75H5665

This useful guide addresses the situation and concerns of Hispanic Americans from many different cultures. The challenges and opportunities of particular focus in this diverse community are summed up in the Issues section, while the bibliography ranges far and wide to identify a wealth of solid resources. Includes indexes.

599   Hispanic periodicals in the United States, origins to 1960: A brief history and comprehensive bibliography. Nicolás Kanellos, Helvetia Martell. 359 p. Houston, Tex.: Arte Publico Press, 2000. ISBN: 1558852530.

015.7303408968   Z6953.5.S66.K36; PN4885.S75

Bibliography including all known United States serials either in Spanish or for a U.S. Hispanic community. Includes approximately 1,700 titles, almost half of which are considered missing and bear the annotation "no extant issues located." Entries are arranged alphabetically by title. Contains three indexes: geographical, chronological, and name/subject.

600   Latinos and politics: A select research bibliography. F. Chris Garcia, Patti Constantakis. xvi, 239 p. Austin, [Tex.]: Center for Mexican American Studies, University of Texas at Austin, 1991. ISBN: 0292746547.

016.9730468   Z1361.S7L365; E184.S75

Drawn from the remarkable resources of the Mexican American Studies Center of the University of Texas at Austin, this bibliography covers the

Latino political scene during the time period up until 1990 in a comprehensive way. Later sources—usually online and often full-text—do not go back over the ground covered here so as to replace this work. Still useful in identifying resources to document a time of awakening political activism.

601   Latinos in the United States: A historical bibliography. Albert
Camarillo. x, 332 p. Santa Barbara, Calif.: ABC-CLIO, 1986. ISBN:
0874364582.
016.9730468   Z1361.S7L37; E184.S75

It would be easy to assume that 20 years after publication this bibliography is outdated and must have been supplanted by a more recent work that includes all that is found here. It would also be wrong. This title provides a window onto research material on the history of the Hispanic American, material which, perhaps from its cross-disciplinary nature, could otherwise well be lost to the serious researcher.

Chronologies

602   Latino chronology: Chronologies of the American mosaic. D. H.
Figueredo. xii, 154 p., ill., map. Westport, Conn.: Greenwood Press,
2007. ISBN: 9780313341540.
973.046800202   E184.S75F543

The numerous and weighty contributions of Hispanic Americans to the development of the civilization of the Americas are highlighted in this remarkably readable reference work. Reaching back into the dim mists of antiquity, and coming up to the present, this extensive chronology identifies major dates in Latino history with well-written explanations of why they are significant. Dates are given in century-year format, and entries are then classified by 40 subject areas, such as education, health, language, religion, and so on. Includes glossary, bibliography, and index.

603   The Spanish in America, 1513–1979: A chronology and fact book.
Rev. ed. Arthur A. Natella. vii, 141 p. Dobbs Ferry, N.Y.: Oceana
Publications, 1980. ISBN: 0379005409.
973.0461   E123.S762

This chronology places an even focus on events across time, and so covers more remote historical periods more fully than some more recent works that focus more strongly on the present. Also includes some full-text documents and a thorough bibliography from a historical perspective.

Dictionaries and Thesauruses

604 **Dictionary of Latino civil rights history.** Francisco A. Rosales.
xi, 513 p., ill. Houston, Tex.: Arte Público Press, 2006. ISBN:
1558853472.
323.116807303   E184.S75R69

Some 900 entries identify significant events in the struggle for Hispanic
American civil rights. Biographical material is included, as is information on important organizations. Even though entries are brief, this is an
important title for both general and research collections. Includes bibliographical references and index.

605 **Notable Latino Americans: A biographical dictionary.** Matt S.
Meier, Conchita Franco Serri, Richard A. Garcia. xv, 431 p., ill.
Westport, Conn.: Greenwood Press, 1997. ISBN: 058538908X.
920.009268   E184.S75M435

Latinos who have made important contributions to American life are represented in 127 biographical essays in this well-researched work. Entries
are usually about three pages in length, and include a photograph of the
person being described. Many politicians, political activists, and educators
are joined by sports figures, musicians, actors, writers, and artists. Writing
is clear and content is suitable to general audiences, including middle and
high school students. Includes bibliographical references and index. Available as an e-book.

Encyclopedias

606 **Encyclopedia Latina: History, culture, and society in the United
States.** Ilan Stavans, Harold Augenbraum. 4 v., ill. (some color),
maps. Danbury, Conn.: Grolier Academic Reference, 2005. ISBN:
0717258157.
973.0468003   E184.S75E587

Some 650 signed essays, ranging in length from a paragraph to some 5,000
words, which cover a broad range of topics describing the experience of
Latinos in the United States. Includes 150 biographical entries. Popular
culture and events have a strong presence. Added features are primary
documents, statistical tables, and timelines. Both historical and modern
times are covered.

Each of the four volumes contains a center section of good color photographs; black-and-white photos are also included. Overall index, and

bibliographical and cross-references throughout. While this encyclopedia is suitable for high school and above, it is also a good solid general Hispanic American encyclopedia for both general and research collections.

607   **Encyclopedia of Latino popular culture.** Cordelia Candelaria. 2 v. (lxxvii, 981 p.), ill. Westport, Conn.: Greenwood Press, 2004. ISBN: 0313322155.
973.0468003   E184.S75E59

All aspects of popular culture concerning Latinos in the United States are covered in the two volumes of this thorough and well-referenced encyclopedia. Some 500 entries range in length from a few paragraphs to some six pages. Includes indexes, chronology, bibliographical references. Suitable for upper-level middle school and high school students, as well as for general collections.

608   **Latinas in the United States: A historical encyclopedia.** Vicki Ruíz, Virginia Sánchez Korrol. 3 v. (xx, 885 p.), ill., maps, ports. Bloomington, Ind.: Indiana University Press, 2006. ISBN: 0253346800.
920.7208968073B   E184.S75.L35

Some 600 signed articles, the majority of which are biographical entries on women who had some significant local or national impact as educators, activists, community organizers, and artists. Although the majority of Latinas included were nominated by scholars on the editorial board, pre-publication publicity resulted in the addition of entries for lesser-known women as well. The introduction is a historical and regional overview of Latinas. Thematic entries cover organizations and major events, plus many standard gender studies topics (violence, education, arts, family, religion). Each article has a brief list of sources, and the final volume includes a three-page unannotated list of selected readings. The encyclopedia is appropriate for both general readers and undergraduates. Available electronically from multiple vendors.

609   **The Latino encyclopedia.** Richard Chabrán, Rafael Chabrán. 6 v. (1821 p.), ill. New York: Marshall Cavendish, 1996. ISBN: 0761401253.
973.0468003   E184.S75L357

Nearly 2,000 entries cover the Latino experience in the United States from numerous perspectives. A few entries are scholarly essays, which are signed and have bibliographies, while many others are brief, sometimes only a paragraph or two, and cover some aspect of Hispanic American culture in a more cursory way. Its breadth enables it to cover topics sometimes left out of more scholarly works because of the magnitude of the subject matter. It is a sound, but for the most part, not scholarly reference work, useful for middle school and high school levels, and in general collections. Includes some bibliographies and index.

610 The Oxford encyclopedia of Latinos and Latinas in the United States. Suzanne Oboler, Deena J. González. 4 v., ill. New York: Oxford University Press, 2005. ISBN: 9780195156003.
973.0468003   E184.S75O97

More than 900 signed entries provide sweeping coverage of the Hispanic American experience in the United States. This population has come from all over the world: Europe, Asia, the Middle East, South and Central America, and especially from Puerto Rico and Mexico. An essential reference set for both general and reference collections. Available as an e-book.

Handbooks

611 Handbook of Hispanic cultures in the United States. Nicolás Kanellos, Claudio Esteva Fabregat. 4 v., ill., maps. Houston, Tex.; Madrid, Spain: Arte Público Press; Instituto de Cooperación Iberoamericana, 1993–1994. ISBN: 1558850740.
973.0468   E184.S75H365

Fifteen years after its original publication, this handbook, which is really a kind of encyclopedia of Hispanic culture from four scholarly disciplines, still provides a set of highly useful classic frameworks to help understand Latino culture in the United States. In a cross-disciplinary and multidisciplinary world, having the basics spelled out in a disciplined way is valuable indeed.

Indexes; Abstract Journals

612 The Chicano database. http://www.oclc.org/services/ brochures/12451chicano_database.pdf. Research Libraries Group. [Mountain View, Calif.]: Research Libraries Group, 1995–.

Comprehensive index covering Mexican-American topics from across the disciplines. Coverage extends back to the 1960s, but records added since 1992 cover the broader Latino community, including Puerto Ricans, Cuban

Americans, and Central American immigrants. The database moved to the OCLC FirstSearch platform in 2007. This database corresponds to the print title most recently known as *Chicano index* (1989–1993) and previously as *Chicano periodical index* (1978–1988). Earlier content was cumulated in *Chicano periodical index: A cumulative index to selected Chicano periodicals published between 1967 and 1978* (G. K. Hall, 1981).

613 **HAPI online.** http://hapi.gseis.ucla.edu. UCLA Latin American Center. Los Angeles: UCLA Latin American Center.

The online version of *HAPI: Hispanic American periodicals index* (UCLA Latin American Center Publications, University of California, [1970?]–). As of 2006, HAPI covered more than 275 peer-reviewed journals with content on Latin America, the Caribbean, Brazil, and U.S. Latinos. Historically, more than 500 periodicals have been indexed. Includes citations to articles, book reviews (through 2001), documents, and original literary works. Initially, indexing began with 1975, but a retrospective project bridged the gap with the cessation of *Index to Latin American periodical literature, 1929–1960* (G. K. Hall, 1962). The database has a thesaurus and provides links to some full text.

614 **Latin American periodicals tables of contents.** Latin Americanist Research Resources Project. Austin, Tex.: Latin American Network Information Center. http://lanic.utexas.edu/project/arl/laptoc.html.
Z1605; PN4930

Searchable database of tables of contents for more than 800 primarily humanities and social science periodicals published in Latin America. It is possible to browse titles by country. Libraries participating in the Latin Americanist Research Resources Project have assumed collecting responsibility for these titles and will supply interlibrary loan requests.

Quotations

615 **Contemporary Hispanic quotations.** Daniel E. Stanton, Edward F. Stanton. xiii, 251 p., ill. Westport, Conn.: Greenwood Press, 2003. ISBN: 0313314640.
973.0468
PN6084.H47C66

Some 200 notable Hispanic persons in the United States are represented by more than 1,000 quotations that come from published works and the media, and also from original sources. Includes indexes and many photos.

616 **A dictionary of Mexican American proverbs.** Mark Glazer. xxii, 347 p. New York: Greenwood Press, 1987. ISBN: 0313253854.
398.961097644   PN6426.3.T4G5

The proverbs of the Mexican American world—by degrees wise, funny, pithy, and always insightful—are a fun read and also offer important insights into the culture they come from, as well as the evolving multiethnic reality that surrounds them.

617 **The fire in our souls: Quotations of wisdom and inspiration by Latino Americans.** Rosie Gonzalez, Edward James Olmos. xiii, 173 p. New York: Plume, 1996. ISBN: 0452276845.
081.08968   PN6084.H47F57

The particular wisdom of Hispanic Americans is reflected in the quotations provided in this thoughtful reference volume. Insight, inspiration, wit, and memory enrich this collection of special words from the Latino perspective.

Native Americans

Bibliographies

618 **Bibliography of Native American bibliographies.** Phillip M. White. xviii, 241 p. Westport, Conn.: Praeger, 2004. ISBN: 0313319413.
016.97000497   Z1209.2.N67W55; E77

Comprehensive master list of more than 800 bibliographies on Native Americans in the United States and Canada, arranged in categories and by tribe. Annotations provide thorough description and evaluation. Overall index to subjects, tribes, and authors.

619 **Bibliography of native North Americans.** George Peter Murdock, M. Marlene Martin, Human Relations Area Files, Inc. Internet Access. Santa Barbara, Calif.: ABC-CLIO, 1992–. ISSN: 1064-5144.
016.970.00497   Z1209.2.N67

Comprehensive bibliography covers a broad range of topics in Native American life: education, political participation, legal issues, and medical care. Materials include books, journal articles, dissertations, and government documents from both the United States and Canada. Reference created by the Human Relations Area Files (HRAF), covers time periods from the 15th century to the present time. Cross-disciplinary perspectives. Subscription access. Also available in CD-ROM format.

Chronologies

620 **American Indian wars: A chronology of confrontations between Native peoples and settlers and the United States military, 1500s–1901.** Michael L. Nunnally. ix, 171 p. Jefferson, N.C.: McFarland, 2007. ISBN: 9780786429363.
973.049700202   E81.N85

At the beginning of European exploration and settlement in America in 1513, Ponce de Leon's ships were attacked by Native Americans of the Calusa tribe. *American Indian wars* provides a chronology of armed conflict for the next 400 years between Native Americans and Europeans. For each entry, geographic location is given, along with a description and origin of the Europeans, the Native American people's tribe, and the number of casualties. European forts are listed as they are established. Chronology ends in 1901, but an appendix provides a brief listing of later related events.

Encyclopedias

621 **Encyclopedia of Native American bows, arrows and quivers.** Steve Allely, Jim Hamm. v. 1, chiefly ill., maps. New York: Lyons Press in cooperation with Bois d'Arc Press, 1999–. ISBN: 1558219927.
688.7920285   E98.A65A45

Bows, arrows, and quivers are both weapons and cultural artifact for Native Americans. They are cataloged here, and their practical and ritual significance is described. A unique source on these weapons systems and their cultural context. Richly illustrated, including maps.

622 **The encyclopedia of Native American economic history.** Bruce E. Johansen. xviii, 301 p. Westport, Conn.: Greenwood Press, 1999. ISBN: 0313306230.
330.973008997   E98.E2E52

Provides some 200 introductory essays, usually about two pages in length, on a wide range of historical and contemporary economic issues among Native Americans. Each includes a bibliography. The entry on the Iroquois is unusually full, covering some 14 pages, and deals extensively with issues of gender in their successful economy. Economic effect of gaming among contemporary Native Americans is described in detail. Bibliography and index.

623   Encyclopedia of Native American religions: An introduction.
Updated ed. Arlene B. Hirschfelder, Paulette Fairbanks Molin,
Walter R. Echo-Hawk. x, 390 p., ill. New York: Facts On File, 2000.
ISBN: 0816039496.

299.703   E98.R3H73

Provides insight into religious ceremonies and rituals, sacred sites, and religious practitioners for many Native peoples from Canada and the United States. Also includes information on Christian missionaries who have influenced Native American spiritual traditions. Does not include cosmologies, stories of deities, chants, prayers, etc. Entries focus on contemporary religious forms, but also include historical information. Details for rituals and ceremonies are not provided, out of respect for Native peoples. The general, but overarching, nature of this work makes it a true introduction. Bibliography.

624   The Gale encyclopedia of Native American tribes. Sharon
Malinowski. 4 v., ill., maps. Detroit: Gale, 1998. ISBN: 0787610852.

973.0497   E77.G15

The four volumes of this encyclopedia provide both detailed history and the contemporary situation of some 400 Native American tribes of North America. Each entry begins with an introduction that covers tribal roots, historic and current location, and data on population and language. Further sections provide information on religious beliefs, buildings, means of income, clothing, healing practices, customs, oral literature, and even extend to current tribal issues. Illustrations are black-and-white. Includes bibliographies and an overall index.

625   Macmillan encyclopedia of Native American tribes. 2nd U.S.
ed. Michael Johnson, Richard Hook. 288 p., ill. (some color),
maps. New York: Macmillan Library Reference USA, 1999. ISBN:
0028654099.

970.00497003   E76.2.J63

In a single volume, the 2nd ed. of this concise reference work provides good basic information on Native American tribes in North America. Volume begins with a useful classification of Indian languages and an overall description of North American tribes. Entries on individual tribes are then arranged by geographic location and languages, and include information on history, dress, housing, politics, current affairs, and population trends. Illustrations, maps.

626   The Native American world. Donna Hightower-Langston. ix, 445 p., ill. Hoboken, N.J.: J. Wiley, 2003. ISBN: 0471403229.
973.0497   E77.H54

Four sections provide ready access to a myriad of information about Native Americans and their world: 1) Culture, 2) Individuals, 3) Nations, and 4) Politics and Post-Contact History. Encyclopedic coverage, arranged alphabetically by key concept. Bibliography. Available as an e-book.

Guides

627   Native America today: A guide to community politics and culture. Barry Pritzker. xx, 453 p., ill., map. Santa Barbara, Calif.: ABC-CLIO, 1999. ISBN: 1576070778.
970.00497   E98.T77P75

More than a directory of North American tribes, this handbook covers their political structure and tribal culture in detail. The social and economic circumstance of individual tribes is spelled out, as well as the relationship of individual tribes with the federal government in the United States. Illustrations, maps. Available as an e-book.

628   The Native North American almanac. Gale Research, Inc. ill. Detroit: Gale Research, Inc., 1994–. ISSN: 1070-8014.
970.00497   E75.N397

This 1400-plus page reference volume covers as much current information on Native Americans in North America as many titles that are called encyclopedias. Useful, far-ranging. Excellent coverage of Canada, as well as the United States. Extensive chronologies, demographics, lots of directories, including non-governmental organizations, and so on. Covers languages, urbanized as well as reservation populations, religions both traditional and cross-assimilated, women, and gender relations. Includes something about everything to do with native peoples in North America.

629   Social work with the first nations: A comprehensive bibliography with annotations. Joyce Z. White. v., 73 p. Alexandria, Va.: Council on Social Work Education, 2001. ISBN: 0872930858.
362.84

Handbook goes into detail about expectations and dynamics of Native Americans, also termed First Nations, and traditionally called American Indians. Social workers who work with client families of Native Americans benefit by having a strong cultural reference to best serve their needs. A useful work in the field.

Handbooks

630 **Daily life of Native Americans in the twentieth century.** Donald Lee Fixico. xxv, 257 p., ill. Westport, Conn.: Greenwood Press, 2006. ISBN: 0313333572.

305.8970730904 E98.S7F59

This thorough and far-ranging handbook covers a list of topics that describe how Native Americans live today and have lived in the 20th century in the United States. Family and women's roles, economics, language and education, clothing-food-autos-housing, politics, military service and tribal government, recreation, religion, art, and nature get the solid treatment typical of this series of *Daily life* volumes. Includes a section on Indian humor over time and a look at gaming. Includes bibliographical references and index.

631 **Handbook of Native American mythology.** Dawn E. Bastian, Judy K. Mitchell. xii, 297 p., ill. Santa Barbara, Calif.: ABC-CLIO, 2004. ISBN: 1851095330.

398.208997 E98.R3B26

Provides an important framework for understanding the culture and social structure of Native Americans. Arranged geographically, covers native peoples from the United States north to the Arctic Circle, describing their history, culture, and values. Roughly 100 encyclopedic entries cover deities, rituals, sacred objects and locations, stories, and characters. These traditions are reflected today in continuing struggles for land rights, economic justice, and the recognition and return of cultural and sacred properties. Relates time concepts of Native American myth to time as told by the clocks of the surrounding culture. Available as an e-book.

632 **The Indian Child Welfare Act handbook: A legal guide to the custody and adoption of Native American children.** 2nd ed. B. J. Jones, Mark Tilden, Kelly Gaines-Stoner. [Chicago]: American Bar Association, 2007. ISBN: 9781590318584.

346.73017808997 KF8210.C45J66

RACE AND ETHNICITY

225

Published by the Family Law Section of the American Bar Association, this handbook provides a history and analysis of the U.S. Indian Child Welfare Act of 1978. The Act spells out requirements for notification of tribes and families when Native American children are to be adopted, placed in foster care, when dependency and neglect proceedings are being undertaken against Native American parents, or other situations affecting the parental rights of Native Americans.

This volume provides guidance for social workers, counselors, and others working with Native American children. Answers questions such as the following: What are the procedures which must be followed? What are the regulations? How does the placement process for Native American children work?

The handbook reports on nearly 20 years of experience with the Indian Child Welfare Act, explaining ways in which it has been effective, and describing where the provisions need to be strengthened. Also includes lists of tribes recognized by the federal government, social service agencies, and Division of Social Service areas of the Bureau of Indian Affairs. In addition, includes a checklist for adoption clearance, sample form motions, bibliographical references, and index.

633 **Native American issues: A reference handbook.** 2nd ed. William Norman Thompson. xx, 329 p. Santa Barbara, Calif.: ABC-CLIO, 2005. ISBN: 1851097414.
973.0497   E98.T77T56

Some four centuries after initial exposure to European culture, Native Americans face complex issues, some of them still unresolved from that contact. How can Native Americans in the United States and Canada maintain their cultural identities, and how can they flourish in the assimilated world which surrounds them? Gambling as a revenue source on reservations is thoroughly covered. A chronology is especially useful, as are statistics and biographical entries. Glossary and bibliography. Available as an e-book.

634 **Native American sovereignty on trial: A handbook with cases, laws, and documents.** Bryan H. Wildenthal. xvi, 359 p. Santa Barbara, Calif.: ABC-CLIO, 2003. ISBN: 1576076245.
342.730872   KF8205.Z9W55

Provides historical background on the relationship of Native Americans in the United States and the legal system begun by European settlers.

Includes detailed chronology of important decisions, including full text of key legal documents. Documents stretch from the 1785 Treaty of Hopewell between the United States and the Cherokee Nation, to the Gaming Compact between the State of California and California Indian tribes in 2000. Focuses on key people, laws, and concepts. Available as an e-book.

635   Native Americans and political participation: A reference handbook. Jerry D. Stubben. xiii, 339 p. Santa Barbara, Calif.: ABC-CLIO, 2006. ISBN: 1576072622.

323.04208997073   E98.T77S78

A thorough and well-researched handbook covering historical and cross-tribal aspects of participation by Native Americans in their own governance structures. The relationship of individual tribes to the U.S. federal government is well documented, and individual Native Americans who have been elected or appointed to office in the world outside the tribal structure are covered. Protest movements of Native Americans are described. A solid reference work on a complex matrix of relationships. Available as an e-book.

636   People with disabilities on tribal lands: Education, health care, vocational rehabilitation and independent living. National Council on Disability (U.S.). vii, 135 p., ill. Washington: National Council on Disability, [2003]. ISBN: 016051438X.

362.40897073   E98.H35P46

The National Council on Disability, an independent U.S. federal agency that advocates for better treatment of the disabled, produced this lengthy report about disabled native peoples living on tribal lands and how they are served, and underserved, by agencies responsible for their welfare. This report was co-authored by several groups of native peoples, and carries the weight of both oversight and tribal concern for disabled members of the native community. Useful for understanding the care needed by these disabled persons, and also as a model for surveying and measuring the adequacy of care for disabled populations.

Also available electronically at http://www.ncd.gov/newsroom/publications/2003/pdf/tribal_lands.pdf.

PSYCH

2

OLOGY

EDITORS' GUIDE

BROADLY SPEAKING, PSYCHOLOGY is the study of the mind and the relationship between mind and body. It involves research into the individual as well as groups, focusing on such diverse topics as human and non-human behavior, cognition, emotion, environment, genetics, intelligence, learning, motivation, perception, personality, and physiology. Straddling the sciences and social sciences, and involving both clinical and experimental approaches, psychology recognizes few boundaries in its development of theories and schools of thought.

The principal reference works supporting the study of psychology at large include the following: General Works, works on History and Theory, works on Research Methodology and Statistics, and summaries of Tests and Measurements. These categories do not address in detail related issues of biology, mental illness, and psychoanalysis.

Psychology has a variety of focal points and interdisciplinary areas:

- Developmental Psychology studies the effects over time of environment and heredity on human beings.
- Educational Psychology focuses on learning processes.
- Social Psychology studies group dynamics and behavior in social and cultural contexts.
- Clinical Psychology addresses mental health and the diagnosis and treatment of mental illness (see also relevant sections of the *Guide* on Psychiatry, and Medical and Health Sciences).

- Cognitive Psychology examines various aspects of the mind such as awareness, judgment and problem solving, intelligence, memory, perception, and thought.
- Physiological and Comparative Psychology is closely allied with biology and zoology, and focuses on the comparison of behaviors across animal species.
- Consumer and Industrial Psychology deals with issues primarily related to employee profiling, job selection, and motivation, as well as factors that can enhance product development and business marketing programs.
- Parapsychology, which is no longer in the pantheon of academic psychology, is the study of phenomena such as telepathy, clairvoyance, and psychokinesis that appear inexplicable by scientific inquiry.

Readers should take note that two topic headings have changed in the general literature: "Cognition and Intelligence" is now "Cognitive Psychology," and "Industrial and Organizational Psychology" is now "Consumer and Industrial Psychology."

Further, psychology reference materials have been subject to many of the same trends that have affected reference publications as a whole: a drift toward online access over print; an overall increase in the number of publications; and an increase in the number of publications specifically devoted to subsets of the larger discipline. As in other fields, online databases have usurped the role traditionally filled by printed abstracting and indexing publications, and there has also been a significant decrease in the number of bibliographies and directories included in the *Guide*. At the same time, the online environment has allowed direct connections to full text in a resource like PsycINFO, an improvement in convenience over its predecessor *Psychological Abstracts*.

Psychology as a discipline has seen significant advances in recent years. New discoveries have been made, new technologies have emerged, and new theories have been proposed. In today's increasingly interdisciplinary scholarly environment, it is more important than ever for psychology scholars to follow research in fields outside of psychology such as biology, chemistry, and sociology. Although the discipline has become more compartmentalized and interdisciplinary, researchers and undergraduate students must still stay abreast of the latest developments while remaining informed of the past.

Undergraduate students studying psychology often come to the library seeking titles that explain particular theories or illustrate the contribution of a specific researcher. Others ask for help locating original research or scholarly articles for class readings. No matter what form the information need takes, the concepts generated by the most famous theorists, experiments, and studies within the field are still likely to be the sources of excitement that stimulate the intellectual curiosity of students. Reference works such as encyclopedias, dictionaries, and handbooks that illuminate historically significant studies and researchers will always be necessary in any library for both practical and inspirational reasons. Students will look to these sorts of resources for guidance when asked to compile reports on Maslow's Hierarchy, *The Interpretation of Dreams*, or the Stanford Prison Experiments for as long as undergraduate programs continue to exist in psychology departments.

Graduate students, and the occasional advanced undergraduate researcher, often have different needs. Advanced psychology researchers seek resources to help them compile sources for literature reviews, locate instruments for testing, and find information from other disciplines about concepts that are relevant to their work. While today's researchers might rely on databases such as Web of Science (www.thompsonreuters .com/ products_services/scientific/Web_of_Science), Scopus (www.scopus .com), or PsycINFO (6) more heavily than print bibliographies and indexes to accomplish their goals, it is largely the tools that have changed, not the research itself.

—THE EDITORS

5 > GENERAL WORKS

Bibliography

1   **The index of psychoanalytic writings.** Alexander Grinstein, John
    Rickman. New York: International Universities Press, 1956–1975.
                                                            Z7204.P8G7

Comprehensive international bibliography of psychoanalytical literature,
covering the period 1900–69, issued in three large sets. Includes more than
200,000 references to books, articles, reviews, and pamphlets, providing
an exhaustive record on the origins and development of psychoanalytical
theory and practice. Continues John Rickman's *Index psychoanalyticus
1893–1926* of 1928.

2   **Psychology: An introductory bibliography.** Susan E. Beers, Salem
    Press. vii, 431 p. Lanham, Md.; Pasadena, Calif.: Scarecrow Press;
    Salem Press, 1996. ISBN: 0810831198.

016.15   Z7201.P79; BF121

Annotated bibliography, arranged in chapters corresponding to the major
subdisciplines of psychology: biological psychology, sensation and perception, emotion, motivation, learning, cognition, consciousness, memory,
language, developmental psychology, social psychology, assessment, personality, stress, psychopathology, and psychotherapy. Most entries date
from the 1970s to early 1990s and include books, chapters of books,
articles, and a few popular psychology books. Includes significant historical works.

Indexes; Abstract Journals

3   **PEP archive.** http://www.p-e-p.org/. Psychoanalytic Electronic
     Publishing. London: Psychoanalytic Electronic Publishing.

The PEP Archive is a full-text, indexed, and hyperlinked collection of more
than 20 premier journals on psychoanalysis since 1920, the full text of the
Standard edition of the complete psychological works of Sigmund Freud, the
complete correspondence of Sigmund Freud with other leading physicians
and psychoanalysts of his time, and more than 20 other classic books by
noted psychoanalytic authors. Also available in CD-ROM format.

4   **PsycBOOKS: Books and chapters in psychology.** American
     Psychological Association. Arlington, Va.: American Psychological
     Association, 1989–1991. 4 v. ISSN: 1044-1514.

016.15   Z7201.P76; BF121

An index to English-language books and chapters in psychology and
related fields that helped fill the gap when *Psychological abstracts* dis-
continued book indexing in 1980. Annual sets consisted of four volumes
covering experimental psychology, basic and applied psychology, developmental psychology, professional psychology, and educational psychology. A fifth volume provided an author/title/subject and a publisher's
index. Complete retrospective contents of this index are included in
PsycINFO (6).

5   **Psychological index . . : An annual bibliography of the literature
     of psychology and cognate subjects . . . .** Howard Crosby Warren,
     Clement Leslie Vaughan, Knight Dunlap, American Psychological
     Association. 42 v. in 41. Princeton, N.J.: Psychological Review
     Company, 1895–[1936].

                                                                    Z7203.P97

Now primarily of historical interest, originally published as an annual
bibliographic supplement to the journal *Psychological review.* Lists books
and periodical articles in all languages, together with translations and new
editions in English, French, German, and Italian. A classified subject list
with an author index, but no subject index.

6   **PsycINFO.** American Psychological Association. Washington:
     American Psychological Association, [n.d.]. ISSN: 0033-2887.
     http://www.apa.org/psycinfo/.

150.5   BF1.P65

The most comprehensive index to the literature of psychology, indexing more than 1,200 English-language journals and reports and providing descriptive, nonevaluative abstracts. Formerly published in print as *Psychological abstracts* (ceased with 2006). Coverage has varied widely over the history of this title, extending back to 1872 in part. Abstracts are arranged by subject categories following the *Thesaurus of psychological index terms* (30). Coverage of books and dissertations, dropped in 1980, was resumed in 1992. Coverage of foreign-language materials was dropped in 1988. The database replaces associated indexes such as *Cumulative author index to Psychological abstracts* (1959/63–1981/83) (American Psychological Association, 1965–1984) and *Author index to Psychological index, 1894–1935* (G. K. Hall, 1960–), and *Psychological abstracts, 1927–1958* (G. K. Hall, 1960–).

Encyclopedias

7   **The Corsini encyclopedia of psychology and behavioral science.** 3rd ed. W. Edward Craighead, Charles B. Nemeroff. 4 v., ill. New York: Wiley, 2001. ISBN: 0471239496.

150.3   BF31.E52

A basic guide to psychology and the behavioral sciences, more than half of the entries are new since the 2nd ed. Most signed articles provide a list of references for further study. Both an author and broad subject index are included. Available as an e-book.

8   **The encyclopaedic dictionary of psychology.** Graham Davey. ix, 484 p., ill., ports. London; New York: Hodder Arnold, 2005. ISBN: 0340812524.

150.3   BF31.E495

Contains more than 1,500 entries divided into eight topical sections covering such areas as biological psychology, cognitive psychology, personality and individual differences, research methods and statistics, and social psychology. Cross-references and further readings are included with each article.

9   **Encyclopedia of applied psychology.** Charles Spielberger. San Diego, Calif.: Elsevier, 2004. ISBN: 0126574103.

Encompasses applications of psychological knowledge and procedures in all areas of psychology. Aimed at professional practitioners and researchers. Includes more than 60 topical sections covering a wide range of psychological issues, from clinical and cognitive to educational and organizational.

10   **Encyclopedia of psychology.** Alan E. Kazdin. 8 v. Washington; Oxford; New York: American Psychological Association; Oxford University Press, 2000. ISBN: 1557986509.

150.3   BF31.E52

Covers methods, findings, advances, and applications in the broad field of psychology from historical topics to new areas of development. Extensive cross-references guide users to related topics among the eight volumes. Each signed entry includes alternate spellings and synonyms, as well as bibliographies and further references.

11   **The Freud encyclopedia: Theory, therapy, and culture.** Edward Erwin. xxvii, 641 p. New York: Routledge, 2002. ISBN: 0415936772.

150.1952092   BF173.F6176.

More than 250 signed entries reflect much of the recent international scholarship on Freud's largely unproven theories, which continue to provide insights and exert tremendous influence. Each entry contains a list of references, and ample cross-references are provided. Available as an e-book.

12   **The Gale encyclopedia of psychology.** 2nd ed. Bonnie B. Strickland. xiii, 701 p., ill. Detroit: Gale Group, 2001. ISBN: 0787647861.

150.3   BF31.G35

Covers the entire spectrum of psychological terms, theories, personalities, and experiments. Designed to be of use to both students and the general public, with signed entries ranging from 25 to 1,000 words. Provides suggestions for further reading and a subject index. Available as an e-book.

13   **International encyclopedia of psychiatry, psychology, psychoanalysis and neurology.** Benjamin B. Wolman. 12 v., ill. New York: Aesculapius; Van Nostrand Reinhold, 1977. ISBN: 0918228018.

616.89003   RC334.I57

Unparalleled resource. Authoritative and comprehensive information provided by 1,800 signed articles in most areas of psychology and many related fields. Emphasizes theoretical, experimental, and therapeutic approaches.

Although coverage of applied psychology and neurosciences is limited, the *Progress volume* of 1983 provides slightly better, updated coverage of neuropsychology through lengthy articles with bibliographies covering theory, historical development, and recent interpretations. Biographies. Cross-references to articles in the parent work. Indexed by name and subject.

An updated but greatly abridged one-volume version of this work was issued in 1996 as the *Encyclopedia of psychiatry, psychology, and psychoanalysis* (New York: Henry Holt, 1996).

14 **International encyclopedia of the social and behavioral sciences.** Neil J. Smelser, Paul B. Baltes, ScienceDirect. Amsterdam [Netherlands]; [Miamisburg, Ohio]: Elsevier; ScienceDirect, 2002–. http://www.elsevier.com/wps/find/bookdescription .cws_home/601495/description#description.

This major reference work is conceived around 37 broad topical sections, including entries from traditional disciplines such as anthropology, economics, education, geography, history, law, linguistics, management, philosophy, political science, and sociology, as well as cross-disciplinary areas of study such as aging, environment and ecology, gender studies, logic of inquiry and research design, and statistics. More than 4,000 signed entries average some four pages in length and provide overviews, reviews of future directions, and bibliographies. Includes 147 biographies of deceased "towering figures." Subscribers have access to ongoing regular updates and additional new articles. Also published in print format in 26 volumes: v. 25 is a list of contributors and name index; v. 26 is a classified list of entries by field and extensive subject index connecting related topics.

15 **Magill's encyclopedia of social science: Psychology.** Nancy A. Piotrowski, Tracy Irons-Georges. 4 v., ill. Pasadena, Calif.: Salem Press, 2003. ISBN: 1587651300.

150.3   BF31.M33

For beginning students, but also a useful ready-reference tool. Updates the publishers' 1993 *Survey of social science: Psychology series* but represents a significant departure with many of the more than 450 entries new or updated. Signed entries include brief definitions of terms cited, followed by discussion (with cross-references as appropriate) and an informative bibliography for further study. Appendixes include a pharmaceutical list grouped by uses, a brief biographical profile of major figures in psychology, and a website directory for support groups and organizations involved in psychology. Comprehensive subject index.

16   The MIT encyclopedia of the cognitive sciences. Robert W. Wilson, Frank C. Keil. cxxxvii, 964 p. Cambridge, Mass.: MIT Press, 1999. ISBN: 0262232006.

MITECS represents the methodological and theoretical diversity of this changing field. With 471 concise entries written by leading researchers in the field, providing accessible introductions to important concepts in the cognitive sciences, as well as references or further readings. Six extended essays collectively serve as a road map to the articles and provide overviews of six major areas: philosophy; psychology; neurosciences; computational intelligence; linguistics and language; and culture, cognition, and evolution. Available online via MIT CogNet as an e-book at http://cognet.mit.edu/library/erefs/mitecs/.

17   The Oxford companion to the mind. R. L. Gregory, O. L. Zangwill. xvii, 856 p., ill. Oxford; New York: Oxford University Press, 1987. ISBN: 019866124X.

128.2   BF31.O94

Arranged alphabetically, covering a wide range of topics, persons, and theories in psychology and related fields including art, language, and mythology. Many of the signed entries have brief bibliographies. Use of cross-references is limited; subject index. Numerous illustrations. Also available as an Internet resource.

18   Popular psychology: An encyclopedia. Luis A. Cordón. xix, 274 p., ill. Westport, Conn.: Greenwood Press, 2005. ISBN: 0313324573.

150.3   BF31.C715

More than 120 entries cover pop psychologists (e.g., Noam Chomsky, Deepak Chopra, Dr. Phil McGraw) and historical theoreticians (e.g., Erikson, Freud, Jung, Skinner). Other entries cover a variety of topics in the field of popular psychology, including acupuncture, aromatherapy, emotional intelligence, brainwashing, chemical imbalance, and seasonal affective disorder. The alphabetical list of entries, topical guide, and index make possible multiple approaches to the volume, while a general bibliography and suggestions for further reading are included after each entry.

Complements and updates Stephen B. Fried's 1994 annotated bibliography *American popular psychology: An interdisciplinary research guide.*

Dictionaries

19   **APA dictionary of psychology.** Gary R. VandenBos, American Psychological Association. Washington: American Psychological Association, 2006. ISBN: 9781591473800.

150.3   BF31.V295

Over 25,000 terms and definitions encompassing such areas of research and application as personality, development, interpersonal relations, memory, motivation, perception, cognition, language, and communication, among others. Provides coverage of psychological concepts, processes, and therapies across all the major subdisciplines of psychology—including clinical, experimental, social, developmental, personality, school and educational, industrial and organizational, and health. Amply cross-referenced, directing the user to synonyms and antonyms, acronyms and abbreviations, related terms and concepts. Four appendixes, each gathering entries thematically into one synoptic listing, covering biographies; institutions, associations, and organizations; psychological therapies and interventions; and psychological tests and assessment instruments.

20   **The concise dictionary of psychology.** 3rd ed. David A. Statt. 140 p., ill. London; New York: Routledge, 1998. ISBN: 0415179394.

150.3   BF31.S62

Updated third edition has added extensive cross-references, charts, graphs, and other illustrations. More than 1,300 brief entries—many less than 100 words—give clear and succinct definitions of psychological terms most commonly found in popular writing and introductory textbooks. Available as an e-book.

21   **A dictionary of psychology.** 2nd ed. Andrew M. Colman. xii, 861 p., ill. Oxford; New York: Oxford University Press, 2006. ISBN: 9780192806321.

150.3   BF31.C65

Over 11,000 entries covering all branches of psychology. Clear, concise descriptions offer extensive coverage of key areas, including cognition, sensation and perception, emotion and motivation, learning and skills, language, mental disorders, and research methods. Entries extend to related disciplines, including psychoanalysis, psychiatry, the neurosciences, and statistics, and are extensively cross-referenced for ease of use, covering word origins and derivations as well as definitions. Also includes appendixes covering over 800 commonly used abbreviations and symbols as well as a list of phobias and phobic stimuli, with definitions. Available as part of Oxford Reference Online (www.oxfordreference.com/).

22   **Dictionary of psychology.** Mike Cardwell. 249 p. Chicago: Fitzroy Dearborn, 1999. ISBN: 1579580645.

Some 3,000 entries, each with a clear, one-sentence definition followed by explanation and examples. Further commentary assists the reader in acquiring a critical understanding of central topic areas. First published as *The complete A–Z psychology handbook* in 1996.

23   **The dictionary of psychology.** Raymond J. Corsini. xv, 1156 p., ill. Philadelphia: Brunner/Mazel, 1999. ISBN: 158391028X.

150.3   BF31.C72

More than 13,000 entries as well as nine appendixes on such topics as terms used by the DSM-IV manual of mental disorders, prescription terms, measuring instruments, and brief biographies of noted psychologists through history.

24   **Dictionary of psychology and psychiatry: English–German/ German–English/Englisch–deutsch/deutsch–Englisch.** 2nd ed. R. Haas. Seattle, Wash.: Hogrefe and Huber, 2003. ISBN: 0889373027.

This two-volume English–German/German–English dictionary is generally regarded as the most exhaustive bilingual compilation of psychological terms.

25   **Dictionary of theories, laws, and concepts in psychology.** Jon E. Roeckelein. xxvii, 548 p. Westport, Conn.: Greenwood Press, 1998. ISBN: 0313304602.

150.3   BF31.R625

Entries present a good baseline for key psychological concepts, theories, and principles. Brief entries include cross-references, and a subject index is provided. Available as an e-book.

26   **Elsevier's dictionary of psychological theories.** Jon E. Roeckelein. Amsterdam, [Netherlands]; Boston: Elsevier, 2006. ISBN: 9780444517500.

150.3   BF31.E44

Psychologists have established various standards for distinguishing between good and not-so-good theories: simplicity, testability, and generalizability. This dictionary includes 2,000 terms for both types of theories, from classical to contemporary. Each entry provides information on the origination and evolution of the theory, including its first appearance in source literature, and also includes a historical definition, analysis, and occasional criticism of the concept(s) presented. Provides suggestions for additional study at the end of each entry and ample cross-references. Available as an e-book.

27   **The Macmillan dictionary of psychology.** 2nd ed. N. S. Sutherland. ix, 515 p., ill. Houndmills, Basingstoke, [U.K.]: Macmillan, 1995. ISBN: 0333623231.

150.3   BF31.S835

Contains over 8,200 entries, many of them new to this edition. Appendixes include important related materials such as a map of the brain.

28   **The Penguin dictionary of psychology.** 3rd ed. Arthur S. Reber, Emily Sarah Reber. xxi, 831 p., ill. London; New York: Penguin Books, 2001. ISBN: 0140514511.

150.3   BF31.R43

Contains over 17,000 definitions used in psychology, psychiatry, and related fields. Explores developments in these fields as well as in neuroscience and social psychology.

29   **Wiley's English-Spanish and Spanish-English dictionary of psychology and psychiatry = Diccionario de psicología y psiquiatría inglés-espan~ol español-inglés Wiley.** Steven M. Kaplan. viii, 593 p. New York: Wiley, 1995. ISBN: 0471014605.

150.3   BF31.K36

The only book of its kind provides concise, comprehensive, and current bilingual coverage of virtually every word or phrase used in the study and practice of psychiatry and psychology. Contains more than 62,000 entries—30,000+ in each language—covering all disciplines and sub-disciplines, both research and clinical. Gender-neutral equivalents are provided, and in cases where the gender-specific term is the norm, both are given. For idiomatic expressions, conceptual equivalents are provided rather than literal translations.

Thesauruses

30   **Thesaurus of psychological index terms.** 10th ed. American
      Psychological Association. xxxix, 400 p. Washington: American
      Psychological Association, 2005. ISBN: 1557987750.
025.4915   Z695.1.P7T48

Begun in 1974, this thesaurus details the controlled vocabulary and subject headings used in APA publications and databases. This reference will
help researchers, librarians, clinicians, students, and lexicographers in the
behavioral, health, and social science fields search the 1.9 million records
in the PsycINFO (6) database. The book contains some 7,800 standard and
cross-referenced terms, scope notes that define terms, historical notes with
information on usage of terms since their introduction, term hierarchies
showing relationships to other terms, and posting notes on how many
times the term has been used in PsycINFO (6) records. This 10th ed. contains 200 new terms from such areas as neuropsychology, psychometrics,
and artificial intelligence.

Directories

31   **Allyn and Bacon guide to master's programs in psychology and
      counseling psychology.** William Buskist, Amy Mixon. 1 v. (various
      paging). Boston: Allyn and Bacon, 1998. ISBN: 0205274366.
150.71173   BF80.7.U6B87

Aims to help students successfully enter advanced study programs in psychology. Arranged in three sections: programs by state, by program type,
and a detailed description of each program by region, covering the U.S.
and Canada. Includes a glossary of terms.

32   **Internships in psychology: The APAGS workbook for writing
      successful applications and finding the right match.** Carol
      Williams-Nickelson, Mitchell J. Prinstein, Shane J. Lopez,
      American Psychological Association of Graduate Students. xii, 142
      p. Washington: American Psychological Association, 2004. ISBN:
      1591470366.
150.7155   BF77.I67

This manual provides needed resources to navigate the internship application process successfully. Designed for doctoral-level psychology graduate
students, it offers general guidelines and specific information for applying

for internship positions, including checklists, examples of real-life application materials, advice on writing letters and CVs, and several sample essays. No index.

33   **Psychology: IUPsyS global resource.** J. Bruce Overmier, Judith A. Overmier, International Union of Psychological Science. 1 CD-ROM. Hove, [England]: Psychology Press, 2000–.

Annually updated and expanded. Provides a more comprehensive and current alternative to the data found in *International directory of psychologists,* published by the International Union of Psychological Science. This CD-ROM comprises multiple independent information files and databases, including an international directory of psychology departments, research institutes, and psychology organizations, as well as a bibliography of international research currently underway in the field of psychology. The CD-ROM is searchable across many of the independent files it contains, using native integrated software, substantially enhanced in the 2005 release. New also in the 2006 release is a revised and reorganized version of the Origin and Development of Scientific Psychology around the World database as well as substantial updates to the "Directory of international psychological associations and related organizations," the "Directory of major institutions for psychological research and training," and the "Bibliography of world and regional psychology 1974–2005" files.

Handbooks

34   **The handbook of humanistic psychology: Leading edges in theory, research, and practice.** Kirk J. Schneider, James F. T. Bugental, J. Fraser Pierson. xxvii, 732 p., ill. Thousand Oaks, Calif.: Sage Publications, 2001. ISBN: 0761921214.

150.198   BF204.H36

Essays and surveys introduce aspects of a diverse field ranging from the historical, theoretical, and methodological to the psychotherapeutic, spiritual, and multicultural. Includes bibliographical references and indexes.

35   **Handbook of psychology.** Irving B. Weiner, Donald K. Freedheim, John A. Schinka. 12 v., ill. (some color). New York: Wiley, 2003. ISBN: 0471176699.

150   BF121.H1955

The first two volumes cover history and research methods; each of the next ten, a particular area of psychology: biological, experimental, personality and social, developmental, educational, clinical, health, assessment, forensic, and industrial and organizational. Leading national and international scholars collaborated to produce each volume, with chapters ranging from established theories to the most modern research and developments. Each of the 12 volumes contains its own author and subject indexes. Available as e-books.

36 **Handbook of racial and ethnic minority psychology.** Guillermo Bernal. xviii, 714 p., ill. Thousand Oaks, Calif.: Sage Publications, 2003. ISBN: 0761919651.

155.82   GN502.H3635

Scholarly overview of the relatively new field of racial, ethnic, and minority psychology in the United States. Thirty-two thematic chapters cover the breadth of psychology viewed through the lens of the racial and ethnic minority experience, incorporating major subfields within psychology and emphasizing those with wide-ranging and current research on racial and ethnic minority issues such as developmental, social, and clinical psychology. Bibliographies accompany each chapter. Extensive subject index provides easy access to related materials. Conceived to support the efforts of the Society for Psychological Studies of Ethnic Minority Issues of the American Psychological Association.

37 **International handbook of psychology.** Kurt Pawlik, Mark R. Rosenzweig. xxxii, 629 p., ill. London; Thousand Oaks, Calif.: Sage Publications, 2000. ISBN: 0761953299.

150   BF121.I56443

Prepared under the auspices of the International Union of Psychological Science. Covers foundations and methods of current psychological knowledge and research around the world. Topics include human behavioral development and information processing, socialization, and applied psychological science.

Part 1 introduces general principles of research design. Part 2 guides students through various research methods and designs, including experimental and nonexperimental designs. Part 3 focuses on describing, analyzing, and reporting research data. Part 4 discusses advanced topics in research methods, such as multivariate design and the role of theory in science. This 4th ed. incorporates coverage of computer-based resources such as databases and the Internet.

Style Manuals

38   **Concise rules of APA style.** American Psychological Association.
ix, 212 p., ill. Washington: American Psychological Association,
2005. ISBN: 1591472520.
808.06615   BF76.7.C66

Compiled from the 5th ed. of the *Publication manual of the American Psychological Association* (39), this handy work covers topics such as concise
and bias-free writing, punctuation, spelling, and capitalization, italicizing
and abbreviating, the use of numbers, metrication and statistics, tables
and figures, footnotes and appendixes, and quotations. Provides very helpful reference examples, including those from electronic and audiovisual
media, a cross-reference to the publication manual, and a checklist for
manuscript submission.

39   **Publication manual of the American Psychological Association.**
5th ed. American Psychological Association. xxviii, 439 p., ill.
Washington: American Psychological Association, 2001. ISBN:
1557988102.
808.06615   BF76.7.P83

Begun in 1952, this manual provides detailed information on writing for publication, with special reference to the use of electronic and
legal resources. Covers the content and organization of a manuscript
in preparation for publication, with appendixes that include a checklist
for manuscript submission. Sections on data sharing and statistics have
been significantly updated since the 4th ed. An electronic companion to
this manual also is available under a different title, APA-Style Helper. At
the end of 2007, the APA published a supplementary *APA style guide to
electronic references,* available digitally in HTML or PDF formats (ISBN:
1433803097; ISBN 13: 9781433803093).

Biography

40   **Biographical dictionary of psychology.** Noel Sheehy, Antony
J. Chapman, Wendy A. Conroy. xvii, 675 p. London; New York:
Routledge Reference, 1997. ISBN: 0415099978.
150.922   BF109.A1B56

Covers 500 significant worldwide figures in the field of psychology for the
period 1600–1970. Signed entries include the person's date of birth, birthplace and nationality, educational background, appointments and honors,

main area(s) of interest and influence in psychology, and a list of principal publications. Provides a list of further readings and an index of key terms and institutions cited.

41   **Models of achievement: Reflections of eminent women in psychology.** Agnes N. O'Connell, Nancy Felipe Russo. v. 1, 3, ports. New York: Columbia University Press, 1983–2001. ISBN: 0231053126.

150.88042   BF109.A1M6

Multivolume collection of autobiographical essays focusing on American education and trends in psychology, especially in the latter half of the 20th century, when women began making significant contributions to what had been a primarily male-dominated profession. Each autobiography includes a list of references, representative publications by the author, and a photo.

42   **Portraits of pioneers in psychology.** Gregory A. Kimble, Michael Wertheimer, Charlotte White, American Psychological Association. 5 v., ill. Washington; Hillsdale, N.J.: American Psychological Association; L. Erlbaum Associates, 1991–2003. ISBN: 0805806202.

150.922   BF109.A1P67

Provides lengthy signed essays and features some 100 major figures in the field of psychology, broadly defined. Essays, both biographical and professional, run about 20 pages and each include a visual portrait of the subject covered. Each essay provides a summary of the subject's work and personal life, along with a concluding paragraph focusing on their contributions to the development of psychology as a discipline. Extensive references are included, as is a subject and author index for each volume. Updates the 1991 edition by the same name. Some volumes available as e-books.

6 › HISTORY AND THEORY

Guides

43   **Evolving perspectives on the history of psychology.** Wade E. Pickren, Donald A. Dewsbury. ix, 608 p., ill. Washington: American Psychological Association, 2002. ISBN: 155798882X.

150.9   BF105.E87

Twenty-seven chapters bring together important historical writings published in APA journals over the past quarter century, covering the founding of the discipline, its development as a natural science and then as a social and behavioral science, and contemporary practices. Situates psychological practices in the larger context of social, cultural, and political history. Includes several seminal papers from the 1970s and 1980s as well as more recent examples of the finest work in the genre. Discusses methods of historical inquiry.

44 **Forty studies that changed psychology: Explorations into the history of psychological research.** 5th ed. Roger R. Hock. xiv, 322 p., ill. Upper Saddle River, N.J.: Pearson Prentice Hall, 2005. ISBN: 0131147293.

150   BF198.7.H63

Closes the gap between psychology textbooks and the research that made them possible, by offering a glimpse into 40 of the most famous studies in the history of the field. Indexes by name and subject.

45 **The great psychologists.** 3rd ed. Robert Irving Watson. xii, 627 p. Philadelphia: Lippincott, 1971.

150.922   BF81.W35

Useful and well-written summary of the development and impact of psychological philosophies and methodologies through the lives and works of more than 50 great psychologists. Indexes by name and subject.

Bibliography

46 **A pictorial history of psychology.** Wolfgang G. Bringmann, Helmut E. Lück. xix, 636 p., ill. Chicago: Quintessence, 1997. ISBN: 0867152923.

150.9022   BF81.P47

Over 100 articles on the roots of psychology, illustrated with black-and-white photos, covering Gestalt psychology, human development and personality, abnormal psychology, various branches, and international developments. Contains 57 translations from an earlier German edition (*Illustrierte geschichte der psychologie*, published by Lück and Rudolf Miller in 1993) and 50 new English-language essays.

47 **Psychology and theology in Western thought, 1672–1965: A historical and annotated bibliography.** Hendrika Vande Kemp, H.

Newton Malony. xiv, 367 p. Millwood, N.Y.: Kraus International Publications, 1984. ISBN: 0527927791.

016.20019   Z7204.R4V36; BL53

Contains 1,047 entries to monographic literature that treats Judeo-Christian religious thought in relation to psychology. Also contains foreign-language works that have been translated into English. Topical arrangement into seven parts. Entries give bibliographical information and annotation. Name, institution, title, subject indexes.

7 > RESEARCH METHODOLOGY AND STATISTICS

48   **Encyclopedia of statistics in behavioral science.** Brian S. Everitt, David C. Howell. 4 v., 2208 p., ill. Hoboken, N.J.: John Wiley and Sons, 2005. ISBN: 0470860804.

150.15195   BF39.E498

Essential reference work for researchers, educators, and students in the fields of applied psychology, sociology, market research, consumer behavior, management science, decision making, and human resource management and a valuable addition to both the psychological and statistical literature. Contains over 600 articles; contributions from eminent psychologists and statisticians worldwide. Emphasizes practical, nontechnical methods with wide-ranging applications. Extensively cross-referenced. Available in print and online.

Guides

49   **Research design and methods: A process approach.** 5th ed. Kenneth S. Bordens, Bruce B. Abbott. xv, 490 p., ill. Boston: McGraw-Hill, 2002. ISBN: 0767421523.

150.72   BF76.5.B67

Part 1 introduces general principles of research design. Part 2 guides students through various research methods and designs, including experimental and nonexperimental designs. Part 3 focuses on describing, analyzing, and reporting research data. Part 4 discusses advanced topics in research methods, such as multivariate design and the role of theory in science. Incorporates coverage of computer-based resources such as databases and the Internet.

Dictionaries

50 **Dictionary of statistics for psychologists.** Brian Everitt, Til Wykes. 187 p., ill. London; New York: Arnold; Oxford University Press, 1999. ISBN: 0340719974.

150.15195   BF39.E927

Defines over 1,500 statistical terms routinely used in psychology and covering the full range of statistical methods that might be encountered by psychology students and working psychologists. Also includes many mathematical details and numerical examples, graphs, and illustrations.

Handbooks

51 **Concise handbook of experimental methods for the behavioral and biological sciences.** Jay E. Gould. 430 p., ill. Boca Raton, Fla.: CRC Press, 2002. ISBN: 0849311047.

570.72   QH315.G66

Covers the philosophy of science, forms of research, steps of methods, variables in designs, initial and final phases, ethics, experimental control, experimental design, sampling and generalization, and hypothesis testing and statistical significance. Outline format. Available as an e-book.

52 **Essentials of research design and methodology.** Geoffrey R. Marczyk, David DeMatteo, David Festinger. xi, 290 p., ill. Hoboken, N.J.: John Wiley and Sons, 2005. ISBN: 0471470538.

150.72   BF76.5.M317

Chapters cover planning and design; controlling artifact and bias; data collection, assessment methods, and measurement strategies; general types of research designs and approaches; validity; data preparation, analyses, and interpretation; ethical considerations; and disseminating research results. Includes bibliographical references and index. Available as an e-book.

53 **Handbook of research methods in experimental psychology.** Stephen F. Davis. viii, 507 p., ill. Malden, Mass.: Blackwell, 2003. ISBN: 0631226494.

150.724   BF76.5.H35

Presents a comprehensive and contemporary treatment of research methodologies used in experimental psychology. Topics covered range from current and future trends in experimental psychology to ethical issues in psychological research. Includes bibliographical references and indexes. Available as an e-book.

54   **The psychology research handbook: A guide for graduate students and research assistants.** 2nd ed. Frederick T. L. Leong, James T. Austin. xvii, 516 p., ill. Thousand Oaks, Calif.: Sage Publications, 2006. ISBN: 0761930213.

150.72   BF76.5.P795

Follows the flow of the research process in 34 chapters from initially choosing a topic to negotiating with journal editors. New topics since the 1996 edition include research conceptualization and data processing—including multilevel research, computational modeling, and meta-analyses—along with such standard topics as bibliographic research, scale development, conducting surveys, statistical analysis, and writing in American Psychological Association style. Includes bibliographical references and index.

55   **Stevens' handbook of experimental psychology.** 3rd ed. S. S. Stevens, Harold E. Pashler. 4 v., ill. New York: John Wiley and Sons, 2002. ISBN: 0471443336.

150   BF181.H336

This revised, updated, and greatly enlarged edition of the definitive resource for experimental psychology offers comprehensive coverage of the latest findings in the field as well as the explosion of research in neuroscience. An entirely new methodology volume has been added with this edition, providing a rigorous tutorial on key concepts of experimental psychology. Each signed essay provides extensive references, and comprehensive author and subject indexes are also provided.

Standards

56   **APA ethics office.** http://www.apa.org/ethics/homepage.html. American Psychological Association. Washington: American Psychological Association, 2002.

Areas covered include but are not limited to the clinical, counseling, and school practice of psychology; research; teaching; supervision of trainees; public service; policy development; social intervention; development of assessment instruments; conducting assessments; educational counseling; organizational consulting; forensic activities; program design and evaluation; and administration. Provides links to full-text ethics information: "Ethical Principles of Psychologists and Code of Conduct"; "Ethics Committee on Services by Telephone, Teleconferencing, and Internet"; "Guidelines for Ethical Conduct in the Care and Use of Animals"; and more. Available online from APA in HTML, PDF, and MS Word formats.

57   **Ethics in psychology: Professional standards and cases.** 2nd ed. Gerald P. Koocher, Patricia Keith-Spiegel. ix, 502 p., ill. New York: Oxford University Press, 1998. ISBN: 0195092015.

174.915   BF76.4.K46

Updated in response to extensive changes in the American Psychological Association's ethics code, this text considers ethical questions and dilemmas encountered by psychologists in everyday practice, research, and teaching. Includes extensive case studies that provide illustrative guidance on a wide variety of topics.

8 › TESTS AND MEASUREMENTS

Guides

58   **Test critiques.** Test Corporation of America. Kansas City, Mo.: Test Corporation of America, v. 1– (1984–). ISSN: 1553-9121.

150.287   BF176.T418

Each volume contains approx. 100 critical reviews of commercial tests most frequently used in psychological assessment, business, and education. Arrangement is by title, and beginning with v. 3, test, title, publisher, author/reviewer, and subject indexes cumulate. Review essays include a description of the development and applications of the test, technical data, a lengthy critique, and list of references. Since it often duplicates entries in *Mental measurements yearbook* (60), this title is best used as a supplement to that work.

59   **Tests: A comprehensive reference for assessments in psychology, education, and business.** 5th ed. Taddy Maddox. xiv, 581 p. Austin, Tex.: Pro-Ed, 2003. ISBN: 0890798974.

150.287   BF176.T43

Covers more than 200 assessment instruments designed for use by psychologists, educators, and human resources personnel. Arranged in three broad topical sections and 90 subsections. Focusing on psychology, education, and business, each test entry provides information on the test's purpose and intended audience, format and scoring information, costs, and availability. Indexes provide easy access by test title, author, and publisher. Also provided is a list of tests not carried over from the previous edition.

Bibliography

60   **The mental measurements yearbook.** Oscar Krisen Buros, Buros Institute of Mental Measurements. Highland Park, N.J.: The Mental Measurements Yearbook, 1941–. ISSN: 0076-6461.

016.1512; 016.159928   Z5814.P8B932

A monumental collection of standardized measurements, now in its 17th ed. Each edition follows much the same pattern and is intended to supplement rather than supersede earlier volumes. References are numbered consecutively and each has cross-references to reviews, excerpts, and bibliographic references in earlier volumes. Information for each test includes title, intended population, author and publishers, scoring, availability of forms, parts, levels, and computer-assisted scoring, cost, time to administer, and a statement concerning validity and reliability. Tests cover English-language materials. Often referred to by the name of its founder, Buros.

61   **Tests in print.** Oscar Krisen Buros, Buros Institute of Mental Measurements. Highland Park, N.J.: Gryphon Press, 1961–. ISSN: 0361-025X.

                                                                                Z5814.E9T47

Helps test users identify and locate appropriate instruments with this comprehensive index to more than 4,000 commercially available tests. Instruments are listed in virtually all areas of testing, including education, psychology, counseling, management, health care, business, career planning, sociology, personnel, child development, vocational interest, social science, research, and dozens of others. Brief descriptions of instruments are given, together with population, administrative and scoring information, and a reference list of professional literature citing articles relevant to individual tests. All available versions of a test are noted, and pricing is provided, along with the name of the publisher. A convenient publishers directory includes current addresses for more than 500 test publishers. Special notations are given for instruments that are out of print or have been combined with other tests, and entries are indexed by title, classified subject, name, and score. *Tests in print VI* also serves as a comprehensive index to the *Mental measurements yearbook* (60) by directing readers to the appropriate volume(s) for reviews of specific tests.

Dictionaries

62   **Dictionary of psychological testing, assessment and treatment: Includes key terms in statistics, psychological testing, experimental methods and therapeutic treatments.** Ian Stuart-Hamilton. viii, 261 p. London; Bristol, Pa.: Jessica Kingsley, 1995. ISBN: 1853022012.

150.287   BF176.S78

Comprises 5,000 definitions of key terms in psychological testing, assessment, and treatment, encompassing statistical procedures, major psychometric and other psychological tests, categories of mental illness, commonly used medical terms, basic neuroanatomy, and types of psychological therapies.

Standards

63   **Standards for educational and psychological testing.** American Psychological Association, National Council on Measurement in Education (U.S.), Joint Committee on Standards for Educational and Psychological Testing (U.S.), American Educational Research Association. ix, 194 p. Washington: American Educational Research Association, 1999. ISBN: 0935302255.

371.260973   LB3051.A693

Updated to reflect changes in law and practice since the 1985 edition. Developed by AERA, APA, and NCME. Covers test construction, evaluation, and documentation. Contents: "Validity," "Reliability and errors of measurement," "Test development and revision," "Scales, norms, and score comparability," "Test administration, scoring, and reporting," "Supporting documentation for tests," "Fairness in testing: Fairness in testing and test use," "The rights and responsibilities of test takers," "Testing individuals of diverse linguistic backgrounds," "Testing individuals with disabilities," "Testing applications: The responsibilities of test users," "Psychological testing and assessment," "Educational testing and assessment," "Testing in employment and credentialing," "Testing in program evaluation and public policy."

9 > DEVELOPMENTAL PSYCHOLOGY

Indexes; Abstract Journals

64   **Psycscan.** American Psychological Association. Arli[n]gton, Va.:
      American Psychological Association, 1980–. ISSN: 0197-1484.
616.89005   RC467.P776

Provides abstracts from a cluster of 38 selected journals representing the world's current literature in developmental psychology and related disciplines. Arranged by journal title. No index. Available in print and online versions by subscription from the APA.

Encyclopedias

65   **Adolescence in America: An encyclopedia.** Jacqueline V. Lerner,
      Richard M. Lerner, Jordan Finkelstein. 2 v., xxxix, 918 p., ill. Santa
      Barbara, Calif: ABC-CLIO, 2001. ISBN: 1576072053.
305.235097303   HQ796.A33247

Broad and practical survey of the social, psychological, and physical development of American teenagers. Presents current information about the physical, psychological, behavioral, social, and cultural characteristics of adolescence. Entries are arranged alphabetically and are cross-referenced. They discuss both normal and problematic development (from medical and physical to social and psychological) as well as policies and programs useful for alleviating or preventing problems. Essays address the diversity of this life period in terms of various physical, behavioral, racial, ethnic, religious, national, and cultural characteristics; also includes key social relationships and institutional contexts affecting today's youth. Available as an e-book.

66   **The Gale encyclopedia of childhood and adolescence.** Jerome
      Kagan, Susan B. Gall. xiii, 752 p., ill. Detroit, Mich.: Gale, 1998.
      ISBN: 0810398842.

305.23103   HQ772.G27

More than 700 signed essays by experts in the field cover key theories and
issues in child development and offer suggestions for further reading. Provides detailed name and subject indexes. Available online as part of Health
and Wellness Resource Center (www.gale.com/HealthRC/).

67   **International encyclopedia of developmental and instructional
      psychology.** Erik De Corte, Franz E. Weinert. xxviii, 882 p., ill.
      Oxford, [England]; Tarrytown, N.Y.: Pergamon, 1996. ISBN:
      0080429807.

155.03   BF712.7.I58

A spin-off from the *International encyclopedia of education* (Pergamon;
Elsevier Science, 1994). Provides a research-based overview of knowledge
and understanding of the conditions, processes, and adaptabilities of
human development and learning. Signed entries in 12 sections address
the central issues in the fields of instructional and developmental psychology from cognitive development to learning styles. References for further
reading. Indexes by name and subject.

DEVELOPMENTAL PSYCHOLOGY

257

Dictionaries

68   **Dictionary of developmental psychology.** Rev. ed. Ian Stuart-
      Hamilton. viii, 168 p. London; Bristol, Pa.: J. Kingsley Publishers,
      1996. ISBN: 1853024279.

155.03   BF712.7.S78

Provides over 2,500 definitions of key terms in the field of developmental
psychology, including explanations of psychometric and other tests of
psychological development. Covers both American and British terms and
systems.

Handbooks

69   **Handbook of child psychology.** 6th ed. William Damon, Richard
      M. Lerner. 4 v., ill. Hoboken, N.J.: John Wiley and Sons, 2006.
      ISBN: 0471272876.

155.4   BF721.H242

This four-volume set reflects the current understanding of child psychology, focusing on the concerns of a new century. Now in its 6th ed., it is the definitive child psychologist's guide to current research findings. It serves as a sourcebook, encyclopedia, and research review.

10 > EDUCATIONAL PSYCHOLOGY

Encyclopedias

70   **Encyclopedia of school psychology.** Steven W. Lee. xxix, 656 p., ill. Thousand Oaks, Calif.: Sage Publications, 2005. ISBN: 0761930809.
370.15   LB1027.55.E523

A "Readers guide" organizes 263 signed entries into categories such as "Demographic variables," "Family and parenting," "Multicultural issues," and "Technology." Each entry provides references and further reading lists, with a detailed index and ample cross-references. Particularly useful for nonprofessionals.

11 > SOCIAL PSYCHOLOGY

Encyclopedias

71   **The Blackwell encyclopedia of social psychology.** A. S. R. Manstead, Miles Hewstone, Susan T. Fiske. xvi, 694 p. Oxford, U.K.; Cambridge, Mass.: Blackwell, 1995. ISBN: 0631181466.
302.03   HM251.B476

More than 300 topical entries can be used easily by students, teachers, and researchers of social psychology alike. Focusing on particular phenomenon, concepts, and theories, signed entries by international authorities vary from brief 50-word definitions to lengthy 3,000-plus-word essays with bibliographical references. Includes a subject index. Available as an e-book.

Dictionaries

72   **The dictionary of personality and social psychology.** 1st MIT Press ed. Rom Harré, Roger Lamb. xi, 402 p. Cambridge, Mass.: MIT Press, 1986. ISBN: 0262580780.

155.2   BF698.D527

Derived from the authors' *The encyclopedic dictionary of psychology* (Cambridge, Mass.: MIT Press, 1986), with many entries and reference lists updated to provide tighter focus on the main theories and issues of personality and social psychology. Extensive cross-references are provided, as is a modest subject index.

Handbooks

73   **The handbook of social psychology.** 4th ed. Daniel Todd Gilbert, Susan T. Fiske, Gardner Lindzey. 2 v., ill. Boston: McGraw-Hill, 1998. ISBN: 0195213769.

302   HM251.H224

Updated to reflect changes in the field since its original publication. New topics include emotions, self, and automaticity, and edition is structured to show the levels of analysis used by psychologists.

12 › CLINICAL PSYCHOLOGY

Encyclopedias

74   **The encyclopedia of phobias, fears, and anxieties.** 2nd ed. Ronald M. Doctor, Ada P. Kahn. viii, 568 p., ill. New York: Facts on File, 2000. ISBN: 0816039895.

616.8522003   RC535.D63

Some 2,000 entries explain the nature of anxiety disorders, panic attacks, specific phobias, and obsessive-compulsive disorders. Entries also detail important research, treatments, and key researchers working in the field. Appendixes list resources and recommended reading.

Dictionaries

75   **The Blackwell dictionary of neuropsychology.** J. Graham Beaumont, Pamela M. Kenealy, Marcus Rogers. xix, 788 p., ill. Cambridge, Mass.: Blackwell Publishers, 1996. ISBN: 0631178961.
612.803   QP360.B577

Extended entries by international contributors provide a broad perspective on the study of neuropsychology. Entries cover key topics. Alphabetical organization and cross-referencing provide immediate access to the complex vocabulary of this field. Enhanced by illustrations and tables.

Handbooks

76   **Comprehensive handbook of personality and psychopathology.** Michel Hersen, Jay C. Thomas. 3 v., ill. Hoboken, N.J.: John Wiley and Sons, 2006. ISBN: 0471479454.
618.9289   RC456.C66

Presents an overview of the foundations of major theories of personality, covering such broad topics as personality and everyday functioning, adult psychopathology, and child psychopathology. Each section compiled by experts in their fields. Available as an e-book.

77   **Handbook of clinical health psychology.** Susan P. Llewelyn, Paul Kennedy. xvii, 605 p., ill. Chichester, West Sussex, U.K.; Hoboken, N.J.: J. Wiley, 2003. ISBN: 0471485446.
616.0019   R726.7.H3542

Comprehensive overview of the practice of clinical health psychology. Provides authoritative summaries of research evidence in health care and demonstrates how findings are put into practice. Useful detailed and integrated reference work for clinical and health psychologists in academic, practice, and training settings. Available as an e-book.

13 › COGNITIVE PSYCHOLOGY

Encyclopedias

78   Encyclopedia of behavior modification and cognitive behavior therapy. Michel Hersen, Johan Rosqvist. 3 v.; xx, 1637 p., ill. Thousand Oaks, Calif.: Sage, 2005. ISBN: 0761927476.
616.89142003   RC489.B4E485

Broader in scope than the *Encyclopedia of cognitive behavior therapy,* this set brings together the expertise of both researchers and practitioners. Includes a volume each on adult and child clinical applications. A third volume on educational applications is particularly valuable for classroom and school contexts. Five anchor articles in each volume summarize current trends and treatment directions. Each volume includes an alphabetical list of its entries, an extensive general bibliography, and a comprehensive index. Each entry contains brief background, description of the treatment strategy, discussion of potential complications, a case illustration, a brief list of recent publications, and, if appropriate, a summary of research. Entries for prominent contributors to the field chronicle their professional careers.

79   Encyclopedia of cognitive science. Lynn Nadel. 4 v., ill. Hoboken, N.J.: John Wiley, 2005. ISBN: 0470016191.
BF311.E53

A massive encyclopedia which aims to capture current thinking about the relatively new field of cognitive science. An excellent overview article, "What is cognitive science?" is followed by more than 400 topical entries written by experts in their field. Essays are clearly laid out and well illustrated, suggesting further readings. Extensive subject index provides easy access to related materials. Glossary. Available as an online database.

80   Encyclopedia of human intelligence. Robert J. Sternberg. 2 v. (1235 p.). New York; Toronto; New York: Macmillan; Maxwell Macmillan Canada; Maxwell Macmillan International, 1994. ISBN: 0028974077.
153.903   BF431.E59

Comprehensive guide to the many theories of the way humans gather and use information, and to the men and women who developed these theories. Topics covered include aging, Alzheimer's disease, aptitude tests, bias in testing, cognitive styles, culture, drugs, dyslexia, ethnicity, genius, illiteracy, intuition, reasoning, schooling and intelligence, test-taking strategies, underachievement, and wisdom. Two hundred and fifty original, signed articles arranged alphabetically, all with bibliographies, some illustrated with drawings, charts, or photographs that are useful in explaining anatomy and function of the brain and nervous system.

81   **The encyclopedia of memory and memory disorders.** 2nd ed.
      Carol Turkington, Joseph Harris. viii, 296 p. New York: Facts on
      File, 2001. ISBN: 0816041415.
153.1203   BF371.N55

More than 800 entries cover such topics as how thinking processes develop and how cognitive disorders can affect us. A revision of the original 1994 edition. Contains a detailed subject index and list of references. Appendixes include a list of associations dealing with memory problems, periodicals that publish research on memory, and a list of helpful websites.

82   **Historical dictionary of quotations in cognitive science: A
      treasury of quotations in psychology, philosophy, and artificial
      intelligence.** Morton Wagman. ix, 271 p. Westport, Conn.:
      Greenwood Press, 2000. ISBN: 0313312842.
153   PN6084.C545H57

More than 400 quotations arranged under approximately 200 topical listings. Includes a bibliography of sources, author and subject indexes. Available as an e-book.

Dictionaries

83   **Dictionary of cognitive science: Neuroscience, psychology,
      artificial intelligence, linguistics, and philosophy.** Olivier Houde´,
      Daniel Kayser, Vivian Waltz, Christian Cav. xxxv, 428 p. New York:
      Psychology Press, 2004. ISBN: 1579582516.
153.03   BF311.V56713

Translation of *Vocabulaire de sciences cognitives* (1998), a collaborative effort of 60 (mostly French) scholars. Presents 130 terms drawn from five major disciplines of cognitive science: neuroscience, psychology, artificial intelligence, linguistics, and philosophy. Instead of merely defining those terms, the editors divide them into sections corresponding to the five areas and explain them within the context of the applicable disciplines. Concluding each entry is a bibliography of selected sources, updated from the original French version. Not as broad and in-depth as its nearest competitor, *The MIT encyclopedia of the cognitive sciences* (16), still a good resource for definitions of basic concepts in cognitive science, making it suitable for students. Available as an e-book.

Handbooks

84   The Cambridge handbook of thinking and reasoning. Keith James Holyoak, Robert G. Morrison. xiv, 858 p., ill. New York: Cambridge University Press, 2005. ISBN: 0521824176.

153.42   BF441.C265

Thirty-two chapters offer a quick overview of core topics, current research, and future areas of interest. Covers a broad range of subjects, from inductive and deductive reasoning to the effect of aging on reasoning. Each chapter is structured similarly, with an introduction to the topic, history of research, and concluding thoughts on future research and trends. Includes bibliographical references and indexes. Available as an e-book.

85   International handbook of intelligence. Robert J. Sternberg. xi, 496 p., ill. Cambridge; New York: Cambridge University Press, 2004. ISBN: 0521808154.

153.9   BF431.I59

A complement to the *Encyclopedia of human intelligence* (80) and a significant update to the *Handbook of human intelligence* (New York; Toronto; New York: MacMillan; Maxwell Macmillan Canada; Maxwell Macmillan International, 1994) compiled by the same editor. The first international handbook of intelligence, covering intelligence theory, research, and practice from all over the globe, including Great Britain, Australia, French-speaking countries, German-speaking countries, Spanish-speaking countries, India, Japan, Israel, Turkey, and China. Each chapter deals with definitions and theories of intelligence, history of research, current research, assessment techniques, and comparison across geographical regions for the area under discussion. An integrative final chapter synthesizes diverse international viewpoints. Available as an e-book.

COGNITIVE PSYCHOLOGY

14 › PHYSIOLOGICAL AND COMPARATIVE PSYCHOLOGY

Encyclopedias

86   **The encyclopedia of the brain and brain disorders.** 2nd ed. Carol Turkington, Joseph R. Harris. ix, 369 p. New York: Facts on File, 2002. ISBN: 081604774X.

612.8203   QP376.T87

Accessible reference about the brain and brain disorders from a medical writer for general readers. More than 800 clear, concise entries; also includes three directories (of self-help, professional, and governmental organizations), a glossary, an extensive list of references, and an index to a wide range of terms. The 1st ed., called *The brain encyclopedia,* was published in 1996. Part of the *Facts on File library of health and living series* (Facts On File, 1999–). Available online via Health Reference Center (www.factsonfile.com/newfacts/DataDetail.asp?SidText=816046964&Pagevalue=Online).

87   **Encyclopedia of the human brain.** V. S. Ramachandran. 4 v., xxxv, 903 p., ill. San Diego, Calif.: Academic Press, 2002. ISBN: 0122272102.

612.8303   QP376.E586

More than 220 signed entries authored by leaders in neuroscience and psychology cover topics ranging from anatomy, physiology, neuropsychology, and clinical neurology to neuropharmacology, evolutionary biology, genetics, and behavioral science. Each entry consists of an outline and definition paragraph, glossary, cross-references, and a list of suggested readings. Detailed subject index is the main point of access. Valuable for life sciences collections and academic libraries. Available as an online database.

Dictionaries

88   **Animal behavior desk reference: A dictionary of animal behavior, ecology, and evolution.** 2nd ed. Edward M. Barrows. xii, 922 p. Boca Raton, Fla.: CRC Press, 2001. ISBN: 0849320054.

591.503   QL750.3.B37

Annotated definitions for more than 5,000 terms in animal behavior, biogeography, evolution, ecology, genetics, psychology, statistics, systematics, and related sciences. Approximately 1,200 new terms have been added to this second edition. Arranged alphabetically in a standard dictionary format with numerous cross-references. Appendixes include a phylum of organisms, a listing of organizations concerned with animal behavior and related topics, and a bibliography of sources consulted in preparing this work.

89   **Physiological psychology dictionary: A reference guide for students and professionals.** George S. Grosser, Carol A. Spafford. x, 259 p. New York: McGraw-Hill, 1995. ISBN: 0070598606.
612.803   QP360.G755

Contains more than 3,500 definitions to words and phrases in the field of psychology, with special emphasis on physiological psychology. Entries include pronunciation, etymology, cross-references, and alternative terminology.

15 › CONSUMER AND INDUSTRIAL PSYCHOLOGY

Encyclopedias

90   **The encyclopedia of leadership: A practical guide to popular leadership theories and techniques.** Murray Hiebert, Bruce Klatt. xxxi, 479 p., ill. New York: McGraw-Hill, 2001. ISBN: 0071363084.
658.4092   HD57.7.H525

Quick reference guide to over 200 business leadership principles, theories, tools, and techniques. Each explanation of a theory or tool is followed by an exercise or worksheet. Leadership concepts are grouped into 15 sections, such as leading change and critical thinking. Cross-references.

Handbooks

91 **The Blackwell handbook of principles of organizational behavior.** Edwin A. Locke. xviii, 445 p., ill. Oxford, U.K.; Malden, Mass.: Blackwell Business, 2000. ISBN: 0631215050.
658   HD58.7.B574

Identifies and explains 29 management principles that can be applied to all types of work situations. Chapters cover a wide range of topics, including selection, turnover, job satisfaction, work motivation, incentives, leadership, team effectiveness, decision making, creativity, stress, and technology. Provides students and managers with a practical resource that shows the application of theory to the real world of organizations.

92 **Handbook of industrial, work and organizational psychology.** Neil Anderson. 2 v., ill. London; Thousand Oaks, Calif.: SAGE, 2001. ISBN: 0761964886.

HF5548.8.H2652

Vol. 1, *Personnel psychology,* focuses on the theories, techniques, and methods used by industrial psychologists. Vol. 2, *Organizational psychology,* concerns research findings on a range of work-related topics. Each of 41 chapters has been written by one or more of the world's leading researchers in each particular field, to provide both an overview of current research and a description of future trends. Chapters are fully referenced and include a short biography of the author(s).

93 **Handbook of research methods in industrial and organizational psychology.** Steven G. Rogelberg. xi, 520 p., ill. Malden, Mass.: Blackwell Publishers, 2002. ISBN: 0631222596.
158.7072   HF5548.8.H2653

Comprehensive and contemporary treatment of research philosophies, approaches, tools, and techniques indigenous to industrial and organizational psychology. Signed chapters cover such topics as organizational survey research, methodological issues in cross-cultural organizational research, and Internet research opportunities for industrial-organizational psychology. Includes bibliographical references and indexes.

94 **The IEBM handbook of organizational behavior.** Arndt Sorge, Malcolm Warner. xiv, 752 p., ill., maps. London; Boston: International Thomson Business Press, 1997. ISBN: 1861521685.
658   HD58.7.I35

Drawing from material in the highly acclaimed six-volume *International encyclopedia of business and management* (Thompson Learning, 2002) of 1992, this work presents in-depth, global coverage of a wide range of organizational behavior topics and approaches. Bibliographical references. Index.

16 > PARAPSYCHOLOGY

Indexes; Abstract Journals

95   **Exceptional human experience.** Parapsychology Sources of Information Center. Dix Hills, N.Y.: Parapsychology Sources of Information Center, 1983–2004. ISSN: 1053-4768.

016.1338; 133   BF1001.P275

Formerly known as *Parapsychology abstracts international* (1983–89). Presents an information resource for literature recording parapsychological, imaginal, mystical, and peak phenomena. Includes profiles of investigators, accounts of experiences, methodological and theoretical articles, and abstracts from a broad range of journals.

Encyclopedias

96   **The new encyclopedia of the occult.** John Michael Greer. xii, 555 p., ill. St. Paul, Minn.: Llewellyn, 2003. ISBN: 1567183360.

133.03   BF1407.G74.

Comprises 1,500 entries arranged in alphabetical order. Topics include magic, tarot, astrology, and other forms of divination; magical orders such as the Golden Dawn; biographies of significant individuals; and spiritual movements such as Wicca, Theosophy, and the modern Pagans. Where appropriate, entries contain *see* references to other entries and to books found in the extensive bibliography. Illustrations include charts, diagrams, and photographs.

Entries reflect Germanic, Irish, Gaelic, Arabic, Hebrew, Greek, Latin, English, and Egyptian occult practices and cover a wide variety of topics, including alchemy, hermetic traditions, runes, voodoo, herbalism, tarot, magical concepts, divination, Masonic lore, witchcraft, numbers, letters, magical symbols, prominent deceased occultists, and pagan terminology.

INDEX

Numbers in **bold** refer to entry numbers. Numbers in light face type refer to mentions in annotations of other works.

You may also be interested in

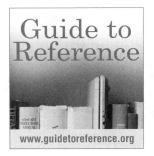

Guide to Reference: This subscription database, published by the American Library Association, takes full advantage of the Web's capacities to connect information sources; it also creates and links to content that makes it a center for learning about and practicing reference librarianship. For more information and to subscribe, visit www.guidetoreference.org.

ALA Guide to Economics and Business Reference: Focusing on print and electronic sources that are key to economics and business reference, this is a must-have for every reference desk. Readers will find information on business law, electronic commerce, international business, management of information systems, market research, and much more.

ALA Guide to Medical and Health Science Reference: This resource provides an annotated list of print and electronic biomedical and health-related reference sources, including Internet resources and digital image collections. Readers will find relevant research, clinical, and consumer health information resources. The emphasis is on resources within the United States, with a few representative examples from other countries.

Annotated Guide to Biographies and Memoirs of U.S. Presidents: Arranged alphabetically and ideal for collection development, each record includes an ISBN, list price, binding, page count, Library of Congress data, Dewey classification, and brief description of the publication. Multiple indices are also included for user convenience.